DYING for JERUSALEM

The Past, Present and Future
of the Holiest City

Walter Laqueur

SOURCEBOOKS, INC.
NAPERVILLE, ILLINOIS

Published by Sourcebooks, Inc.
P.O. Box 4410, Naperville, Illinois 60567–4410
(630) 961–3900
Fax: (630) 961–2168
www.sourcebooks.com

Library of Congress Cataloging-in-Publication Data
Laqueur, Walter
Dying for Jerusalem : the past, present and future of the holiest city 3 / Walter Laqueur.
p. cm.
Includes index.
ISBN-13: 978–1-4022–0632–0
ISBN-10: 1–4022–0632–1
1. Jerusalem—History. 2. Jerusalem—Politics and government. 3. Arab-Israeli conflict. 4. Laqueur, Walter, 1921- I. Title.
DS109.9.L325 2005
956.9405—dc22

2005025006

Printed and bound in Canada
TR 10 9 8 7 6 5 4 3 2 1

For Susi

CONTENTS

INTRODUCTION

Young Man on the Road to Jerusalem, 1938

I FIRST ARRIVED IN JERUSALEM AROUND NOON ON NOVEMBER 15, 1938. Sometimes, with a little effort, it seems like only yesterday. The sun was shining. The bus rolled slowly towards the center of town. It was an armored vehicle with wire mesh covering the windows. We passed numerous military checkpoints on our way from the coast. This was the time of the riots. I remember feeling impatient, not (to paraphrase the great Napoleon) because thirty centuries were looking down on me from the hills of Judea, but because the trip had taken a very long time. I was hungry and thirsty. I faced a great many uncertainties. Where would I go first, where would I sleep that night and the next? I was age seventeen and for the first time in my life I had to confront such unknowns. Ten days earlier I had been in Nazi Germany. The train to Trieste crossed the border as *Kristallnacht* took place in what had been my home.

When I tried in later years to find out more about the day of my arrival, I learned that the weather had been fair, the temperature sixty-eight degrees Fahrenheit (more in the sun), that there had been a great deal of diplomatic activity in New York and London. There were protests against Germany. In addition, some seven hundred thirty Palestinian Arabs had been rounded up by British military units, which successfully put an end to the riots. According to an official communiqué, eight people were killed and, following the shooting of two British soldiers in Gaza, eight houses were demolished. The violence would come to an end just as the Second World War broke out. On that day I arrived in Jerusalem, Mr. Elie Eliachar gave a lecture at the Fast Hotel about the future of aviation in Palestine, Dr. M. ben David was talking about "our neighbor the moon," and the newspapers ran advertisements for "wireless sets," especially short-wave models. These were critical days in world politics; the radio was the only way to keep abreast of affairs. What was the news that day? Ben-Gurion, head of the Jewish agency, warned that the Zionist budget would have to reach one million pounds (sterling) in order to cope with the urgent problems of settlement and defense. On the night of my arrival the radio aired a performance of the "Bartered Bride" from Sofia. Later, you could hear BBC Symphony Orchestra, conducted by Basil Cameron at Queen's Hall, London. At the Eden cinema, *Personal Property* with Jean Harlow and Robert Taylor was playing. On the day of my arrival to Jerusalem G. B. Shaw said Hitler would not go to war.

I have since visited in Jerusalem often, sometimes for weeks at a time, sometimes for months, but I have also worked there for a number of years. My children were born there.

When I returned to Jerusalem in the winter of 2004, my first stop was Rehavia, a part of town I liked best and that was once my home. What did I expect to find there? Hardly anyone I knew there was still alive. The streets go by the same names, and even some of the old shops have survived. The pharmacy is still there, even though it has changed hands four or five times; so have the small coffeehouses at the intersection of Metudela and Gaza Streets. Yomtov, the greengrocer next door, is still in business, but today his sons are running affairs. The Jerusalem stone structures, off-white or yellowish, two or three stories high, International style or Bauhaus, could do with a cleaning. The fences are more or less the same as I recall them, and as I walked slowly along the streets I could hear music from some of the balconies. But it is TV now, not the music of the forties or the fifties, when they transmitted the concerts from the YMCA. Nor is the language the same; it used to be German and Hebrew, now it is predominantly English and French.

The population of Rehavia has grown elderly, but these are not the offspring of the Jews from Central Europe who once lived here; today's residents mostly belong to the national religious camp and are often parents who want to be near their children who settled in the country. The apartments built in the nineteen thirties were small, the second and third generations of Rehavia's settlers wanted more space as their families grew. They moved to Nayot and other suburban destinations. Not many professors from the Hebrew University still live here; they now reside in places like Bet Hakerem and Mevasseret Zion, the suburbs to the west of the city.

When I lived in Rehavia, hardly anyone had a car; now there is no empty space for parking and traffic jams form during all hours of the day. Down in the Valley of Crucifixion, the massive old Georgian monastery looks deserted; not far behind it the scouts have their evening meetings. Once upon a time Gaza Street was surrounded by rocky terrain where tufts of grass grew here and there. During the winter and spring months, wildflowers and bluish-red cyclamen. Today this land had all been developed.

At one time I knew every street and many of the houses, I knew Rehavia in both war and peace, most of my friends and acquaintances had lived here: the grocer to whom we usually owed money towards the end of the month, the lawyer from Berlin who worked as a taxi driver, the good old physician who drove a Fiat Topolino, and who could always be counted on in an emergency, the two sisters next door—one of whom would marry Moshe Dayan; the other who was the future president of Israel.

Some of my erstwhile neighbors have little streets named after them, but I strongly doubt whether any of the present residents know who Yohanan Boehm was (a conductor) or Dr. Siegfried Moses (the first Israeli state comptroller).

There was no air-conditioning when I first came to Jerusalem, and there were no swimming pools either. On summer days, with the viciously hot khamsin blowing, the few-hundred-yard walk to the Number 4 bus stop seemed endless. Sixty years ago neither the Israel museum nor the parliament building could be seen on the horizon.

Rehavia looked shabbier on the morning after my return. Some of the old houses were deserted, others had been replaced by new and bigger buildings that lacked character. The beautiful front gardens of yore had shrunk when the roads were widened to accommodate increasing traffic.

What could I reasonably have expected to find? A landscape, a view, a building without the people who once lived there, all unsettling. The key element is missing. It is an unsatisfactory trip into the past, like watching a new and strange play against the background of a old play's scenery.

I have lived in a variety of places on three continents, in big cities and very small villages. Some no longer interest me and I feel no inclination to revisit. Some I remember vividly and in detail even though many years have passed, while others are only a vague memory. My feelings about Jerusalem have been ambivalent since the day I first arrived there more than sixty years ago. Yet I still return. I would not call Jerusalem's attraction magnetic. But the years I spent there were some of the most interesting and formative of my life (which isn't to say that there weren't boring intervals when I was less than happy). Today I visit primarily to recall people I knew, some well, others only from a distance or by reputation.

There are reasons for my ambivalence about Jerusalem: born into an assimilated German-Jewish family, I had limited interest in things Jewish. The religious services for the young were boring. Fortunately, I had to attend them only up to the age of thirteen, when bar mitzvah took place. The weekly lesson in religion was neither entertaining nor inspiring, though the caliber of the teachers was high. I accompanied my father to synagogue on New Year and the Day of Atonement, but at home the festivals were celebrated in a cursory way, matzo (but not a full-fledged seder) at Passover, candle lighting on Hanukkah.

Nazism and anti-Semitism led to a renewed commitment to Judaism among the older generation and even some of my peers, but I did not feel an irresistible urge to engage in the search for my roots. I read a great deal of literature and history but did not find Jewish history of paramount interest. The stories of persecutions and unredeemed misery over many centuries were too depressing. I had the same reaction to contemporary Jewish literature. Many of the books I read by Jewish authors did not deal with specific Jewish subjects, or did so only tangentially. The great issues as I saw them when I was an adolescent were fascism and communism as they gave rise to the struggle for freedom and a better world. True, I did belong to a Jewish youth group, which over the years embraced Zionism and life in a kibbutz. I read the basic writings, Theodor Herzl and Judah Leib Pinsker, and even Ber Borochov who tried to provide a synthesis of Zionism and Marxism. I took part in discussions along these lines, but there was never much passion.

In 1938 I arrived to what was then Palestine by lucky accident. There were very few escape routes left that year. I could have equally landed in the United States or in Shanghai (had I been less lucky). Or I could have missed the last train and found myself in a trap without exit as so many did.

My encounter with Palestine on the eve of World War II did not carry any shock of recognition. It was a strange and unfamiliar country—the sights, the people, the smells, the language, the climate, the work. This was true especially with regard to Jerusalem, an exotic though rather rundown and ugly place. The Wailing Wall and the Temple Mount meant little to me. What the psalms said about the "faithful city" (*kirya ne'emana*) and the "city knit together" did not make much sense given the stark contrarieties of Jerusalems in 1938. Rabbi Natan said some eighteen hundred years ago that there are ten portions of beauty in the world: nine are in Jerusalem, one in the rest of the world. And he added, there are ten portions of suffering in the world: nine in Jerusalem, one in the rest of the world. I found both statements exaggerated.

My heart was not beating faster when I listened to "From the Peak of Har Hazofim" (Mount Scopus) and other Zionist songs of the thirties. The lyrics, "For one hundred generations did I dream about you, O Jerusalem," did not resonate with me. Jerusalem had not appeared in my dreams, and I doubt whether it appeared in the dreams of my father or my grandfathers. The same was true, incidentally, with regard to the majority of newcomers from Europe at the time. Few of them settled in Jerusalem, only twenty-five hundred new immigrants went there during the thirties. There was an aversion against Jerusalem even on the part of the Zionist leaders, who preferred Tel Aviv or Haifa. Herzl wanted the capital of his Jewish State to be on Mount Carmel, not on Mount Zion—he found Jerusalem too depressing, Weizman wanted it to be in Rehovot, and Ben-Gurion had no preference for Jerusalem either. True, he invoked Jerusalem in his speeches—but he did not want to live there. I think that until recently no Israeli prime minister (with the exception of Moshe Sharett) had his main residence in Jerusalem before he became prime minister, and the same is true with regard to most ministers, left or right. Jerusalem symbolized the old, the traditional, the conservative. The Zionists had come to build a new society and a new country. This contempt toward the Diaspora character of Jerusalem expressed in the work of Uri Zvi Grinberg, the poet laureate of the far right, was even more emphatic. In the early summer of 1948, about the time of the siege of Jerusalem, Ben-Gurion wrote in his diary: "20 percent of the Jerusalemites are normal people, 20 percent belong to the university (but not really to the city). The rest is weird..."

At seventeen and eighteen my preoccupations were not mainly with ideology, politics, and religion but with personal problems— friendship and first love, finding a new home and new friends. I learned Hebrew fairly quickly, and also a little Yiddish and some Arabic. Before eight years had passed I wrote my first book in Hebrew. But the young Saulus did still not become a Zionist Paulus, and did not spend much of his time trying to rediscover his Jewish roots. It was not a case of opposition and rejection. It was a question of indifference. Of course there was a feeling of shared interests, emotions and values, even of solidarity but this was mainly with those of a similar background and of the same generation.

I met many people my age from Eastern Europe and also Oriental Jews and for years I lived among them. I learned to sing and to curse in their languages; I laughed with them and I fought with them. I found some of their customs and their mentality interesting and the encounter certainly broadened my horizons. They became my friends. But it still did not make me one of them.

I was struck by the extent to which the people I met had been shaped by their surroundings abroad, their places of birth and education; the same was, of course, true of myself. Those who came from small towns in Poland still bore unmistakable traces of the shtetl.

Those from Warsaw and Lodz were the product of a Polish-Jewish culture, they were familiar with the Polish classics and recited Julian Tuwim. Zionism was the revolt against the miserable Jewish existence in the shtetl, but even those who joined the revolt had been shaped by their origins—how could it have been different? The new man and the new woman had not yet been born. It goes almost without saying that it could not be found in Jerusalem at the time.

It did not take me long to realize that Zionism had been more far-sighted than other ideologies in anticipating the difficulties of assimilation and the coming disaster in Europe. The problem was that it could offer refuge only to relatively few.

I began to read books in Hebrew, but more out of a feeling of duty than deep interest and conviction. I discovered that there were genuine poets and writers among them, perhaps even great ones, but again I did not feel an exhilarating sense of identification. The subject matter seemed not of overwhelming interest. (My interest, I should add, increased in later years.) I went to exhibitions and concerts but found it difficult to discover a specific Jewish content in the paintings and the music of local composers and painters. The Jewish religion, with its heavy emphasis on the observation of ritual, remained almost as alien to me as Christianity or Islam. Some of my contemporaries went hiking in an attempt to know better the new homeland and also to develop a feeling of communion with the land and with nature. I often joined them, but found the effort a little artificial—the love of the homeland could not be acquired by an act of will.

In other words, I was still not a good Jew and as far as Zionism was concerned, I remained an agnostic.

And yet, over the years there developed something akin to deep sympathy, perhaps even identification with the new home. There was, to begin with, a feeling of gratitude as I realized that I owed my survival to those who had come before me to start building a home for their fellow Jews. I joined a kibbutz, and while it did not take long for me to realize that this was not the kind of life in which I would find satisfaction and fulfillment, I also understood that the kibbutz was a unique attempt to build a new form of social life. Whether it ultimately succeeded or failed, it was an important social experiment, and I felt privileged to see it firsthand.

There was more than that. When I met in later years some of my contemporaries, especially in the academic world, who had emigrated to the United States or Britain or some other Western country, I came across a syndrome that greatly puzzled me. That they had no interest in Israel was understandable, but it was perplexing to find that many of them should make a point of dismissing their own heritage—especially if they happened to be historians. Some of them were writing books about their "German problem," but I suspect what really bothered them, not always consciously, was their "Jewish problem," or to use an overworked phrase, the question of their identity. When I met these people or read their work, I often had the feeling that this, but for the grace of God, would have been my fate too if the years in Palestine and Israel had not provided an excellent antidote against any self-consciousness I might have fostered about being Jewish.

Subsequently I worked for a number of years as an Israeli newspaper correspondent and came to know the country and the people rather well. I met most of the leading political and cultural figures of the day. I developed respect, sometimes grudging, for some of the leaders, almost all of them self-made men, provincial as far as their background was concerned, but people of vision, character, and intellectual curiosity. I did not necessarily share some of their ideological beliefs, but I was still impressed by their idealism and unselfishness, the modesty of their lifestyles, and their disdain for what they considered luxuries. Sometimes I wished I could share their sense of purpose and their unquestioning faith in the cause.

The achievements were remarkable. Those who built the country were neither saints nor geniuses; they could be narrow minded, clannish and hostile vis-à-vis those not belonging to their circle. But there was a great deal of heart and the positive features of this vanguard outweighed the negative ones.

I was also impressed by the generation of 1948, those my age or a few years younger, the native-born Israelis, who played a decisive role in the events that led to the establishment of the state. They were extroverted, aggressively anti-intellectual, provincial, often superficial. But they were fearless; they felt a solidarity for which I envied them, and their instincts were good. They were very different from the young Jewish intellectuals I had known in Europe. My own generation, which had gone through the neo-romanticism of youth movements in Central Europe, was a little closer to them, but it had taken us an effort to adapt ourselves to the things that had come naturally to them. I do not want to idealize them; they were excellent companions in a time of emergency, with the back to the wall. In normal times, I would find many of them less than congenial company.

And then, in 1948, the state came into being. I belonged to those who had doubted the wisdom of building a Jewish state. I sympathized with a binational solution. I lost my illusions while touring the country with a UN commission (UNSCOP) and talking to Arabs of all walks of life. They were quite unwilling to accept a binational state based on equality.

The first years after 1948 were difficult, even depressing. The political and economic outlook was bleak. Food and other essentials were rationed. Jerusalem was a divided city and thousands left it because it seemed to have no future. The idea of a Jewish state had been based on the assumption that millions of Jews from Europe would eventually join those who had acted as pioneers. But these millions had been killed. Was a state still needed in these circumstances?

The alternative was to be part of Greater Syria or something of this sort and it was not for this that three generations had worked, giving their sweat and blood.

But the demographic base of the new state was not broad enough to ensure its survival and thus the ingathering of the exiles got underway, the arrival of the sad remnants of European Jewry and hundreds of thousands of Oriental Jews.

Few of those who came after the end of the war were Zionists. Those from the displaced persons camps in Germany and Austria came because, for many of them, there were no other opportunities. Those from Romania and Bulgaria and Poland came mainly because life in Israel seemed preferable to an existence under Communism. Some of the Jews from Oriental countries came because their situation had become untenable following the pogroms and the anti-Jewish politics in countries such as Iraq. Others came from Morocco and Yemen because of a messianic religious belief (or because their neighbors went) rather than because of Zionism. Before 1948, it had been difficult enough to develop among the Jewish community of Palestine a feeling of belonging to one people. Following the mass immigration of 1948, the task became even more difficult, even though attacks from the outside provided some national cohesion.

The people who arrived after the foundation of the state were not pioneers, and their expectations were well above what the new state—any new state—could give them. Regardless of how poor Israel was, these newcomers still would have experienced discrimination, paternalism, and a general lack of respect for their respective cultures and traditions. Zionism was an European affair; it had never been a strong draw among the Jews of the Middle East and North Africa. Feelings of solidarity with their Ashkenazi coreligionists was strictly limited, and the European Jews did not feel too close to them either (though some of them went out of their way to help to overcome the difficulties).

Seen in retrospect, it is not at all clear if the Jews from countries such as Morocco (and later Ethiopia) had been in any sort of mortal danger. Was Israel right to encourage non-European Jews to come to Israel? I doubted it at the time and these doubts have not diminished over the years. The situation was further aggravated by the fact that the North African Jewish middle-class did not come to Israel, only the leaderless masses.

"We are a people, One people," Herzl had exclaimed in a famous speech in an early Zionist Congress to stormy acclaim, but was it still true? We shall return to this question later on. There certainly had been a Jewish people at one time, but Zionism had come too late to reunite it, its various branches had gone their own ways. They still shared some common features and traditions and felt a certain responsibility for each other at a time of crisis. But most of them no longer felt an urge for redemption and the building of a new kingdom of Israel.

Many Western Jews had left the community; others had remained Jews mainly out of a feeling of piety toward their ancestors and the conviction that it was immoral to flee from a fortress under siege. Hitler in particular and anti-Semitism in general did much to forge the Jewish community in the latter half of the twentieth century. But after 1945, there was no Hitler and while anti-Semitism continued to exist, multicultural societies developed in Europe and America in which Jews could find their place with greater ease than ever before.

I felt solidarity with Jews who were under attack; we were members of a community of fate. I knew that part of my heart was in Israel, and would be there as long as I lived. But when Nazism was defeated, this community of fate was replaced by a much vaguer feeling of solidarity, atavistic perhaps, rooted in the distant past but nonetheless quite real. I had nothing to do with nationalism, and it was devoid of a specific cultural content. The fate of the country was close to my heart, and I followed events in Israel even while I lived in London and Washington.

I found it puzzling and painful how a people showing so much intelligence in other respects should show so little political maturity and wisdom. How to explain the decline in the quality of leadership, the growing shortsightedness, and parochialism? I knew that much of the criticism of Israel emanating from Jews and non-Jews was unfair or uninformed or both and that it involved applying standards to Israel that would not be—and indeed never have been—applied to any other country. Of late these voices have become fashionable, almost deafening, but with all my criticism I felt that I did not belong *dans cette galère*.

But these feelings were paired with a growing sense of unease as I walked the streets of Jerusalem on frequent visits in the sixties and seventies. What exactly did I have in common with the people I met? I felt myself alone with these doubts, but today I know that they were shared by many of my contemporaries. I knew that such disappointment faced every national movement in the twentieth century, every new country that came into being (from Yeats, "Romantic Ireland's dead and gone").

"Hayu zemanim," which freely translated means "Those were the days, my friends." But Jerusalem had never been associated with "the days." It somehow fell outside the new world that was built in Palestine during the 1920s and 1930s and then again in 1948. I shared the nostalgia up to a point, but since my hopes concerning Romantic Israel had not been that high, despair was not that deep.

During its stormy economic development, the face of the young nation changed; those who had not been in the country in 1950 would hardly recognize it twenty years later. Hundreds of new settlements had been established; the towns had grown. Israel had become a modern country. Work had been found for everyone, even the many hundreds of thousands of Russian Jews who had arrived with training or professions that did not make their absorption in Israel very likely. Modern technologies had been developed in industry and agriculture, and in some respects Israel was considered a leading source of innovation in the world. Experts from other countries came to learn from the Israeli example. The very fact that a small society of about six hundred thousand had managed to absorb an influx several times that number was without parallel in history.

All countries change over time; most European countries today are no longer what they were after World War II. But Israel has changed much more than any of them. It is a different country in more than one sense. Today, I am told the number of those now alive who resided in the country before 1948 is no more than fifty thousand, a small minority. Before 1948, the settlers had comprised an elite. That is no longer the case. Normalization led to polarization, economically as well as socially. Once upon a time it was one of the most egalitarian societies. If a family had a three-room apartment and a small car, it was considered wealthy. Today, among the developed countries Israel has the most pronounced disparities between the rich and the poor. This is a major source of trouble. Israel is a small country, a face-to-face society and great disparities are bad for the democratic character of the country.

The ideological polarization has been equally pronounced. No matter what country you look at in the world, there is a left and a right and there is also an extreme left and extreme right (whether or not the old labels are still in use). The issue at stake is no longer socialism versus capitalism; the rich suburbs vote Labor whereas the poor development towns opt for the right-wing parties. As long as extremism is confined to relatively small groups, it is politically irrelevant. But if the extremes grow in influence and if the center that holds society together shrinks too much, society faces a crisis. Over the last twenty years, the belief has gained ground on the right that the whole of historical

Palestine is theirs "by divine right." This has occasioned (among other things) the mushrooming of settlements in the areas occupied in 1967. Most of them do not make sense militarily or economically, but it is a major obstacle on the road to some form of peaceful coexistence between Arabs and Jews.

At the other extreme, anti-Zionism in various guises has gained ground in Israel, even though its cultural influence has been greater than its political impact. This is the school of thought that states that Israel was conceived in sin, for the Jews had no right to invade a country that they had left two thousand years earlier. The message was not new, it had been preached by critics of Zionism since its inception, most vociferously perhaps by the Communists during the 1920s and '30s. Following the ideological demise of Marxism-Leninism, anti-Zionism reappeared among a new generation of native Israelis who had never experienced anti-Semitism, for whom the Holocaust was about as real a historical experience as Napoleon, all this being under the influence of various neo-Marxist schools of thought popular in France and the United States. I never was a Zionist if this implied the ingathering of all the exiles, but I could not possibly be an anti-Zionist, for it would have meant turning against those who had saved my life. The anti-Zionists would have me believe, in effect, that I should have committed suicide together with thousands belonging to my generation rather than immigrate to a country that was not altogether empty.

I organized my thoughts on Zionism and the State of Israel in a history of Zionism written during the early 1970s. I argued that the historical tragedy of Zionism was that it appeared too late on the political scene while it could not have come earlier. Arguments about the essentially sinful character of Zionism and its violent essence seemed to me disingenuous. It is, of course, true that Palestine was not empty in 1897 when Herzl convened the first Zionist Congress in Vienna.

But it was sparsely populated at the time. Even later when the British mandate was established the populated was small. *Baedeker's Guide to Vienna,* published in 1896, reports a population of 1,364,500. The total number of Arabs in Palestine that year was perhaps one-third of that number. The next sentence in *Baedeker's Guide* helps to explain why the idea of Zionism occurred to Herzl in the first place. It says "including 118,000 Jews and 22,651 soldiers." There lived in Vienna at the time tens of thousands of Poles and Czechs, Croats and Hungarians, Italians and Slovenians, and many other nationalities. But only the Jews were listed in a separate category. Were they thought to be transients like the soldiers?

No state has ever been established in history by friendly persuasion or some legal contract. There has always been violence involved and invasion, in Europe and North America as well as in Africa and Asia, and there was no reason to assume that Israel would be an exception. The tragedy of Zionism was not that it was morally wrong but that it came too late; as I argued in my history of Zionism (1972). Thus a conflict was inevitable, but Zionism and Israel could have defused it by offering massive compensation to those who had lost their homes.

Zionism came too late—in the nineteenth century only part of the Jewish people felt the urge to build a state of its own anymore and, in any case, the Turks ruling the Near East would have never accepted the emergence of a Jewish state in their midst. With the establishment of the state and the great immigration waves, the historical function of Zionism had ended and a new, post-Zionist age had dawned. Approximately one-quarter of the population of Israel and almost one-third of the population of Jerusalem (not counting the West Bank) was Arab. Since such a state was bound to be Israeli, not exclusively Jewish, it could not expect that its non-Jewish citizens would accept the Star of David and the blue-and-white flag as an expression of their deepest feelings, or that they would sing a national anthem about the Jewish hope of two thousand years that had at last been fulfilled. Attempts were made to preserve the Jewish character of the majority of society while respecting the rights and aspirations of the non-Jewish citizens. But such attempts never went far enough.

As for the consequences of the great victory in the Six Days War, I wrote at the time (*The Road to War,* 1968) that there was no greater potential disaster than a great victory—except perhaps a crushing defeat. And what happened in the following years only strengthened my belief.

Having left the country in the middle 1950s, I became by necessity an outsider despite the frequent visits, long stays, and the intellectual interest in the country. I was reluctant to offer political advice, even though the temptation was always strong. Advice from abroad (especially advice given in public) seemed to me problematic when the issues concerned the very survival of the country.

Even as an outsider I could not fail to notice the changes that were taking place in the country. My sympathies were naturally with the generation of pioneers. Most of the achievements before 1948, and after, had been their work. Without the pioneers, Israel would have never existed in the first place, nor would it have been able to defend itself. The left wing enjoyed a great ascendancy; all other political forces were marginal. I noted with sadness their decline; they lost their original role and did not find a new one. But I had always tried to be fair to the right in Israel inasmuch as it was a democratic and rational right. However, this right in the Jabotinsky tradition also largely disappeared and in its place there came the fanatics and blind believers talking not only about redemption, but about a new kingdom and the building of a new temple. Every nation needs its national symbols and mythology but these people were grossly overdoing it. I had been convinced all along that the admixture of fundamentalist religion and politics was explosive and potentially suicidal.

The emergence of those on the other extreme of the political spectrum, the school of postcolonialism, was in part a manifestation of generational revolt akin to the students' revolt in Europe and the U.S. during the late 1960s. Their rejection of Zionism (and sometimes also of Israel) is psychologically understandable, for this generation did not have to confront persecution and the danger of destruction, and they did not have to flee Europe to save their lives. Their desire for peace and close relations between Jews and Arabs is laudable, but they hardly have a monopoly when it comes to this aspiration. As for the rest of their ideology, there is nothing specifically Israeli about it, the inspiration comes from the gurus of postmodernism. But postmodernism is not, and cannot be, a political force. Whereas the fanatics of the right are willing not only to demonstrate but to fight and perhaps give their lives, the anti-Zionists of the academic world are not even willing to endanger their tenured positions in the universities.

Originally, I lived not only among Jews but also among Palestinian Arabs, villagers and simple people, not their upper class and intellectuals. I lived among bedouins and fellaheen in the Esdraelon Valley; I made my home for a year in Issawiya, an Arab village close to the old Hadassah hospital on Mount Scopus; and for another year in the old German Colony. At one time I spoke their language tolerably well and learned to behave according to their customs. I went to Arab restaurants, I watched some Egyptian movies, and smoked Arab cigarettes (I never liked the *nargileh*). In later years, being a journalist, I read *Falastin* and *Al Difaa* or at least scanned the headlines. I felt that conflict between the two peoples was inevitable given the unwillingness of the Arabs to compromise. But why should they have compromised, was it their fault that the European Jews were persecuted and threatened with extinction?

So they went to war for their rights and they lost. The Palestinian Arabs had been wronged just as the many millions in Europe and Asia have been wronged who were forced to leave their homes after World War II. Many Israelis found it difficult to understand the Palestinian Arabs reaction. Did they not live much better than before? Was their lot not preferable to that of their fellow Arabs in the neighboring countries? Of course, this showed an astonishing lack of imagination. Had these same Israelis been born Palestinians, would they have reacted any differently?

But the fact that the Palestinians were wronged did not make them better men and women. Perhaps it was inevitable, but the defeat brought out the worst in them, like it did among many Germans after World War I, when many came to believe in the Protocols of the Elders of Zion and to admire the Nazis. They never quite understood that there would have been no State of Israel without Adolf Hitler. If Israel were a major power, those insisting on the right of return of the Palestinian refugees would be branded as revanchists and warmongers. But Israel is not India or Pakistan, not Poland or Czechoslovakia, from which millions of Germans were expelled.

It has been the misfortune of the Israelis that their country is located in a part of the world which has shown particular ineptitude in establishing civil (let alone civilized) societies, engaging in economic and social progress, and making a notable contribution to world culture. I do not know why this should be the case. I am simply noting a fact. As a student of history I know that this was not always so, Arab civilization in the Middle Ages was greatly superior to that of Christian Europe. But many centuries have passed, and the Arabs have fallen steadily behind in comparison not only with the West but also the rest of the world, and the resulting frustration may be at the bottom of their resentment, their violence, and their unwillingness even to avow the sorry state of affairs in which they find themselves. Instead of self-criticism there is self-pity. This is their business, not ours, but it could explain to a certain extent why many find it difficult to feel sympathy for many Arab causes even when they are just. Nor is there any reason to believe that democratic Arab societies would have been any more friendly disposed towards the state of Israel.

Back to Jerusalem, its walls and monuments and its strange mixture of people. It is there in the streets of Jerusalem that the problems besetting the whole area can be viewed in their most extreme form. It has been said that Jerusalem is a microcosm of all that is wrong in the world. It is an exaggeration. Many of the Jerusalemite problems are unique, *sui generis*. Almost one-third of the city is Arab; some 130,000 residents belong to various *haredim* or Jewish ultraorthodox sects, which are for the most part anti-Zionist. Prior to the 1980s, virtually no *haredim* (ultraorthodox) lived in the Jewish Quarter of the Old City; today they constitute the overwhelming majority. There is concurrently a substantial exodus of young secular residents from Jerusalem, which is by now truly a post-Zionist city. It was not on a mere whim that Uri Lupoliansky, then interval mayor of Jerusalem (who belonged to the ultraorthodox community), refused to participate in the Independence Day celebrations in 2003. A month later, in June 2003, he was elected mayor of Jerusalem. My right-wing friends are fond of saying that Jerusalem, the eternal capital of the Jewish people, must never again be divided. They fail to understand that the city is already divided, and does not even have a Zionist mayor.

The orthodox live in a ghetto of their own (as did, *mutatis mutandis,* the German-Jews in Rehavia at the time. As did—and do—the various Oriental-Jewish communities from Bukhara, Kurdistan, Georgia, Shiraz, Urfa, and a few dozen other places). And there are no mixed Jewish-Arab neighborhoods now as there were before 1948. Jerusalem is still the poorest of the big cities in Israel and culturally the most backward, despite the presence of Hebrew University, Bezalel (the arts school), and other cultural institutions. It is socially the least integrated city. It is the most picturesque city and has some of the ugliest neighborhoods to be found in the country. With many ultraorthodox rejecting the Jewish state as a matter of principle, it is the most anti-Zionist city, and it is home to the most fanatic religious-nationalist militants willing to launch a major religious war. It is a most interesting city for painters, photographers, and political scientists specializing in the study of conflict. It is an obvious home for the fundamentalists of all religions who want to be near the holy sites, to be at hand when *Messias* comes.

For many of the secular it has become a nightmare.

This is a book of recollections, of impressions, and reflections about Jews and Arabs and the conflict between them, about nationalism and religion, about Zionism and post-Zionism, about the kibbutz, about extreme movements of the left and right, about the fate of German and Oriental and Russian Jews, about war and peace and the uncertainties of the future, and about people I have met over the years. It is also a book about streets and buildings and sights, holy and unholy. But mainly it is about human beings, including myself.

It is not a systematic overview. My starting point is neither the Bible nor the kabbalah but the Jerusalem telephone directories of 1940 and 1946 and the *Who's Who* of 1947, the last published under British mandate. Obtaining these books in order to refresh my memory proved to be surprisingly difficult. Eventually I found an English-language telephone directory published by the British Mandatory government in 1940 and one in Hebrew that appeared in early 1946. Many people had been in the possession of this book at the time, but no one keep old telephone books forever; even libraries and intelligence services discard them after a number of years.

The Jerusalem telephone directories of 1940 and 1946 were skimpy, a mere thirty pages, of which a page or two were instructions on how to dial. On the front cover Martell cognac and Peugeot cars were advertised, as well as Packard automobiles, "the new masters of

the world's highways." There were all together twenty thousand telephones at the time in the whole of Palestine. The present directories,
in contrast, are formidable books. That Jews use the telephone often
and at length is well-known, but the same is true for Arabs. Since the
invention of cell phones, Israel has probably achieved a per capita
world record as far as frequency of use and the duration of calls is concerned. In the 1940 directory, a mere five Husseinis appeared; in the
year 2000, there are too many to count.

These reference works are interesting both for the people you can
find in them, and for those you cannot find. The locations, the
addresses of individuals, and institutions are not devoid of significance
either. The same applies to the names of streets, especially since some
of them have changed. At one time I lived on Gaza Street. It is now
known as Rav Berlin street.

My first home was Workers Housing Development Number 2 in
Rehavia, an unremarkable place then, but one that later became an
important address for students of architecture as a landmark of
Bauhaus design. I also lived on the Street of the Prophets, one of the
oldest and most famous outside the Old City; near the market of
Mahane Yehuda (which has been the target of many bomb attacks in
recent years; in Hebron Way; in Issawiya, the Arab Village; and in
Arlosoroff Street. When I visit Jerusalem now, my address is Street of
November 29, referring to the U.N. resolution to divide Palestine in
1947. All things considered, there have not been that many name
changes. Agrippas is still Agrippas, King George Street is still there
(even though he was not a king of the Jews), but Princess Mary is now
Shlomzion Hamalka, another princess and queen who lived almost
two thousand years earlier. Queen Melisande Street has become Queen
Helene, who was an Assyrian, but her two sons converted to Judaism.

This is not primarily a book about political, cultural, and religious
conflict, even though conflict, in a wider sense, is never far from the

surface. Jerusalem the golden has been known for a long time as the city that kills its prophets, but this has not prevented a multitude of prophets from near and far from going ahead with their predictions. Nothing is further from my intention than prophecy. But shall I be able to persevere or is this Saul also among the prophets? There may be something conducive to prophecy in the Jerusalem air, difficult to resist. In any case, it is my aim to note some of the changes that have taken place during my lifetime. These are personal impressions and recollections; others, of course, may have had different experiences.

Walter Laqueur

Jerusalem-Berlin-London-Washington, D.C.

July 2000–December 2005

CHAPTER 1

SUKENIK AND THE WAR OF THE ARCHAEOLOGISTS

THE 1946 JERUSALEM TELEPHONE DIRECTORY IN HAND, I looked for Sukenik, Eliezer Lipa, professor of archeology at the Hebrew University. I did not find him. He was born in Bialystok (then Russia) in 1889, received his education first at the Lomza and Slobodka *yeshivas* (rabbinical college would be the closest comparison), arrived in Palestine in 1912, and qualified as a teacher in 1914 at the newly founded teachers' seminary in Bet Hakerem.

During World War I he was expelled from Palestine like most Jews who were not Ottoman citizens. He later served in the Jewish Legion (established in Egypt), fighting on the side of the Allies. After the war he studied archaeology at Berlin University, Dropsie College, Philadelphia, and the Dominican Biblical Seminary, Jerusalem. He was employed by the Hebrew University as a field archaeologist, but not until 1935 did he became a lecturer. Three years later he was made professor and head of the University Museum of Jewish antiquities.

My first encounter with Dr. Sukenik was as a student in my home-town in Germany. He gave a lecture about recent excavations in

Palestine. The next meeting was ten years later, in December 1947. Serving as an official of the Jerusalem journalists' association, I invited him to address one of our background meetings. These meetings always took place on early Friday afternoons at the Café Palatin, owned by the brothers Warshawski. There had been reports that Prof. Sukenik had obtained some very important scrolls, possibly the earliest ever found. But two weeks earlier the riots had broken out in Jerusalem in reaction to the U.N. decision to partition Palestine. The armed attacks and counterattacks continued throughout 1948 and eventually, after the departure of the British, led to full-scale war.

This was the backdrop of our meeting in December 1947. We were all preoccupied with the military situation and whether we would reach home safely. Thus we missed the full significance of what Sukenik was telling us. The single most important archaeological discovery in Palestine of the twentieth century was eclipsed by the dangers that surrounded us all.

Sukenik was married to Hasia Fainsod, as lively and dynamic a character as her husband. She was one of Palestine's leading kindergarten teachers, an organizer, and a second-to-none fighter for women's rights.

Eliezer and Hasia Sukenik had three sons. Yigael, the eldest, attended the Rehavia gymnasium (high school *cum* junior college) and joined the hagana or the Jewish defense force (where he was given the name Yadin). When war broke out in 1948 he became chief of staff of the newly founded Israeli army. He was not yet thirty. Yadin married Carmela Ruppin, the daughter of a leading Zionist official who lived across the street at 30 Ramban Street.

The Sukenik's second son was Matatyahu. He served in the air force and was killed in the War of Independence at the age of nineteen.

The third son, Josef (Yossi) became a leading actor and one of the founders of the Cameri Theater; he died in May 2001. He began acting while still a kindergartner and continued to appear on the stage up until the month before he died. He had eleven thousand appearances on the stage ranging from Tevye the milkman in *Fiddler on the Roof* to the eponymous role in *Zorba the Greek* to Willy Loman in *Death of a Salesman.* He was one of the most popular actors in the country. Hanna Maron, his ex-wife and co-star (she was the little girl dancing on the pavement in Fritz Lang's *M*), said, after his death, that there was no single actor who did not delight in working with him.

Eliezer Sukenik was an indefatigable excavator, above all in Mandatory Palestine. He oversaw the digs of the Third Wall in Jerusalem and other excavations in the City of David, the town of Samaria, Bet Alpha, Afula, Hadera and, of course, the immediate vicinity of Jerusalem. He excavated synagogues (including the Dura Europos synagogue in Syria) and tombs. He found a bronze age site and Chalcolythic remains. Sukenik founded and belonged to countless associations: the Palestine Historical and Ethnographic Society, the Committee of Jewish Palestine Exploration, the Palestine Oriental Society. He lectured at the British Academy in London and chaired a meeting of the International Archaeological Congress in Berlin. He was not the greatest theorist of his time, but he was an enterprising man, open to new ideas and findings, with a good all-around knowledge of the field. He was someone who had learned his profession largely through working in it.

The story of the Dead Sea Scrolls is now a familiar one. It begins in early 1947 in the caves of Qumran, when three bedouin boys of the Ta'amira tribe were searching for a stray goat. They came across pottery containers in one of the caves. Inside them they found rolls of parchment. The boys took them to Khalil Iskander Shahin, a shoemaker in Bethlehem who was also a part-time antiquities dealer. Shahin contacted Mar Athanasius Samuel, the metropolitan of the Syrian Christian church, who wanted to buy them. But when the boys went to the Monastery of St. Mark, the gatekeeper turned them away. They were offended, and so they instead got in touch with a dealer in the Old City of Jerusalem named Salahi, who phoned his old customer Professor Sukenik. Sukenik, realizing that the scrolls were very old indeed, bought them.

Consulting with colleagues, Sukenik established that the scrolls contained half of the book of Isaiah and many psalms. They also contained a story of the war of the sons of light against the sons of darkness, which obviously was not part of the Bible. The oldest Hebrew texts available in 1947 dated to approximately AD 900 and had been found in the Cairo *genizah,* whereas the Dead Sea scrolls, as was clear even from this cursory examination, had been written during the period before Christ. In a first attempt to date these manuscripts Sukenik estimated that most were written in the two centuries before Christ and that they emanated in all probability from the Essenes, a proto Christian chiliastic sect. This is the general consensus to this day.

To say that the Dead Sea Scrolls caused a sensation would be an understatement. There was reason to assume that there were more scrolls and immediately a search began. But the war engulfed the country, and Jerusalem was divided. Communication between the two parts of the city became virtually impossible. After hostilities ceased, the search continued for many years.

It was learned that Mar Athanasius Samuel had in fact acquired four more scrolls for one hundred ten dollars. He too suspected that these scrolls were very valuable, if not unique, and he tried to sell them in the United States for three million dollars. They were eventually bought by Yigael Yadin for a quarter of a million dollars.

Ultimately some eight hundred scrolls were found, the great majority in fragments. Why are they so important? Any artifact two thousand years old is important. These were the oldest known manuscripts of the Bible, a work of profound meaning to millions of people. In addition, the scrolls contained nonbiblical material that no one had ever seen before, or even imagined to exist. The scrolls, most in Hebrew, some in Aramaic, were of equal interest to historians specializing in the origins of Christianity.

However, as is usual with important archaeological discoveries, there were controversies about origin and meaning of the scrolls almost from the beginning. Some of the quarrels were rooted in personal antagonism. For instance, John Strugnell, head of the team working in the Rockefeller Museum in the Arab part of Jerusalem, once called Judaism a horrible religion, the only antidote being a conversion to Christianity.

But the main complaint was that work on the scrolls and their publication was proceeding too slowly. According to some conspiracy theorists, publication of the scrolls held by the Rockefeller museum in Jerusalem was deliberately delayed because it was feared that they might do irreparable harm to the Christian religion. But the real reasons were far more prosaic. The material consisted of many tens of thousands of little pieces, a giant jigsaw puzzle that had to be put together, frequently by people without a sufficient knowledge of the language in which the scrolls were written. (Keep in mind that languages change over time, and this was Hebrew from two thousand years ago. In addition, people had stopped speaking Aramaic thirteen thousand years before.)

The vanity of the editors also caused delays; every one insisted that he and only he had to right to publish first. By 1990 only 20 percent of the fragments had been published. Only the advent of the computer helped to speed up the process. As of today almost all the material has appeared, the only exception being a volume with some Aramaean fragments.

The scrolls fascinated not only the experts, they also caught the imagination of the public. Tens of thousands of people not previously interested in early manuscripts or archaeology streamed to see these extraordinary exhibits in the Jerusalem Museum and elsewhere. Sukenik did not live to witness the endless disputes—or the endless excitement—concerning his great discovery.

The disputes spread, leading to a wider confrontation among archaeologists and biblical scholars during the 1980s and 1990s. This series of battles began with the publication in Denmark of two essays demanding a basic rethinking of the Bible and biblical archaeology. The authors' basic assumption was that the Bible was a literary document, not a historical one, and that it had been composed many centuries after the events it described. There were major discrepancies between what the Bible said and what the archaeologists had found. For this reason the Bible should not be the compass guiding the archaeologists; they ought to forget about it or consult it only after they had finished their work. The Bible, it was argued, was not a primary source but merely tradition, legend, and folklore. Among the discrepancies between what the Bible said and what the archaeologists had found (or failed to find), was the fact that references to the palaces of King David and King Solomon or the walls of Jericho, which figure so prominently in the Old Testament, had not been discovered.

These assertions were not as revolutionary as the proponents of the Copenhagen School (or "minimalists") may have thought. The historical accuracy of the Bible had after all been questioned or negated for many centuries by nonbelievers and scholars alike. Even the most pious Christians and Jews among the archeologists had difficulties with the report that two million Israelites had crossed a suddenly receded Red Sea, nor did they take the claim literally that Methuselah lived some 960 years. They did not believe the story of Noah's ark and had doubts whether Lot's wife was really transformed into a pillar of salt.

The critical school among the Bible exegists in nineteenth-century Germany had also drawn attention to the many contradictions in the

Bible, and the fact that it had been produced by a variety of authors at various times. Among the archaeologists doing research in the Near East there were few (if any) Christian or Jewish fundamentalists who believed the world was created in six days some six thousand years earlier. If so, what was the novelty in the arguments of the Copenhagen School?

The Copenhagen critique condemned biblical archaeology, claiming that it had done only harm. It had led archaeologists to preoccupy themselves not with determining what actually happened but with trying to prove that, at least broadly speaking, the Bible was correct. Three examples of how biblical archaeologists had been led astray were Jerusalem, Jericho and Megiddo, they said.

Israeli archaeologists had claimed all along that Jerusalem was the city of David, and a royal capital of a kingdom united. Throughout history pictures and maps had been produced of the alleged capital, its walls and other buildings which, the minimalists claimed, were pure fantasy. The archaeological findings from the golden era of the Israelites were few and far between and also ambiguous. In all probability there was no united kingdom, there was no proof that David and Solomon ever existed, and Jerusalem, if it had been inhabited in the tenth century BC, was a small and unimportant highland village, not a capital of some mighty kingdom.

The excavations in the City of David in Jerusalem did result in findings dating to the middle Bronze Age (fourth or third century BC) and the Iron Age (first century BC) but very little from the tenth century. And this was, according to tradition, the period of the kingdom of David and Solomon. If so, Jerusalem was not a rich center of trade and the seat of a bureaucracy ruling a great empire, but at best the residence of a few hundred peasants. Thus, because the existing accounts of Jerusalem and the history of ancient Israel are not born out by scientific archaeological evidence, they are a mere invention, an ideological construct.

As for Jericho, if the Bible were "true," there would be traces of the mud brick wall that fell down when Joshua sounded his trumpet. Some expeditions in the 1930s indeed found traces of a destroyed or collapsed wall, but more intensive searches showed that this wall belonged to a much earlier period and could not possibly have been the one that appears in the Bible. Yigael Yadin developed a theory that those who had built the wall of Joshua had probably used the remnants of the earlier wall, but a number of things made this version appear unlikely. There was no trace of a settlement in the thirteenth-century BC Jericho, when the invasion of the children of Israel was reported to have taken place. There had apparently been a settlement one hundred years earlier but it was small and, like other places in Canaan, it had not been fortified. In other words, the stories about the Israeli invasion were based on legends not historical facts.

Some cities of Canaan (such as Hazor) had undoubtedly been attacked and destroyed, but it was by no means clear when exactly and by whom and whether there had been one attack or a whole series. To follow this logic, the children of Israel had never been in Egypt, never crossed the Red Sea, never erred for many years in the desert. Instead, a network of highland villages came into being in the central hill country of Canaan around 1200 BC, populated by nomads who gradually became farmers, and these (as a leading archaeologist put it) were the first Israelites.

Megiddo, located halfway between Haifa and Nablus, has been, next to Jerusalem, the most intensively studied place in Palestine, beginning with a German expedition launched by an amateur archaeologist in 1903. The diggings continued in the 1920s and '30s and after a long interruption were resumed by Yadin and teams from the universities of Jerusalem and Tel Aviv as well as American universities such as Pennsylvania State. These diggings resulted in a multitude of findings and theories. Yadin had gone to Megiddo because he believed that King Solomon's stables had been located there. He did find the remains of a big palace but it belonged apparently to a later period, fifty or one hundred years after Solomon's reign, that is to say, to King Ahab or King Omri. Some leading archaeologists believed with Yadin that the building served as a stable whereas others thought that they were store houses or markets or barracks for troops. The debates about Megiddo continue to this day. But so do the debates about Troy; the archaeologists claim that it was a very important trading center whereas some historians deny this.

The minimalists believing that the Bible is either worthless or almost worthless as a historical source are not a monolithic camp, nor are they all concentrated in Copenhagen; some can be found in England and Scotland, others in Israel. In their extreme form, their views are openly politically motivated. Thus one recent book belonging to this school appeared with the title *The Invention of Ancient Israel: The Silencing of Palestinian History.* It was written not by an archaeologist but a professor of biblical studies whose main authority is Edward Said, a literary scholar who developed an interest in stones late in life but could not by any stretch of imagination be called an archaeologist. According to this author, biblical studies are a subdivision of "Orientalism," that is, imperialist and colonialist ideology. Biblical studies have not only falsified history, they have dispossessed the Palestinians of their land and their past. To correct this injustice and to put the record straight, the ancient history of Palestine should be studied in the future within the framework of "cultural" and "subaltern" (post colonial) studies.

Statements of this kind (and the jargon in which they are put) may lead one to dismiss this whole school of thought out of hand. For a number of reasons this would be a mistake. Nationalism has had an impact on archaeology all over the world, and furthermore there was indeed a "Bible bias" in view of the central importance of the Old Testament for both Christians and Jews. In Nazi Germany, where I had the misfortune to attend school for a number of years, the official version formulated by linguist-turned-archaeologist Gustav Kossinna claimed that all European civilization, including ancient Greece and Rome, had been created by the Germans. In the Soviet Union, the so-called Norman theory of the foundation of a Russian state was out-lawed because it would have meant that the founding initiative had come not from Slavs but from foreigners.

Nationalist and even chauvinist bias was by no means limited to fascist and communist regimes. In one form or another it can be found to the present day in virtually every part of the world. It is now partic-ularly strong in many former colonial countries such as India and Pakistan countries in search of identity and continuity. Some question whether the "Aryans" were the original inhabitants of the Indus valley and of Punjab, or whether they were the invaders. Indians and Pakistanis cannot even agree on the terms used in their polemics; Pakistanis call the river Indus, whereas the Indians talk about the river Sindhu or, more recently, Saraswati and its Harappan civilization.

The impact of nationalism on archaeology has been pronounced in contemporary Greece and the smaller European countries as well as among the national minorities, because they feel the need to prove their historical rights even more acutely than the bigger countries. Macedonia is an excellent example, but there are hundreds of others. As Ernest Renan wrote more than one hundred years ago, historical error is a crucial factor in the creation of a nation. If archaeology were the decisive criterion for national borders in the modern world, virtu-ally everyone would have to pick up and move. Humankind would be in perpetual motion, since the question as to who was where first can never be answered in a satisfactory way.

Archaeology has become, as a Palestinian archaeologist has put it, the second religion for Israelis and Palestinians alike. This was not true for Herzl's or Weizman's generation, who were preoccupied with the plight of the Jewish people rather than the excavations in the City of David. But in later years, archaeology became something like a national hobby with Moshe Dayan taking the lead, followed by many other eager amateurs.

And it is certainly true that in their enthusiasm to discover Jewish roots in Palestine religious-nationalist extremists as well as, on occasion, those experts who tended to overlook the Bible's discrepancies, got carried away.

In the heat of battle these archaeologists are blind to the fact that their studies have limited relevance to the present situation. Both Hindus and Muslims have lived on the Indian subcontinent for a very long time and it does not really matter whether the Indus Valley civilization between 3000 and 1500 BC (and in the Saka Parthian period and under Kushan rule) developed separately from India or not. The children of Israel lived in Palestine for a long time and it will probably never be established who came first, them or the others. But whether the history of the Jews can be traced back twenty-eight hundred years as opposed to a full three thousand—what European country dates back that far?

Those who launched the modern archaeological exploration of the Near East were neither religious Jews nor nationalist Arabs but rather Englishmen like Austen Layard and Flinders Petrie, and Americans like J. H. Breasted and W. F. Albright, the father of biblical archaeology. They followed many wrong tracks, as do archaeologists everywhere, but their accomplishments were enormous. Even if they did not find Noah's ark on Mount Ararat, or the Tower of Babel, they made decisive progress in exploring the history of the region and its ancient civilization. Some of them were decidedly romantic, and often embellished the past. Gertrude Bell and T. E. Lawrence (of Arabia), both leading Arabists of their time were, after all, archaeologists. Instead of erecting statues in their honor, they are now denounced for their "Orientalist" aberrations.

To what extent does all this affect current debates? It has been argued that wide sections of the Israeli and Jewish public simply cannot accept the idea that their traditions may be rooted in myth rather than scientific fact. Of course the distant origins of every people and nation are rooted in myth. Why should the Jews be an exception? The minimalists have overstated their case. While it is true that parts of the Bible are not easily borne out by research, other parts bear a strong resemblance. If biblical archaeologists have misdated certain events and trends by fifty or even two hundred years, if the palace at Megiddo was built by King Omri and not by Solomon, this fact (if fact it is) should not cause any sort of collective depression in the state of Israel or the Jewish world.

For a long time there was no direct archaeological evidence of King David and his kingdom. But then, in 1993, a stela was found in Tel Dan, a victory monument erected by Hazael, King of Aram, referring both to the house of David and his kingdom or, to be precise, to a King of Israel named Jehoram who lived about 840 BC. This caused unhappiness among the minimalists. Some of them accused those who had found the stela of forgery, whereas others thought that David could be a place name. As usual there was no absolute certainly, but there was a very high degree of probability. The minimalist attacks on Israeli archaeologists are unfair. Most of them hail from the left of the political spectrum, or are at least neutral; they are not trying to buttress any specific ideologies with the fruits of their excavations.

But let us assume for argument's sake that David and his kingdom were indeed a figment of the imagination, that they were at best a poor tribe originating in Mesopotamia, what if Jerusalem at the time was not a mighty capital but a desolate hamlet at the border of the desert? What impact would it have on Jewish identity three thousand years later?

It might well be true that Jerusalem in the year 1000 BC was a very small place and that the whole population of the Judean hills was no more than perhaps one hundred thousand (out of an approximate Middle East population of nine million at the time), and that neither Israel nor Judea was a mighty empire by the standard of later ages. There is the Hebrew language, which can be traced back some three thousand years, considerably longer than any of the languages in which the quarrels of the archaeologists take place. There is the appearance of monotheism and the place of Jerusalem in the Jewish liturgy, from "If I forget thee, Jerusalem" to the "Next Year in Jerusalem" prayer in the Passover Haggada. In other words, there was a settlement there, which is more than can be said about, for instance, Washington and Moscow.

Berlin, for another example, only came into being two thousand years later. Copenhagen, where some of the minimalists reside, erstwhile a tiny fishing village called Havn, was given by King Waldemar I to Absalon, archbishop of Zealand, in 1167, again two thousand years after Jerusalem. Paris, first called Oppicum, later Lutetia, seems to have been founded by Caesar in 54 BC. (There was a settlement there in the Neolothicum, around 2000 BC, but there is little evidence of continued human settlement during the following periods.)

What we know about the emergence of Rome and Athens was largely based on mythical figures such as Romulus and Remus and Theseus. Rome did exist as an Etruscan village in 575 BC but not much earlier. Athens was a tiny village with the earliest traces on the Acropolis dating back to the thirteenth century BC. And it was only over a number of centuries that the villages of Attica grew together to form something like a state (a process called *synoikismos*). It could well be that a similar process took place in the hills of Judea between the three hundred or so small villages, remnants of which have been found.

In brief, to say that a place was old or not so old, big or small, is a statement that makes sense only by comparison, in a historical context.

What if it were true that the Bible in its Hebrew text dates back only to the Hellenistic period? What impact does such a fact have on current political debates? Whenever the Bible was composed, it was still considerably earlier than any of the comparable religious texts in Europe or the Near East. It remains a historical, theological, and literary document of great importance in the annals of mankind.

Only when Palestinian Arab archaeologists begin to engage in systematic research might they be able to prove or disprove various theories; for instance, that they are descended from the ancient Philistines, and if Philistines were invaders or native inhabitants of the country. The native Philistine theory faces problems, among them being a perceived break in cultural tradition—Philistine pottery is different from late bronze or early Iron Age. Explanations will doubtless be found for this and other unsolved questions. Regardless, no one doubts that the Palestinian Arabs have been in Palestine for a very long time.

That Israeli and Palestinian archeologists have become so passionately involved is to be expected. It is decidedly less obvious why other archeologists have become equally emotionally involved. Is it just because they care deeply about their work, or are there ideological issues in play? One deeply concerned archaeologist who came down squarely on the Arab side was Albert Glock, an American Lutheran, who was eventually head of the archeology department at the Palestinian Bir Zeit University. Glock was killed there in January 1992 in circumstances that appeared at first mysterious. He was not one of the leading figures in the field, and he was about to retire. It seemed odd that anyone could have had an interest to remove him from the scene. Gradually it appeared that an overzealous local cell of Hamas had been involved. For Hamas, every foreigner, however strongly pro-Palestinian, is automatically suspect.

It could well be that the ideological battlefield will migrate from archaeology to the genetics, as scientists will try to establish whether there has been biological continuity and how far back it dates. Attention is shifting from pottery and stelae to the Y chromosome and mitochondrial DNA. Promising as it may sound, such a practice is bound to be as inconclusive as the archeologists' attempts to find answers. Research shows that Ashkenazi priests have a distinctive set of genetic markers, but it also shows that Jews in Europe, as well as those still in North Africa, have many genetic markers in common with the non-Jews among whom they live. Miscegenation in the Near East over the centuries and millennia has been such that it is impossible to talk about one race as being distinct from another. There are no "pure races" in the modern world, and for all we know there hasn't been since Adam and Eve had to leave paradise.

Fifty-eight years have passed since the emergence of the Dead Sea Scrolls. Eliezer Sukenik died in 1953, well before the scrolls were published. Yigael Yadin left the army to finish his studies in archaeology and, following in the steps of his father, became a professor. He was in charge of many excavations, and had yet another career as a politician when Shinui, a new political party, was founded in the 1970s. After a promising start it fell apart. Yadin was a success neither as a minister or deputy prime minister. He died in 1984. A street is named after him in northern Jerusalem leading from the Nablus Road to Ramot. Yet another road bears his name in a new settlement outside Jerusalem.

The Dead Sea Scrolls can be viewed at the Israeli Museum in a domed building called the Shrine of the Book. The white dome is shaped like the lid of the clay vessel in which the scrolls were found. In the middle of the building is a drum that contains a facsimile of the Isaiah scroll (the original scroll was displayed in the early years, but it showed signs of disintegration and now is kept in a special humidity- and temperature-controlled environment).

But what of the history of ancient Israel, the story that never was, as some have been claiming? What of the patriarchs, Abraham the man from Ur in Mesopotamia, Isaac, Jacob, Joseph, and the others? Are they legends, or were they real historical figures? Alas, we shall never know—archaeology is about civilizations, not about the biography of individuals. The consensus of the scholars was that while the first eleven chapters of Genesis belong to the realm of myth, the later chapters, including the story of the patriarchs, may well be rooted in history and were first recorded in the tenth century, not so long after the events they describe.

What of David, his kingdom, and Jerusalem, his residence? Historians have become more cautious in their conclusions than a generation ago, but most serious scholars tend to believe that there was such a king who, using a favorable international constellation (the eclipse of Egypt and Assyria) made his country, albeit for a short time only, one of the great powers in the Near East. In the meantime, biblical archaeology continues to be of fascination to a great many people all over the world; the bimonthly *Biblical Archaeology Review* published in Washington, DC, has a circulation of 190,000. Archaeology continues to be the national hobby in Israel and soon, no doubt, it will be in the territories under the Palestinian Authority. Perhaps we shall have one day a minister of archaeology.

CHAPTER 2

GOLDA MEIR AND THE
POST-ZIONISTS

G OLDA MABOWITZ TOOK THE NAME MEIR IN 1956 when she became foreign minister. She was born Kiev, Russia, on May 3,1898. After migrating to Israel, she lived in Rosh Rehavia; the official address was 6 Keren Kayemet Street. She worked at the Jewish Agency building just across the road. Like other leaders of the Jewish community, she also had a small apartment in Tel Aviv. Rosh Rehavia was a collection of apartments, big and small (hers was on the small side) built in the 1930s on land belonging to the adjoining Ratisbonne monastery. It was U shaped, Bauhaus style, and in the courtyard there was an art deco glass fountain which, as I recall, seldom if ever operated.

The Jewish Agency building, which also housed some other Jewish institutions, had been built at about the same time; the architect had been told to design something that was impressive but no higher than two floors—not an easy assignment. It took him eight years.

Meir's father was a poor carpenter. The family migrated to the United States when Meir was eight and settled in Milwaukee,

Wisconsin. She attended school and a teachers' seminar and did some war work. In 1915, she joined Poale Zion, the Zionist socialist party. She married Morris Meyerson in 1917 and went to Palestine in 1921. In a letter to her sister she wrote that her husband was no beauty, but that he had a beautiful soul. They had a son, Menahem (later a musician in America), and a daughter, Sarah (later a member of a kibbutz in the Negev). They remained officially married until Meyerson's death in 1951, but they were separated in the 1930s, partly because Morris fell ill and was not up to manual labor, partly because Mier throughout her life always gave priority to her public duties rather than her obligations to her family.

Golda Meir and her husband went first to Merhavia, a collective settlement in the Jezreel Valley, where she spent three happy years despite the heavy and unfamiliar work, and after that four unhappy years in Jerusalem where she felt very lonely. Eventually she was offered work in Tel Aviv, where she worked first for Solel Boneh, the union building enterprise. Later she became an organizer for the Women's Labor Council and the Histadrut executive (General Federation of Jewish Labor). She served on the union sick fund and on more boards than can possibly be enumerated. During the late 1920s and early '30s, she went to America six times on lengthy missions for her party, and from 1932 to 1934 she stayed there as the emissary of the Hechalutz (Pioneer's organization).

At the end of World War II she became active in Zionist diplomacy. The first time I visited her in her busy and crowded kitchen in Rosh Rehavia (where many meetings took place and important decisions were made), she had just become acting head of the political department of the Jewish Agency, something like deputy foreign minister. The meeting took place in her small apartment because the British Mandatory government had closed down the Jewish Agency building suspecting the Jewish leadership of collusion in a terrorist campaign that culminated in the bombing of the King David Hotel in July 1946. Almost one hundred British nationals, Jews, and Arabs were killed in that attack.

Golda Meir's Hebrew was slightly accented and she was no great stylist (she was a much better public speaker in English and Yiddish). Despite the fact that she had a heart condition, she continued to chain-smoke; she used to say "I won't die young," and this proved to be correct. She had many sterling qualities: she was fearless and proud, she was purposeful, she made a formidable appearance, and on occasion she could have a good sense of humor. ("Why did Moses have to lead the children of Israel to the one country in the Middle East that had no oil?") She disliked formality, and was wholly unpretentious.

And yet I was not particularly taken with her. I found her to be strident, and too rigid for someone in public affairs. There was a certain coldness in her, but those who knew her better insist that she was a passionate, impulsive woman with a warm heart. I regret that I had no opportunity to know that part of her. I had the impression that she did not like, and perhaps distrusted, Jews of German origin; she thought they were too soft and lacked backbone.

Golda Meir acquitted herself well during that summer of 1946 when the political leadership of Palestinian Jewry was detained by the security forces or, like Ben-Gurion, were forced into exile. The immediate crisis passed within a few months, and she again took her place in the second rank of the leadership.

Golda Meir enjoyed a spectacular career after the establishment of the Israeli state.

Earlier still, in November 1947, and again in May 1948, still deputy head of the political department of the Jewish Agency, she had dressed as an Arab woman and met King Abdallah of Jordan inside Arab territory. Revisionist historians regarded this as proof of

Jewish-Jordanian collusion to divide Palestine among themselves in violation of the United Nations decision. Such collusion would not have been the worst crime in history, but the historical truth seems to be less fanciful. Although the two sides talked, they distrusted each other and there was no agreement. Meanwhile, the Jewish Agency building was severely damaged by a car bomb; an Arab driver working for the local U.S. Consulate general had entered the courtyard and detonated the explosives.

Meir was a signatory of the Declaration of Foundation of the State of Israel on May 15, 1948, and soon afterwards became the first Israeli ambassador to the Soviet Union, warmly welcomed by Moscow Jewry, considerably less cordially by the Soviet leadership. After her return in 1949, she became minister of labor and introduced Israel's social security system. In 1956 she was appointed foreign minister and remained in office for ten years. Between 1966 and 1968, she was the secretary-general of the Israeli Labor party. After Israel's brilliant victory in the Six-Day War, and following the sudden death of Levi Eshkol in 1969, she became prime minister.

Golda Meir became a legend in her own lifetime—the mother of the nation, one of the greatest women of the century, a role model for thousands. Her autobiography was widely read and praised; after her death streets and schools were named after her, not only in Israel. Her likeness was on stamps and coins. *A Woman Called Golda,* a three-hour docudrama, marked Ingrid Bergman's last film appearance and she won an Emmy for it.

But history has not dealt kindly with her since her death in 1978. The initially successful Egyptian attack in 1973 occurred on her watch. It is probably unfair to place all the blame for the early Israeli setbacks on her; others in the government, including the military, had ignored the warnings that had been received in Jerusalem. There had been too much self-confidence, even hubris, in high places in

Jerusalem. Golda Meir is to blame, however, for the lack of political initiatives during her years as prime minister. She was a disciple of Ben-Gurion, but without Ben-Gurion's vision. Her years in power were years of stagnation. She should never have been prime minister.

After the Six-Day War, Israel and the subsequent Israeli governments were flushed with the unexpected magnitude of that victory. They were slow to realize the enormous problems of occupation, and of governing the hostile populations of West Bank and Gaza. For the first time in the history of Israel there was a chance for negotiations with the Palestinians and the Arabs in general; previously the Arabs had been unwilling to even accept Israel as established by the borders of 1948. But no one took advantage of the opportunity. Minister of Defense Moshe Dayan, among the more cautious elements in the government, waited for a telephone call which never came.

True, the Arabs were not ready to negotiate either, and neither side was psychologically ready for a compromise. This is beyond dispute. But there still should have been a unilateral Israeli withdrawal. There would have been a tremendous outcry in Israel and enormous resistance to overcome: why give up territories that Israeli soldiers had given their lives for? Some of Golda Meir's deputies, such as Yisrael Galili, even claimed that the possession of Gaza was essential for Israel's security. Yigal Alon and Shimon Peres were among the dubious pioneers of the ill-starred settlements on the West Bank.

The West Bank should have been given up because Israel would be better off in the long run without millions of hostile subjects. And given the fact that it would have to withdraw anyway in the end, why not from a position of strength rather than under pressure? This pattern was to repeat itself in Lebanon, when, under Ehud Barak, Israeli forces were withdrawn. It came more than ten years too late and was interpreted as a sign of Israeli weakness. The Israelis were running, the Palestinians thought, so why make concessions to them?

Neither side was ready for a compromise. The willingness and ability to force through unpopular but necessary measures is always the measure of true leadership. There is no way to know for certain, but I believe that the majority of Israelis, kicking and screaming, would have put up with a unilateral withdrawal. Unfortunately, neither Meir nor her predecessors saw the necessity of doing so. Unlike Ben-Gurion, she did not understand that there was a Palestinian people and a national movement; like Menachem Begin and the leaders of the right-wing Likud, she thought that perhaps somehow one day they would vanish.

She shared, in retrospect, responsibility for yet another failure: the decline and fall of Labor Zionism. She and the other members of the old guard of Mapai, the ruling party, should not have clung to power but passed it on to a younger generation of leaders. They were getting on in years and could not provide dynamic leadership. By failing to do so, she helped to bring about the victory of Begin and Likud just one year before her death. Again, there are no certainties. Perhaps Mapai had been in power for too long, perhaps there was no successor generation to take over. All we know is that no attempt was made.

Golda Meir belonged to a highly idealistic generation of pioneers. In their mental and emotional make-up, they were the progeny of the young Russian revolutionaries, motivated by dreams of a new society in a new land, working toward a solution of the national and social question, committed to living in dignity and to creating a home for the many millions that would come after them. Had they been motivated by gain, the young pioneers from Eastern Europe would have been better advised to emigrate to what was then called *di goldene medine,* America the golden. Meir, who was already there, would no doubt have had a brilliant career even though she would not have become president or secretary of state. What impelled these pioneers to forgo the many amenities of the United States for the poverty, the disease, and the personal suffering in a faraway, backward country?

It was the dream of Zionism.

Golda died in December 1978, and by that time Zionism was under siege. In Russia it had become a synonym for fascism. Communist anti-Zionism was in fact Russia's particular brand of anti-Semitism. That the Arabs regarded Zionism as an abomination goes without saying. For the European left it was, with some exceptions, viewed as a subspecies of Western imperialism. The United Nations had passed a resolution branding Zionism as racialism.

Thus it was not surprising that a few years after Golda Meir's death a new movement of young Israeli academics appeared on the scene calling itself post-Zionist. The Zionist dream, as many of them saw it, had been a nightmare since it caused so much unhappiness for so many people. This new movement had a variety of motives. It emerged at a time when Israeli governments and also sections of society gravitated more and more to the right. As a result, the intellectual opposition to this new status quo became increasingly radical in the opposite direction. Marxism as a serious intellectual force had disappeared in Israel, and the Communist party, such as it was, became almost entirely Arab in composition. Thus a new ideology was needed.

But there were also other influences, intellectual trends mainly from the United States that, as so often happens, reached Israel after some delay (the famous cultural lag). The main American imports were the critical school and, later, postmodernism. Above all the ideological shift was a revolt against the generation of parents and grandparents, who had been among the founders of the state. The post-Zionists were almost entirely confined to the universities, and their attacks were directed mainly against Labor Zionism, that is, the movement to which Golda Meir had belonged. They shared no common language with the right wing and the ultraorthodox. Immigrants from the former Soviet Union or Morocco would not have understood their discourses about para-history and meta-narratives; they had not heard about hegemony and did not know what an imagined community was.

The post-Zionists were not a monolithic group. Some were anti-Zionist and anti-Israeli, others were more moderate. Some regarded themselves as loyal citizens of the state, provided the state kept its democratic character. Some came from the Young Communist League (Banki) or the Trotskyites (Matzpen), but others were not socialists at all. Some found their inspiration in postmodernism, an intellectual fashion that originated in France and later gained popularity in the English literature departments of American universities. Others were followers of postcolonial studies, another academic fashion whose gurus were American professors, more often than not expatriates of Arab or Indian origin. Some post-Zionists are against all kinds of exclusionary nationalism, others support progressive Arab nationalism but reject Zionism which they see not as the national liberation movement of the Jewish people but as merely reactionary.

By and large, the post-Zionists agreed on the following basic tenets. They argued, to begin with, that the historical connection between the Jews and Palestine had been much more tenuous than commonly believed. They did not go as far as the mufti of Jerusalem who argued (in 2001) that no single stone had been found in Jerusalem that proved that the Israelites had ever been in Palestine. But they asserted that most of the essential elements in Zionist ideology, from Massada (the last stand of a group of Jewish zealots against the Romans in about AD 70 that ended in collective suicide) to the death of Trumpeldor in 1920 (a Zionist who was an officer in the Russian army and who died defending a Jewish village in Galilee against Arab attackers), belonged to the realm of mythology. According to this mythology Trumpeldor's last words were, "It is good to die for one's country."

As for the Zionist settlement in Palestine, beginning in the 1880s the post-Zionists claimed that it had been in the deplorable tradition of

Western colonialism in Asia and Africa. This comparison was not very convincing because colonies are traditionally acquired to make money—to exploit the native population and to extract raw materials. Palestine, from an economic point of view, was always a losing proposition.

The post-Zionists further argued that the very concepts used by the Zionists such as *aliyah* (immigration to Israel, literally, "ascent"), *haluziut* (pioneering), *geulah* (redemption of the land), and *tekumah* (rebirth), were ideological constructs, as was the so-called myth about the War of Independence in 1948—the Jewish community had never been faced with a real military danger or destruction, since the armies attacking it were so weak.

During World War II, according to the post-Zionist version, the Zionist leadership did little to save European Jewry; they were focused instead on establishing a Jewish state. As for the mass immigration after 1945 from Europe as well as Iraq, Morocco, and other countries, the post-Zionists said it was generated partly by coercion, partly by deceitful propaganda and false promises. Above all, the Jewish state was born in sin inasmuch as it was established through violence and caused the exodus of hundreds of thousands of Palestinians. That atrocities were committed by the Israelis during the fighting but also during the years after goes without saying. Many Arab villages had been depopulated and were razed to the ground. The state which came into being was not only capitalist but produced a militarization of society.

The post-Zionists reject what they call the "Judaeocentric, exclusionary categories" of the Zionists, such as the Law of Return, and they believe that Jewish claims on Israel are no more legitimate than, say, English claims on India.

The post-Zionists are not quite explicit with regard to what *should* have happened—whether, for instance, victims of Nazism should have stayed in Germany and Austria, and they certainly disagree on the details. But by and large there seems to be a consensus that it would have been much better if the state of Israel had never come into being. Once it existed, it should be fully democratic rather than Jewish in inspiration. This implies not just equal rights to Palestinian Arabs but the return of refugees. Such a state would no longer be Jewish in character, and Jews would be in the minority.

Some of the post-Zionist critique is political propaganda using pseudoscientific terminology. The Jewish settlement in Palestine prior to the establishment of the state has as much to do with colonialism as colonialism has with colonoscopy. Some of the critique is factually correct, but its conclusions are farfetched and naïve, at least as naïve and provincial as the Zionist ideology so much resented by the post-Zionists. To give one example, it is perfectly true that the "five Arab armies" which invaded Israel in May 1948 were not very strong or well organized or highly motivated. It is also true that the Jewish community was better educated and organized, and had the advantage of inner lines of communication. But on May 15, when the invasion took place, the Jewish state had neither a navy nor an air force, neither tanks nor artillery, so education and organization per se were not decisive strategic factors.

That much of Zionism rests on myths is beyond doubt, though not more than other national movements. Herzl, Max Nordau, and the other early Zionist leaders were secular liberals and rationalists who seldom, if ever, invoked the Bible and historical rights. The post-Zionists ignore the fact that the beginnings (though not just the beginnings) of all nations, from ancient Greece and Rome to China to the Native Americans, are rooted in myth and in folklore. This is true with regard to France from Vercingetorix onwards, to Britain, to the country of the Nibelungen, to the Scandinavian countries with their sagas, and of course the United States. It is particularly true with regard to the smaller nations from the Irish to the Basque. Wilhelm Tell and

Arnold Winkelried, the great heroes of Swiss history, probably never existed, or if they did, were very different people from what tradition says. Yet how many statues were erected in their honor during the last hundred years, and what central place do they play in Swiss history? Was there ever a Ruetli Oath, the Swiss declaration of independence, in 1291? It is quite doubtful, but in the last two centuries, following Schiller's play *Wilhelm Tell,* it became the cornerstone of the saga regarding the democratic origins of the Swiss confederacy.

Post-Zionists could argue that this happened a long time ago. True, but the myths persist everywhere. The Czech national movement was one of the most democratic but this did not prevent some of its fervent supporters from engaging in blatant forgeries (the Koeniginhofer manuscript) to reinforce its legitimate claims. And this happened at the very time the Zionist movement arose in Vienna, Prague, and Budapest. The history of Eastern Europe, the Balkans, and Russia is largely mythical. Take away the mythology, and what remains?

The early history of Islam and the Arab countries, beginning with Muhammad and the caliphs Husayn and Ali, is it not all based on well-established historical facts. The belief that the origin of any nation is rooted in more or less scientific, objective, historical facts that have been established beyond reasonable doubt is just that, a belief, and there is no reason to assume that Zionist history could have been different. Every people needs its heroes, from Siegfried to El Cid to Joan of Arc to Alexander Nevsky to Bar Kochba and the Maccabees. It is only much later that revisionist historians appear on the scene to deconstruct and debunk, proving that the heroes really were not that heroic, or did not exist in the first place.

What of the contention that the state of Israel was born in sin, that violence was used, that Arabs were expelled—whether as a matter of policy or in the course of fighting—that atrocities took place? The

Zionists bought Arab lands, and it was not unnatural that suspicious Palestinians, resentful of the arrivals from abroad, should attack them in 1920, in 1929, between 1936–39 and then again in 1948. What people will not defend its homeland? All this is true, but it disregards that every state is born in sin. It is difficult to think of a single state that came into being on the basis of a peaceful contract rather than through violence.

Post-Zionists would be more persuasive if they argued that since nation states cannot be built except through violence, the Zionists should never have dreamed of one. This position has been traditionally taken by critics of Zionism from various ideological vantage points—liberal internationalists, orthodox religious believers, the Communist party—that is, at least until 1948. Nationalism, especially in its most aggressive forms, gives rise to misery and bloodshed, and the world would be better off were it not divided into warring nation states. But it is divided, and the Jews have often been a persecuted minority. How relevant is the post-Zionist argument (along with that of the Arabs and other critics of Zionism) that were it not for the Nazi persecutions, a Jewish state would never have come into being? They are perfectly right—without Hitler, Zionism in all probability would have remained a small, uninfluential sectarian movement. But there *was* Hitler, and he was not the only one in his time to kill Jews on a massive scale.

The Zionists saw the coming disaster, though they did not think it would assume such enormous proportions and lead to the destruction of most of European Jewry. Owing to their work in Palestine, which led to the foundation of the state, many thousands of Jews were saved who otherwise would have perished. Later, hundreds of thousands who could not remain in their host countries would find shelter in Israel.

Let's perform an exercise in counterfactual history. What if there had been no Zionism? The post-Zionists could argue that since

Zionism was not capable to save the great majority of European Jews, it does not matter, from a world historical point of view, if more Jews were killed rather than immigrated to Palestine. And as for the postwar situation, they might argue that the Jewish survivors of Europe and those living in Arab countries would have eventually found a place in America or Australia, or would have remained to live in Iraq, Libya, Iran, or Syria—though perhaps not very comfortably, or with much dignity.

Such noble altruism, nay, self-sacrifice, among these Jews would have been admirable. But it would have been unique in the annals of humankind. Most groups of people are motivated by the instinct to survive—and at least some egotism—and it would have been a miracle were the Jews to have behaved differently once they had a chance to do so.

Should post-Zionism be taken seriously? The brief answer is no; intellectually it contains very little that was not voiced fifty or one hundred years ago by the critics of Zionism. Politically it is a negligible force; most citizens of Israel are probably unaware of the existence of this school of thought. It is of psychological interest as a manifestation of antipatriotism such as is found occasionally on American campuses but seldom if ever in Europe, let alone in other continents. The British poet George Canning wrote about the anti-patriots, "A steady patriot of the world alone, / The friend of every country but his own." But Canning wrote about the Jacobins, and he did them a grave injustice; the *Marseillaise,* after all, invokes *l'amour sacre de la patrie.* It can be endlessly discussed whether in retrospect patriotism has done more good than evil, but this is outside the field of interest of these critics preoccupied with one sort of nationalism alone, that of the Jews.

As some of the post-Zionists saw it, the early Zionists, and especially the Labor Zionists like Golda Meir, were not so much wicked people as they were foolish, narrow-minded nationalists, worrying only about the problems of their own people and disregarding all others. True, they were not internationalists. But how would internationalists have survived in an age of aggressive nationalism?

There was the reprehensible slogan (according to the post-Zionist narrative): "Land without people to the people without land." It was never an official slogan, and in fact it had been coined by a non-Zionist. But it is true that in the early days there was a tendency among Zionists to play down the presence of the Arabs in Palestine. This was a mistake and there were warning voices within the Zionist camp from the very beginning. But let us stop for a moment. The country was not empty, but how many people lived there? There are no exact numbers for the early twentieth century, but four hundred to five hundred thousand is not an underestimate as far as the territory of the future state of Israel was concerned. Of these, not all were Arabs, and of the Arabs thousands were bedouins, that is to say, nomads.

Thus it cannot be argued that the country was heavily populated or intensively cultivated. Four hundred thousand (if there were that many), is roughly three percent of the present population of greater Cairo. True, not many Jews came, or could come, to Palestine between 1900 and 1948, and the Arab population was growing fast. But even in 1948, when the British mandate ended and Israel came into being, the Arab population of Palestine was less than half the population of Vienna. It is perhaps understandable that, seen in this light, Herzl and his colleagues should have thought that the problem was soluble, especially in view of the fact that, in 1900, a modern Palestinian national movement did not yet exist.

A critique of Zionism has to start elsewhere. Theodore Herzl's prediction, in 1898, that within fifty years a Jewish state would come into being was amazingly correct. Neither Herzl nor anyone else could foresee that the Jews of Europe did not have much time. A Jewish state that could have absorbed millions of Jews did not exist when it was needed most—in the 1930s and '40s. In other words, the Jewish state came too late. But it could not have come earlier.

Is it permissible to criticize the state of Israel? This is a rhetorical and, in the final analysis, nonsensical question. No government and no political movement is beyond criticism. But are not critics of Israel, some argue, automatically dismissed as anti-Semites even if they are Jewish? Such arguments are unacceptable, but it is also true that behind the cover of "anti-Zionism" lurks a variety of motives that ought to be called by their true name. When, in the 1950s under Stalin, the Jews of the Soviet Union came under severe attack and scores were executed, it was under the banner of anti-Zionism rather than anti-Semitism, which had been given a bad name by Adolf Hitler. When in later years the policy of Israeli governments was attacked as racist or colonialist in various parts of the world, the basis of the criticism was quite often the belief that Israel had no right to exist in the first place, not opposition to specific policies of the Israeli government.

Traditional anti-Semitism has gone out of fashion in the West except on the extreme right. But something we might call post-anti-Semitism has taken its place. It is less violent in its aims, but still very real. By and large it has not been too difficult to differentiate between genuine and bogus anti-Zionism. The test is twofold. It is almost always clear whether the attacks are directed against a specific policy carried out by an Israeli government (for instance, as an occupying power) or against the existence of Israel. Secondly, there is the test of selectivity. If from all the evils besetting the world, the misdeeds, real or imaginary, of Zionism are singled out and given constant and relentless publicity, it can be taken for granted that the true motive is not anti-Zionism but something different and more sweeping.

In retrospect, Zionism can be criticized for a number of reasons, among them the belief in the impossibility of assimilation. The fact that assimilation had been impossible in some countries during certain periods did not mean that it was doomed forever. On the contrary, assimilation and the eventual disappearance of Diaspora were inevitable. Nor was there any reason to assume, with Jacob Klatzkin and other Jewish thinkers, that there was a "spirit of Judaism." The Jewish religion has always been one of laws, observations, and taboos, not one of philosophical ideas. A national spirit might develop through living together in a land, a community of fate, speaking the same language and sharing (to a greater or lesser extent) the same beliefs, but there can be no "Jewish" spirit.

Herzl declared at the Zionist Congress that "we are one people." To what extent is this still true? Jews had lived for too long separated from each other in different parts of the world to share a great many common features. Hence the dubious character of the automatic Right of Return law, which had been passed soon after the establishment of the state. While one can see the wisdom and morality in granting citizenship to every Jew persecuted as a Jew, should citizenship be granted to every Jew as an intrinsic right? And is the state of Israel better off today as the result of the indiscriminate immigration of hundreds of thousands, most of them lacking the inspiration and the motivation of the early Zionists?

Herzl's basic intention was to restore dignity and security to the Jewish people, but how could security be achieved in a part of the world so highly charged with nationalist and fanatic religious emotions like the Middle East? (And whether it could be achieved anywhere else is equally doubtful.)

The post-Zionists' discussion along these lines has been modest. With the establishment of the state, a new age has dawned. The post-Zionists did make a contribution towards demythologizing Zionist and Jewish history; the state and society were by then strong enough to survive without all kinds of mythical constructs about historical rights. In the final analysis, a Jewish state had come into being because of the existential needs of the Jews, not because of the many Zionist precursors ranging from Shabbetai Zevi to *Daniel Deronda*.

Academics are accustomed to arguing in a universe of abstractions. Hence it was no surprise that the post-Zionists should tend to ignore reality to some extent. They were inclined to forget that they were not teaching in American or Swiss universities (in secure countries recognized by their neighbors and the rest of the world), situations very much in contrast to that of Israel, which was and is a country still under siege. The anti-Zionists decried the militarization of Israeli society and it was of course true that such a process had taken place. But it was also true that there was no real prospect of peace. This militarization had not taken place by choice: Israelis did not enjoy spending so much on their defense budget and so much of their time serving on reserve duty. Post-Zionists decried the dubious moral character of Zionism and Israel, as if morality had been a factor in the emergence of nation states or in the migrations that have been a crucial factor in the history of mankind since time immemorial.

Golda Meir and the others of her generation were not the near saints Zionist hagiography has made of them. But they were, as a leading post-Zionist has noted, idealistic and modest people who were not out for personal gain. They worked for the good of the community as they saw it. They sacrificed careers and an easy life in the pursuit of their dreams. Above all, they had their convictions. The Israeli proponents of postcolonialism had no such sacrifices to make; in fact, they could be accused of a certain duplicity. For they seem not to be bothered by the fact that many of them live and teach in countries that (they believe) are not theirs by right, that one hundred fifty years earlier had belonged to another people, in universities which would never have come into existence but for the Zionists. Some of them have moved on to Oxford, New York, and San Diego (places which, alas, also belonged to other nations at one time), but most have not.

Perhaps I have given too much space to a group of academics (with an admixture of poets, actors, and artists) who have been given publicity out of proportion with their numbers and political influence. The real backlash from the demise of Labor Zionism comes not from the assistant professors but from the right wing and the religious Orthodox. Their ideas have little impact, partly because they speak in jargon. They do this, it seems, because if they were understood, the great majority would reject it in disbelief, above all the Middle Eastern Jews on which the postcolonialists pin such high hopes. (In the elections of 2001, marginalized Beersheva with its Mizrachim—Jews of Middle Eastern and North African origin—and other fairly recent immigrants gave Sharon 72 percent of the votes; in wealthy establishment, Ashkenazi Kfar Shmaryahu, got 28 percent.) They will have no influence because, unlike the fanatics of the right, they will not fight for their ideas, such as they are, and this is always decisive in politics.

After Golda Meir had retired, three years before her death she wrote her autobiography. She observed:

"When it became fashionable [in later years] for young people to deride my generation for its rigidity, conventionality, and loyalty to the Establishment, it was about intellectual rebels like A. D. Gordon [a Russian-Jewish Tolstoyan who in middle age went to work the land in Palestine] and [the poet] Rachel [Bluwstein] and dozens of others like them that I used to think, —No modern hippie, in my opinion, has ever revolted as effectively against the establishment of the day as those pioneers did at the beginning of the century. Many of them came from the homes of merchants and scholars, many even from prosperous assimilated families. If Zionism alone had fired them, they could have come to Palestine, bought orange groves there, and hired Arabs to do all the work for them. It would have been easier. But they were radicals at heart and deeply believed that only self-labor could truly liberate the Jews from the ghetto and its mentality and make it possible for them to reclaim the land and earn a moral right to it, in addition to the historic right."

Just as Frantz Fanon believed in the redeeming value of violence, the pioneers believed in manual labor, which became almost a fetish. The same cannot be said of their critics, the self-proclaimed friends of the toiling and exploited masses. Some of the pioneers were poets, some were cranks, some had stormy personal lives; but what they all had in common was a fervor to experiment, to build a good society in Palestine or at least a society that would be better than what had been known in most parts of the world.

All this sounds very naïve, and it is certainly no longer politically correct. It is also anachronistic. Who needs self-labor on the land in the age of automation and agricultural surpluses? Of course this was not the state of affairs one hundred or even sixty years ago. Golda Meir and her generation of pioneers could not have known this, but perhaps the post-Zionist critics will grant that there were at least mitigating circumstances.

Meir also wrote in her autobiography about crossing Beersheba in 1947 to visit her daughter in the Negev. What was then a small, dusty Arab village (there were probably more camels and sheep than people at the time), is today a city of 165,000. It even has a university. If Golda Meir were to visit the university she would be given a refresher course on Zionism by the local post-Zionist teachers. They would berate her for not being a feminist, for never engaging in a systemic critique of the Zionist patriarchal hegemonic discourse, for failing to tell Israeli women that they were marginalized and that they should recognize their moral kinship with Palestinian Arabs. She would also be told that Zionism had been a colonialist enterprise and that the Mizrachim were also victims of exclusion and subordination. Golda Meir might well ask how, in the circumstances, this institution is still called the Ben-Gurion University of the Negev rather than the University of Southern Palestine.

Golda Meir was laid to rest on Mount Herzl in Jerusalem. At the entrance to Rosh Rehavia, where she lived when I knew her back in 1947, is now a post office, a small mini market, an electronics shop, and a fashionable boutique. When she became prime minister her private residence was again in Rehavia, but she lived in Ben Maimon Boulevard in a building (now derelict) with a far bigger kitchen. The Jewish Agency is still located where it then was but no one seems to know what role it should be playing now that the state exists.

CHAPTER 3

KIBBUTZ: UTOPIA PLUS
NINETY

KIRYAT ANAVIM IS SEVEN MILES WEST OF JERUSALEM, 2,130 feet above sea level. Its telephone number in 1947 was 4072. Number of inhabitants at the time, about three hundred. Founded as a kibbutz in the 1920s, Kiryat Anavim had little land and virtually no water; drinking water had to be bought from a nearby monastery. The community kept some cows and they had a poultry farm. They tried to grow grapes, and planted apple, peach, and plum trees. There was a small metal workshop that produced garbage containers. The kibbutz established a little guesthouse for outside visitors, the first of many kibbutz hotels to emerge during the 1960s and '70s.

Today Kiryat Anavim has a hotel with fifty rooms. There is a restaurant called Dining Room Opposite the Cowshed, a coffee house, and a nightclub that is open on Friday nights. There still is not much land for agriculture, but kiwis are grown, and in place of the small garbage container workshop there is now a large factory that makes insulation material for pipes and another that produces components for the silicon technology industry. There is a magnificent swimming pool and a music school named Tzlile Harim (Melodies of the Mountains), in which students receive private tutoring on an instrument of their choice, including organ, piano, guitar, darabukka (an Arab drum), percussion, violin, cello, saxophone, oboe, and bassoon.

It is a beautiful place, but the members of the kibbutz do not want it to remain a nature reserve. As their spokesmen say, their settlement has been aging, the crisis in agriculture has worsened, and in contrast to city dwellers they have no private property or pensions. Therefore, they want to establish shopping malls, gas stations, industrial hi-tech areas, a power center, and American-style wholesale warehouse outlets.

Kiryat Anavim now has one hundred ninety-six members, one hundred ten youths and children, ten soldiers, some parents of members, and a handful of volunteers. The name Kiryat Anavim goes back to a settlement that is said to have existed there some three thousand years ago, and which appears in old maps as Qiryat el Anab (the Village of the Grapes).

Ramat Rachel (so-called for its proximity to the tomb of the biblical Rachel), is on the southern outskirts of Jerusalem and was founded in 1926. In 1947, its population was roughly the same as Kiryat Anavim, but it had less land. Most of its members worked on construction sites; they were instrumental in building Talpiot, Rehavia, and other Jerusalem neighborhoods. Some were employed in the Dead Sea Potash works. They had a few small orchards and chicken coops. The kibbutz was destroyed in the riots of 1929, was later rebuilt, and came frequently under fire between 1936 and 1939.

The founders of Ramat Rachel were from the Gdud Avoda (or Labor Legion). These were the most radical of the pioneers, the hippies of the 1920s. The old photographs show them in the streets of Jerusalem bearded, in ragged clothes, barefoot. They wanted to set up one countrywide Palestinian commune. Out of this gang of daring, Wild West-type revolutionaries emerged a future mayor of Jerusalem (Ish Shalom), a governor of the Bank of Israel (David Horowitz), and one of the founders of both the Palmach (the elite strike force of the Haganah) and the Israeli army (Jizhak Sadeh). One group, led by David Elkind, gave up in despair and returned to Russia where they intended to build a real Communist settlement—these unfortunates ended their lives in Stalin's gulag. What remained of the group found-ed Ramat Rachel in 1926.

A little while ago a pictorial history of Ramat Rachel was pub-lished—apparently for members and former members only. Perhaps the most moving and most interesting pictures are those brought together under the heading "couples." Marriage was frowned upon in the 1920s. It was considered an outdated institution, not in line with socialism and the ideals of a new society. It seems one couple got married furtively so that their comrades would not know. But now there are the pictures of radiant young women and their bridegrooms dressed immaculately. The pioneers of the 1920s would have choked of laughter, just as their grandchildren smile when they see the pictures of the founder genera-tion, unkempt and in rags. Yet the kibbutz still exists, and the investiga-tive journalists who claim that kibbutz children grow up desperately unhappy must have had another settlement in their sights.

The Judean hills have not been auspicious ground for kibbutzim, and so Ramat Rachel has fared worse than Kiryat Anavim in the years that passed. Ramat Rachel was destroyed a second time during the War of Independence. After the armistice, forty members returned and slowly rebuilt it. For another twenty years it remained a border settle-ment, exposed to periodic shooting. Four participants in an archaeo-logical conference were killed there in 1956. It was again heavily shelled in 1957, but after the Six-Day War of 1967 it ceased to be a border settlement. There still are some three hundred residents, and it still has no land except a few orchards with apple and cherry trees. A little corn and wheat are grown there.

It is now mainly known for its hotel and swimming pool, which serve guests from Israel and abroad. The hotel (originally a youth hostel, now a four-star establishment) has one hundred sixty-four rooms. It houses a health center, an "exclusive country club" (according to the brochure), an awning that has been permanently erected in the gardens to provide ample space for seminars, exhibitions, conferences, and the Project Oren, which is for long-term visitors from abroad ("three thousand years of history and spirituality through studies of the Hebrew language, hikes through the landscape, and visits to Jerusalem").

The resort promises spectacular views of the Old City of Jerusalem, Bethlehem, and the Judean Hills. The hotel is employee-owned and staffed by kibbutz members who, again, according to the brochure, treat every guest as a member of their extended family. It can be reached by the Number 7 bus, but there is a sizeable parking lot, as befits a country club. There is a hairdresser and a beautician, Jacuzzis, a souvenir shop, a sauna, a center for alternative medicine, a synagogue, and VIP rooms.

Are these typical kibbutzim? Not really, given their proximity to a major town. When kibbutzim were first founded they were meant to be agricultural settlements for ideological as well as practical reasons. But as agriculture was modernized and became more productive machinery replaced human labor and inevitably the pioneers had to look for other enterprises both as a source of income to safeguard a decent living standard and to provide employment for their members. Seen in this perspective the problems facing Kiryat Anavim and Ramat Rachel are not so different from those confronting settlements at locations more distant from the big cities.

The story of the kibbutzim goes back to the years just before World War I, when small groups of young people from Eastern Europe established a few collective farms in what was then a province of the

Ottoman Empire. In December 1938, when I first visited a kibbutz to meet friends from my hometown, there were some seventy such settlements with a total population of twenty-five thousand.

It was not easy at the time to reach these places. They were not on the main roads, so you went, at least part of the way, by horse-drawn cart or by truck. Fares were paid in kind, by helping the driver to unload milk churns and boxes of vegetables. There was an element of adventure on these trips—you never knew where you would land and when. But time was not that important then; you could always count on a bed somewhere, or at least a pile of straw in a barn. Tea and bread, with or without jam, were available in the communal dining hall at almost any hour of the day or night.

As far as their political orientation was concerned most kibbutzim identified with the non-Communist left; some were Marxist, others not, and there were also a number of religious settlements. However, kibbutzim differed from each other also in other respects. What should be the form and the content of communal life? Originally kibbutzim had been something like extended families of twenty or twenty-five. By the 1930s, however, the conviction prevailed that a settlement of fewer than one hundred members might not be viable. Others thought that a kibbutz should not be much bigger if members wanted to live according to the original kibbutz ideals.

What were these ideals? It was unanimously agreed that they consisted of practical socialism (in contrast to merely studying Marxist tracts), a return from the Diaspora to Zion, and a life dedicated to the soil. All shared the conviction that this form of life represented a new and more exalted form of human coexistence; as one of the ideologists expressed it, "even the weakest collective has an infinitely richer and more meaningful content than life in the towns."

Strict equality reigned in the communal settlements, where a member's sole possessions comprised a bed, cupboard, table and chair, a tablecloth, and a few books. Until the mid-1930s, individual members did not even own their personal clothing. It was not until years later that the Sabbath clothes they collected from the laundry on Friday afternoons were the same they had worn the previous week. As for working clothes, even when I was a member, everyone received different sets each week, often consisting of patches of cloth clumsily stitched together.

Some of the members lived in tents, others in wooden huts; the first stone houses were the communal dining hall and the children's house. Kibbutz members had no money or luxury articles such as radios or phonographs. There was neither the money nor the leisure to indulge in spare time hobbies. Food ranged from poor to inedible and was eaten off aluminum plates. Since there was a shortage of crockery and cutlery, the main course was served first and the soup, on the same plate, afterward. Small rations of meat and fish appeared on the table once a week. Two prerequisites had to be fulfilled before a kibbutznik would see a piece of chicken: both he or she and the bird had to be sick. Half a glass of wine was issued once a year, at Passover, and cigarettes, the cheapest variety only, were strictly rationed. So were the number of airmail letters members were permitted to send. Sanitary arrangements were deplorable and, as is so often the case, kibbutz women suffered more in this respect than men.

The older kibbutzim were on the whole somewhat better off. But in the newer ones, which constituted the majority, conditions were often worse. Young families did not get a tent or a room of their own but had to share it with a third person (called, for some obscure reason, a "primus") to their, and his or her, mutual embarrassment. The general level of health was poor; malaria and other diseases claimed many victims. A number of settlements were so indigent that they could not pay membership dues to union sickness benefit funds and were cut off from medical aid. Once I had to tie the soles to my shoes with string because there was no money for new boots.

Work in the newly founded settlements was generally unrewarding and their financial position often disastrous. They were all in debt, and a kibbutz secretary's main task was to obtain short-term loans on unfavorable terms. Since there was no cultivable land, many members were employed in the towns, mostly in housing and in public-works projects such as road building or, at best, forestry. These were jobs for which they earned a minimal wage.

Fields were usually scattered between Arab villages and so had to be guarded against invading herds day and night, which tied up a great deal of manpower. Most settlement members had worked on farms for a year or two prior to their arrival in Palestine, but qualified agriculturists, not to mention technical experts of any kind, were very rare. Proper planning scarcely existed, and many mistakes were made. There was, for instance, the belief in absolute self-sufficiency, of baking one's own bread and tailoring one's own overalls. Projects were undertaken that were not and could never become profitable. Members who wanted to leave were at liberty to do so. They were given $5 or $10, the clothes they wore, and possibly a bed and a mattress.

There was considerable turnover. People joined the kibbutz and left, some after a few months, some after years. Agricultural work in this pre-mechanized age was not to everyone's liking or physical ability. Others left because the idea of putting the collective's needs above their own appealed to them more as an ideal than as a practical reality. For everyone, life in the kibbutz was materially infinitely worse than what he or she had been accustomed to. And yet I do not recall manifestations of despair. Members in most settlements were between twenty and thirty years of age, young, idealistic, and carefree. Often on Friday nights there was singing and dancing in the dining hall or in the open air. The kibbutz movement was small; there was certainly nothing of the anonymity of big-city life. We knew what went on in our own settlement (and indeed in the neighboring room or tent). We made friends with members of other settlements, and something like a family atmosphere prevailed.

The kibbutz movement was elite and had considerable weight within the Jewish population, which then numbered only half a million. Reinforcements arrived from abroad almost every week—groups of pioneers and parties of young people from Eastern and Central Europe as well as from the Balkans, all eager to found their own kibbutzim. Despite the bad news from Europe, there was a certain mood of optimism. Furthermore, the successful defense of the many kibbutzim which had been attacked during the riots of 1936–39 instilled a sense of security. Those living in the kibbutzim felt safe, and unlike the Jews of Europe they could at least defend themselves against attackers.

Some time ago, I received a bundle of letters written during World War II from friends in kibbutzim that for some reason had never reached me. They reflected the state of mind that prevailed among the very young people who had left their sheltered homes in Europe and looked upon the kibbutz as a sort of continuation of the summer camps they used to attend as members of youth movements. As everywhere else, the older comrades thought and acted more seriously and responsibly, while the younger ones had not yet recognized the gravity of life.

I remained a member of a kibbutz for five years. Twenty years were to pass until, in the 1960s, I paid an extended visit to the settlement that had once been my home. It had greatly expanded and I had a hard time finding my bearings. Gone were the tents and wooden huts and the watchtower, gone the horses, donkeys, and sheep, gone the shabby shorts and shirts. Perhaps the only reminder of the old kibbutz was the tall fence around the perimeter. There were gardens, expanses of lawns and many trees, the sound of splashing and children's voices from a large swimming pool. Families were sitting on the grass, deck chairs, and garden benches. Gone were the iron bedsteads and the straw-filled mattresses, the tables and chairs hammered together out of packing crates. The living quarters had considerably increased in size, replaced by two-room suites, each with a kitchen and bathroom.

Members could now wash at home, whereas in the olden days we had to make the long trek to the communal showers, returning bathed in sweat in summer or drenched with rain in winter. Amenities in these corrugated iron sheds were primitive in the extreme, the water was never quite warm in winter and everyone tried to avoid the rush hours. However, like the well in the neighboring Arab village, the shower was an important meeting place, where deals were transacted, political and social problems discussed, and gossip exchanged.

Had communal life ever recovered from the change? Well, my hosts replied, people's needs and desires at forty-five are different from those of younger people. They wanted privacy. Surprises awaited me in the dining hall too: The meal was excellent, and the kitchen equipment equal to that of a modern hotel. The huge trays with aluminum plates had vanished. Now there was a choice of several dishes, which were wheeled around on small trolleys, designed to keep the soup, meat, and vegetables warm. With all this made available to guests, most people had at least one meal a day at home.

What was the economic basis of the newfound prosperity? People had learned from their early mistakes, I was told. Agriculture had been rationalized and mechanized. Productivity had increased fourfold in two decades. Unprofitable lines of activity, such as sheep breeding, had been discontinued, as had the idea of being self-sufficient at any price. Many settlements had built large fishponds or were growing cotton or bananas and all kinds of tropical and subtropical fruit that had not existed in my time. Almost every kibbutz boasted some form of industry, and in some almost half of the income was derived from industry rather than farming. This meant that little survived of the old Tolstoyan back-to-the-land ethic, and that some outside labor had to be employed to work in the kibbutz industries. Most kibbutzim were still deeply in debt, on average a sum three or four times the value of their net annual income. But few seemed to spend sleepless nights worrying about it.

What of politics? There had been the bitter ideological struggles of the early 1950s when kibbutzim split and old friendships broke over such questions as the role of Stalin in history and the viability of Marxism. Only two decades had passed, but these quarrels had already receded into history and they no longer seemed important. What of the young generation that formed the backbone of the older kibbutzim? They were no longer debating the Spanish Civil War, the Moscow trials, and the Chinese revolution. Even the term Zionism had attracted a certain opprobrium—it meant everlasting speeches, newspaper articles, and classes of instruction in school. They were far more pragmatic, better workers than their parents, and their interest in politics was strictly limited.

But there was a price to be paid for normalization. They had also shed much of the optimism and idealism that had made the generation of their parents so interesting and attractive. When I asked some of the young people whether they themselves would have opted for life in a kibbutz as their parents had done, or merely accepted that they had been born into one, their answer was "We do not give much thought to this problem." I suspect many would consider this a reassuring answer, but I was not so sure.

My impression at the time was that most kibbutz members were either reasonably contented or had ceased to ask themselves why they belonged. What kept them was not politics but principally the satisfaction they derived from their work—or inertia. I also noted that it was difficult for women to find rewarding work in the kibbutz and that, in a majority of cases, women rather than men were the driving force behind the decision to leave. But there was also a sense of security that accrued from living in a collective. The living standard of the average kibbutznik was by then comparable with that of an urban worker, and in addition there was the feeling of belongingness that tends to grow on individuals after ten or twenty years.

At this time, the 1950s and early '60s, the kibbutz was at the height of its prestige and influence. More than twenty members of the Knesset, the Israeli parliament, were members of a kibbutz, and each of the early governments included at least three or four kibbutzniks. Eight percent of the total population lived in kibbutzim on the eve of the War of Independence, and their share in the higher ranks of the army was fifty percent or more. But then a slow decline set in, which became a deep crisis in the 1980s, when the very existence of individual kibbutzim and the whole movement was questioned.

Numbers tell only part of the story. There are, as these lines are written, some two hundred seventy kibbutzim with a total population of about one hundred twenty thousand, about five times as many as there were in the days when I was a member. Furthermore, the kibbutz has outlasted most other socialist experiments. Communists look down on these "allegedly socialist islands in a capitalist ocean." But the *kolkhoz* (and the whole Soviet Union) have disappeared, whereas the kibbutz still exists. The number of kibbutzim that failed and disappeared can be counted on the fingers of two hands.

True, there are no kibbutzniks in government, and only one or two can be found in the Knesset, but this was a natural process. Their specific weight in Israeli society has shrunk. True again, the kibbutz did not play any significant role in absorbing the great immigration waves, especially from North Africa and the Soviet Union. But how could it have been different? These late arrivals were not moved by the same spirit as the early pioneers. Anything smacking of socialism was anathema to émigrés from Odessa. The same can be said for émigrés from North Africa. To them, the kibbutz was a secular, Ashkenazi abomination.

While the crisis of the kibbutz was economic in character, a graver socio-cultural crisis became apparent when about half of the first-generation kibbutzniks began to leave the settlements. There was the very real danger that the kibbutzim would become old-age homes. The question arises, Why? Given the relatively high standard of living at most kibbutzim, it was hard to understand what great attraction urban existence held for young people.

There is no clear answer: at best there are several explanations. The kibbutzim made the fatal mistake of borrowing money from banks and government at a time when borrowing was easy in view of their fine economic performance in the past. In 1988, the kibbutzim were about $4.5 billion in debt, whereas their annual income was slightly in excess of $3 billion. They would have been able to service these loans if the prosperity had continued, but it did not. Galloping inflation ensued, and the kibbutzim had to be bailed out from bankruptcy by their creditors.

Why had they engaged in irresponsible borrowing? It is, to a certain extent, understandable in retrospect—they wanted to invest in new industrial enterprises and to modernize existing factories. The whole world was undergoing an industrial (or postindustrial) revolution, and the kibbutzim had to adjust to changing conditions. But the choice of new projects was often erratic and unprofitable. As for why the banks engaged in irresponsible lending, the motive was simple. At a time when it seemed everything was going up, they were interested in making an easy profit.

While the kibbutzim were bailed out from immediate collapse, the long-term consequences were severe. New lines of credit hardly existed anymore, and living standards declined. The self-confidence of the kibbutzim was shattered and for some of them prospects seemed nearly hopeless, even after the consolidation. As late as 1969, a kibbutz was defined in an encyclopedia as a "voluntary collective community, mainly agricultural," and this was, broadly speaking, true at the time. About half of the kibbutz population was engaged in agriculture and fishing. But by 2000, agriculture had declined to 10 percent or even less, and many kibbutzniks found themselves working in industry, tourism, public and community service, and even commerce.

Today there are almost four hundred industrial plants operated by the kibbutzim. They produce plastic and rubber goods, electronic and optical appliances, printed materials, chemical and pharmaceutical products, metal products, and textiles. Recorders and car windshields, medical-recording paper, and furniture for synagogues are all made on kibbutzim. Naot, a sandals manufacturer, and Plasson, a plastics manufactory, have become world leaders in their fields. Some kibbutzim arrange wedding and bar mitzvah celebrations on their premises. One established a water park, and fifty-two other kibbutzim run hotels and holiday villages. More than 70 percent of kibbutz income now accrues from kibbutz industries, which account for 8 percent of total Israeli industrial exports. So what had gone wrong, and why are there even now complaints about insufficient (or even declining) productivity?

All too often one kibbutz or another simply failed to do their market research prior to establishing a new enterprise. Other kibbutzim were simply unlucky. Unforeseen competition from abroad impinged on market share. Products became obsolete due to technological progress. But these risks are faced by entrepreneurs all over the world. The weaknesses of kibbutz industry were manyfold. It was not adaptable enough, not alert to changing demand in the country and abroad, not quick enough to shift to new products and to update strategies, equipment, and marketing. If a kibbutz industry succeeded, there was the tendency to rest on one's laurels. With a few exceptions, kibbutzim were slow to understand the full implication of the high-tech revolution, especially in the field of computers, which could have offered many opportunities. The democratic structure of the kibbutz—important decisions were made by the general assembly—was not conducive to quick, creative, and effective management. In a world of specialists, only a few had the training, the knowledge, and the experience to make valuable contributions to the decision-making process.

Some of the kibbutz enterprises did exceedingly well, but by and large, a decrease in labor productivity was noted throughout the 1990s. This had to do in part with bad management, but more perhaps with the very structure of kibbutz, where there is a relative lack of motivation and the absence of a system of rewards. The egalitarianism of the early decades arose out of the young pioneers' idealism and their eagerness to build a new society in a new country. But as the young pioneers grew old and the country was established, the second- and third-generation kibbutzniks began to exhibit marked differences from the character and motivation of the founders. In recent years, the fortunes of many kibbutz industrial enterprises have changed for the better. Productivity is also up, but it is too early to say whether this is a lasting trend.

And this leads to the issues involved in the crisis that were not primarily economic in character.

From the very beginning, the negative aspects of collective life had been obvious. As a cynical observer once noted, kibbutz was a wonderful way of life for the very young and the very old, but not so great for those in between. A woman once said that the kibbutz was a creation for men rather than women. The implication was that the number of opportunities for female kibbutzniks to find congenial work were more restricted than elsewhere. The main psychological problem dating back to the early days was the limited personal choices available to members, whether it concerned work or leisure, food or clothing. The founders, and up to a point their children, had been willing to accept these privations.

With the third generation, the conflict became aggravated. These were not recent immigrants from Europe; their ideal was not to reclaim the country and to build a new society. The country was already in existence, and so was the communal society into which they had been born. While performing mandatory service in the army (and as they were doing a year of service in new kibbutzim or youth movements), they came in touch with a world they had known only imperfectly, one that greatly appealed to them. Many of them ached for a year of freedom from the kibbutz after release from the army, and virtually all kibbutzim granted their wish. The older generation seemed to understand that without this concession, their children and grandchildren would be forever lost from the kibbutz. And so it happened that a whole generation of kibbutz children made their way to the most remote quarters of the world from Nepal to Bolivia.

Still, allowing some time away from the kibbutz was not enough. Many of the youngsters wanted to attend a university or technical college. In the early days of the kibbutz, that would have been quite unthinkable—the aim was to redeem the land. They had no use for a new class of intellectuals. There had been enough of them in the Diaspora.

Eventually these wishes were also fulfilled, partly for fear of losing the young generation, but also because the kibbutzim realized that more highly trained members would be needed in the age of technological sophistication. Of course, these young people were again exposed to the attractions of a wider world than the one they had known all their lives. Thus, the kibbutzim faced the risk of losing those whose higher education they had financed.

Was there no way to retain the loyalty of the third generation kibbutzniks? Would greater privatization do the trick? There had been creeping privatization in the kibbutzim even earlier on. Whereas in the beginning there had been absolute equality (in theory, if not always in practice), certain breaches gradually occurred. When kibbutz members returned from army service in World War II, they were permitted to buy or keep certain amenities such as a little radio, record player, and a coffee maker from the pay that had accrued during their years of service. Then, in the late 1950s and early '60s, restitution from Germany created new problems. Those receiving money from Germany gave the bulk of these funds to the kibbutz, but there was the possibility that many would leave unless at least part of these funds were put at their disposal.

The dilemma was how to make these concessions without creating a new class society in the kibbutzim. Those less fortunate were to be gradually recompensed, and eventually everyone received a private radio and later a television set, as well as new furniture, a private little kitchenette (and later a full-scale kitchen), and other amenities. One thing led to another—a kitchen did not make sense unless the kibbutz family could get food for home consumption free of charge. Members of the settlements had the right to get two weeks paid vacation and also a trip abroad every few years. Private ownership of cars was not yet permitted, but each kibbutz bought a number of cars and members could use them whenever they pleased. Some services were free, others rationed. Gradually living space expanded. Instead of one room, a family was given two rooms, and once it was decided that children would stay overnight with their parents rather than in the children's home, a third room became necessary.

Other changes included a gradual weakening of kibbutz democracy.

Once upon a time all important—and many unimportant—decisions had been taken by the general assembly. But as the settlements became larger and as the issues involved became more intricate, decision making shifted from the general assembly to small committees or individual managers. In some kibbutzim the general assembly was no longer convened at all and was replaced by occasional ballots and referenda.

Once upon a time the very idea that outside labor would be employed by a kibbutz would have been considered anathema, but by the 1990s kibbutz members constituted only forty percent of the workforce in kibbutz industries. Outsiders were also employed in nursing and other services. Some of these workers came from nearby development towns, some were Arabs, but there was also imported labor from abroad. At the same time, members working outside the kibbutz was no longer frowned upon, especially if it was well paid. Some kibbutz members worked as lawyers in Jerusalem, Tel Aviv, and Haifa; others were architects, managers, or business consultants.

Industrialization and other trends outside the kibbutz caused some of these changes, but other reforms, no less profound, were generated by internal dynamics. For instance, the upbringing of kibbutz children changed. For many years, kibbutz children belonged to the collective as much as to the family. Children saw their parents for at most an hour or two in the late afternoon or evening; the question of whether the parents were entitled to keep toys at their home was hotly debated. But in the 1950s and '60s, the center of gravity shifted from the children's house to the parents' apartment. The family proved stronger than the collective, the influence of the peer group became weaker, and eventually kibbutz children lived with their parents. The influence of socialist ideology and of Zionism also became weaker among the young generation and was replaced by an interest in pop culture, and even experimentation with alcohol and drug use.

The financial and the social crisis of the 1980s greatly damaged morale among the kibbutzim. More important was the fact that so many of the young people were leaving despite every effort to keep them. Had the kibbutzim failed to impart the values of the founders? It seemed plausible that the causes ran even deeper, the result of embourgeoisement and what sociologists call routinization. Young people were bothered by the lack of freedom at the kibbutzim. They wanted more privacy, and they wanted to make money. There can be no doubting the fact that the younger generation was more materialistic than the earlier generations. In addition, the defection of young people from the countryside to the cities was more generally the manifestation of certain global trends.

Decollectivization made rapid strides among the kibbutzim. It began with the allocation of household budgets and the advent of charging kibbutzniks for services such as electricity, food supplied for private consumption, and so on. This eliminated a considerable amount of waste. But far more important were the changes that took place when a gradual system of rewards was introduced. The question as to why those who worked hard and contributed greatly to the economic success of the kibbutz received the same rewards as the "free riders" who contributed minimal effort or even shirked their duties became an important one.

It will be recalled that the Soviet Union and the other communist countries had practiced openly or discreetly a system of differential wages with often very substantial differentials. Stalin had condemned "excessive egalitarianism" even in the 1930s. The equality of the kibbutz was an exception among socialist societies, and it was argued that only highly motivated groups of people could practice it since human nature craved rewards and abhorred its opposite. When the possibility of paying higher wages to those making a greater effort was first discussed, a majority of members approved extra pay for those working extra hours. And there was also a majority in favor of taking sanctions against those who did not pull their weight. But there still was considerable resistance to paying higher salaries to those making a greater contribution to the kibbutz economy.

This was in total violation of the basic kibbutz concepts—solidarity and mutual trust. What difference would remain between kibbutz life and the rest of the world if the model of a classless society was abandoned?

By 1997, seven kibbutzim had adopted a differential system of paying wages. More and more kibbutzim decided on *hafrata* (privatization), which included providing a safety net of essential services rather than a pension. By 2004, less than half of the kibbutzim were still collective settlements in the traditional, historical sense. However, the populations of many kibbutzim are over-aged, and it is not clear whether they will be able to meet the cost of a safety net in the years to come. It seemed that this was to be merely the beginning of the transition towards full differentials—within reasonable limits and while retaining minimum wages. Whereas equality was now a thing of the past, essential communal services such as food, education, health care, and provisions for old and infirm members would continue. In 2001, kibbutzim were given the permission to privatize their houses without losing their legal status as cooperative associations. It was proposed that from then on members of the kibbutz should have the right to sell their houses, but the kibbutz had to be given the right of first refusal.

These debates concerning fundamental values lasted for years, and different settlements reached different conclusions. Previously there had been solidarity between kibbutzim, and the older ones had felt an obligation towards the younger and poorer ones. But over the years a cleavage had developed between wealthy kibbutzim and those tottering on the brink of bankruptcy. Not surprisingly, the willingness for radical reform was much greater in the kibbutzim that suffered most from the crisis, whereas among those who were comparatively well-off (perhaps half of the total) there was initially more resistance to privatization.

Since 1990, the population of the kibbutz movement has been slowly declining, and there have been many predictions that the day of the kibbutz has passed. But the number of kibbutzim that were actually dissolved is very small; there was, in fact, a slight increase in 2004. It is also true that the impending demise of the kibbutz has been predicted since the beginning.

It is sometimes argued by the enemies of the kibbutz, of which there are now a great many, that it survives only thanks to very substantial government subsidies. This is not true. Government subsidies amount to 5 percent in Israel—as compared to 22 percent in the United States and 34 percent in the European Union. In addition, the kibbutzim with 2 percent of the total population account for a much higher percentage of industrial production and 14 percent of total Israeli exports.

The kibbutz as a social laboratory attracted, somewhat belatedly, the attention of social scientists. Some of their observations and conclusions were shrewd, but most suffered from the ignorance of the specific Palestinian-Israeli conditions. In other instances their *obiter dicta* belonged to the realm of fantasy, such as the statement made by the Polish Jewish sociologist Henryk Infield, who claimed that kibbutz members had sex, on average, only once a month.

During the last two decades, more authoritative studies have come from kibbutz-sponsored academic centers for the study of the settlements. Even among these insiders there has been considerable pessimism regarding the future, where talk about the end of the communal dream, or, at the very least, about the necessity for a drastic reappraisal of the kibbutz as a communal and economic entity is common.

Much of this was probably inevitable. In many ways, trends in the kibbutz reflect developments elsewhere in Israel and in the developed world in general. Fewer and fewer people in developed countries are employed in industry and agriculture. This trend has implications for the kibbutz. Once one of the most egalitarian societies, Israel is now home to greater discrepancies in income than almost any European country. Retired politicians and senior army officers opt with much success for a second career in business. It is difficult to imagine the generation of Ben-Gurion (or even Begin and Shamir) mingling at ease with the wealthy entrepreneurs of West and East, earning what they do, and sharing their lifestyle. This social polarization, the growing discrepancy between rich and poor, may pass without major upheaval in the anonymity of big countries and cities, but it does not go down well in a small country where so many people live below the poverty line. The spirit of idealism and volunteerism has faded, and materialist values are as prominent in Israel as most other countries.

But the zeitgeist tends to change, and while the kibbutz in its historical form will not have a revival, it is not unthinkable that communal settlements set up even vaguely along the lines of the kibbutz may some time, somewhere, have a second flowering. The attractions of suburban existence are not greater in Israel than elsewhere in the world, and communal settlements keeping some of the values and traditions of the kibbutz have much to offer as far as the quality of life is concerned.

With all this, there are new challenges and opportunities. Agriculture can no longer be a decisive factor in making the kibbutz a viable economic entity, and kibbutz industries have to make great efforts to be competitive. Nevertheless, the settlements have certain advantages that have not been fully utilized. In view of their relatively high educational standards, they constitute a reservoir for the development of high-tech work in computers field and related enterprises. This will involve cooperation not only among different settlements but also investors and international companies. Such cooperation has been in existence for years as far as the kibbutz industries were concerned. This is a field in constant change in which there still exist many niches for creative and enterprising groups of people, and there is no reason why these should be based only in the cities.

Of course there is increasing dissatisfaction with the quality of life in the big cities—the lack of security, constant traffic jams, noise and dirt, and also the frequent lack of human contact. The kibbutz is certainly a better place to bring up children, and a growing number of young couples have moved to these settlements without becoming members. Once the city had a monopoly on culture and entertainment, but this too has changed. Every year thousands of volunteers from Europe and America used to come for short and long periods to work in the kibbutzim. This influx has dwindled, but it has not disappeared, showing that the settlements still have their attraction and that this attraction might be rediscovered in the volunteers' countries of origin.

Which takes me back to my starting point, to Kiryat Anavim and Ramat Rachel. The other day I read a letter written by a member of Youth Aliyah in 1936, soon after his arrival in Palestine and Kiryat Anavim. He was very critical about the kibbutz; he did not like the red flags and the banners proclaiming "Workers of the World Unite" that flew proudly on May Day. He wrote that the members of the kibbutz were real "proletarians" in the derogatory sense—they did little but work and sleep and eat, with no interest in the higher things in life.

If he were to visit his old kibbutz now (which recently celebrated its eightieth birthday), he would find most of the farmers and blue-collar workers replaced by engineers engaged in the production of bio-imaging systems. True, this kibbutz has stagnated but it is less in debt (about $4.5 million) than are most other settlements. He would be able to listen to melodies from Pergolesi, Johann Christian Bach, and even Orlando di Lasso emanating from Tzlile Harim, the music school. In the kibbutz hotel the members of the Fritz Haber conference on chaos and related nonlinear phenomena would be engaged in hot debate. Earlier there had been a global seminar on spinal deformities, and the next international conference was to be on multiparticle dynamics, not to mention the European conference on computational learning theory and the international seminar for young diplomats. The young man of 1936 could acquire a higher education of sorts simply by listening in from time to time.

If he were to proceed to Ramat Rachel, he would find not much farming left except a big plant nursery also teaching artistic flower interweaving, hydroponics, and bridal arrangements (be it noted—for brides-to-be, the epitome of bourgeois society, something that was quite unknown in Palestine in the 1920s and '30s). But most of the action is in the hotel and conference center; a workshop on dielectric spectroscopy, the Mediterranean conference on medical and biological engineering, a seminar on Database theory, and also the First International Bible Conference sponsored by the Adventists. Ramat Rachel boasts one of only two big open-air swimming pools in Jerusalem, open summer and winter to the general public, and there is plenty of spiritual fare with a heavy emphasis on archeology, because some important excavations were made there in recent years.

Thus, the complaints about a proletarian existence and the lack of culture are no longer justified. But there are other fundamental questions. What has become of the original ideas underlying the kibbutz— a mere cooperative owning a hotel, a country club, and a few other enterprises? The present tendency is to belittle the role of ideology, yet what is a kibbutz devoid of a vision?

When revisiting my old kibbutz in the 1960s, returning just before midnight to our seashore hotel, I noted in my diary:

"A party of teenagers has just arrived but I could not tell at first glance whether they hailed from Brooklyn or Golders Green. Their behavior suggested that they were hell-bent on enjoying themselves in the next few weeks. Some bemoaned the fact that the bar was already closed, others complained that the air-conditioning in their rooms was not working efficiently. The girls were too heavily made up and I found the boys too loud. They were about the same age as the leather-jacketed pioneers whom I had seen disembarking in Haifa harbor in 1938. The pioneers of 1938 had not expected four-star hotels, let alone air-conditioning or whisky and soda. They were bubbling over with dreams of a new Jerusalem and a utopian idealism that in retrospect seems quaint and touchingly naïve. To most of the party of boys and girls, products of our society and mass culture, the kibbutz must have seemed an antiquated relic from a forgotten world, something to be visited on a sightseeing tour in an air-conditioned bus, something like a museum. But who wants to live in a museum?"

These young visitors from New York or London were no doubt decent enough human beings, and it was reasonable to assume that within a year or two they would shed some of their crudity. But what a gulf separated them, rebel and conformist alike, from the youngsters of 1938, inspired by Hermann Hesse's *Demian* and Romain Rolland's *Jean Christophe,* by Martin Buber and the Communist Manifesto. True, some of the intellectual fare disappeared rapidly in the harsh Palestinian realities. Whether the pioneers of 1938 were more talented or more decent is a moot point, but one thing is certain—they had a chance that comes very rarely, the chance to make a radically fresh start and try to mold their lives in a different way. Perhaps they failed; they certainly did not succeed in lifting the world off its hinges. Out of three or four who joined the kibbutz, only one stayed; there was a great turnover. I am not so sure, however, that the question of success or failure is the decisive one. As the Latin poet said, "*in magnis voluisse sat est*" (as far as great things are concerned, it is enough to have wanted).

Since I wrote these lines, another generation has come and gone. The student radicals of the 1960s are now respectable citizens. Some have become ministers or professors and others are now computer millionaires. The kibbutz still exists—but will it survive in a world that is so different? Its failure would be a great pity, for viewing it in broader perspective it is the only truly unique achievement that Israel has produced. All the rest can be found elsewhere, left-wing and right-wing parties, shrewd business people, good and bad restaurants, traffic jams, holy places, religious fanatics, postmodern intellectuals, terrorism and anti-terrorism, modern methods in agriculture. Even the revival of a language that was more than half dead has been attempted elsewhere. But the idea of the kibbutz is something unique.

CHAPTER 4

ELIACHAR AND THE
SEPHARDI ARISTOCRACY

J EWS WHO GREW UP IN ENGLAND AND RECEIVED THEIR education there have little in common with Jews who emigrated to
Israel from the former Soviet Union. The differences outweigh the
similarities. This rule of thumb should be observed when one feels the
urge to generalize about Sephardim (or Mizrachim, as they are sometimes called). Jacques Derrida, the deconstructionist from Algeria with
an enormous following at American universities and child of Sephardi
parents, has little in common with Rav Ovadya Josef who enjoys an
equally impressive following among the Jerusalem religious proletariat. In fact, the only thing they have in common is their Sephardic
roots.

Take the case of one well-known family I knew during my years in
Jerusalem. Menashe Eliachar (1901–93) belonged to a clan of the
Sephardi aristocracy that had lived in Palestine since the fifteenth century. The family, as far as can be established, had left Spain seven or
eight years before the expulsion in 1492. Menashe Eliachar was born
in the Old City of Jerusalem near Yohanan Ben Sakai synagogue. His

grandfather had been the chief rabbi of his community. His father was a businessman and later deputy mayor of Jerusalem. They lived together in a two-story house with spacious rooms and marble floors. As customary in those days, three generations of Eliachars lived in this building as well as some nephews, uncles, and aunts. Large as the building was, it finally proved to be too small for the family, so they decided to move. The story of the Eliachars exodus from the Old City actually resembles the story of the Alamis, an upper-class Palestinian Arab family, which I will tell later on.

When Menashe Eliachar married at the age of twenty-nine, he moved to Rehavia. He lived at 24 Alharisi Street (phone 3290) but later bought a second house at the corner of Ben Maimon and Arlosoroff Street. Elie, his older brother, lived at 40 Ben Maimon Street, a stone's throw away. It was customary for the sons and daughters of these upper-class Sephardi circles to marry someone from within those circles. Eliachars's mother was a daughter of Josef Bey Navon. Menashe married Rahel Kukia, who belonged to another old and substantial Jerusalem family that owned half of Jaffa Road, Jerusalem's main thoroughfare. Rahel's sister married a Valero, yet another Sephardi clan, prominent in banking and import-export trade. Elie married a young Ashkenazi lady named Bialik who, obviously, came from a different background. Such "mixed marriages" were however not infrequent; his own grandfather, Josef Navon, had married Gisha Frumkin, who emigrated from Russia as a child. It is reported that she quickly conformed, and while she spoke little Hebrew and continued to read Yiddish, she learned to speak pure Ladino (Judeo-Spanish) and even developed a love for the language.

The world in which Elie and Menashe Eliachar grew up before and during World War I was very different from the world of the young Zionists who arrived from Eastern Europe. When the Eliachars and their contemporaries reminisced in later years about the city of their birth, their feelings were mixed. Relations with their non-Jewish neighbors had been cordial, sometimes even close. Arab friends visited their parents' home and vice versa. At the same time, the call of the muezzin from the nearby mosque and the bells from the Christian churches made it only too clear to them that Jerusalem really belonged to others and that the Jews were there on sufferance: They should not stand out. They should not attract attention, envy, or enmity.

The education of the two brothers was traditional. Menashe was first sent to a Sephardi yeshiva in Jerusalem, later to a school sponsored by the Alliance Israelite, and eventually to the Reali Gymnasium in Haifa. He received a fairly good Jewish and general education. In those days, the secular culture of the Eliachars was French, as it was for other Sephardi families in Europe and the Near East. The younger Eliachar was named Henri (in addition to Menashe). His father's home was designed in the French style, and their clothing was European.

What was their attitude to the Zionists who came from Eastern Europe? The older generation had their reservations about the pioneers and their freewheeling attitudes. It was not entirely clear to the Sephardim why Jews should engage in unprofitable manual labor such as working the land. Elie, Menashe, and their contemporaries shared these doubts about the newcomers. By and large, these people were strangers. But having watched them dance and celebrate, they were fascinated by the pioneers' idealism, vigor and enthusiasm. In other words, they became Zionists, even though their motivation and background were quite different from that of the Eastern European émigrés.

When Jerusalem was occupied by the British in late 1917, Menashe Eliachar was no longer a child. Soon after, he went to a good French school in Cairo to finish his studies. The coming of the British meant that he had to become fluent in English, which he did. Upon his return to Jerusalem, he began his career as a businessman. He imported cigarettes and tobacco (but never smoked himself) and was also a leading importer of wines and spirits but seldom drank.

Elie was studying medicine in Beirut. When the war broke out in 1914, he was forced to join the Turkish army. He served as a junior officer in a Nazareth hospital. After the war, Elie went to law classes in Jerusalem and later became an official in the British Mandatory government. Ten years later, after the death of his father, he too went into business. He owned rice mills in addition to managing various investments, including aviation and the purchase of land in Southern Jerusalem.

Generally speaking, the Jerusalem (and Jaffa) Sephardim were active and successful in trading. They knew many languages, and the banks trusted them—in fact, some of the banks were owned by them. They had the right connections, first within the Ottoman government and then with the British authorities who, on the whole, preferred "native Jews" to the Zionist newcomers. (As the British noted, the Sephardim, like the upper-class Arabs, also had better manners.) But even the most successful, except a very few, were not wealthy. In fact, the majority of the Sephardim were poor. World War I profoundly affected imports and exports. This had a profound negative effect on Eliachar's income, given the fact that he had found it difficult to afford a good education for his sons well before the war.

Having said this, some of the Sephardim were not just traders but also entrepreneurs of vision who contributed to the economic development of the country. The most ambitious was Josef Bey Navon, Eliachar's maternal grandfather. More than anyone else, he helped realize the construction of the Jaffa-Jerusalem railway, which was completed in September 1892. This earned him the title "Bey." As Josef Bey Navon, he had to be addressed as "His Excellency" on official occasions.

Navon also planned the building of the harbor in Haifa, he developed the big indoor Mahane Yehuda market, and had a hand in many other projects. When he heard of Herzl, he was one of the first to look him up him in Paris to persuade him, without success, to support the economic development of Palestine. As it turned out, a few of Josef Bey's schemes misfired, and, compelled to take substantial loans at high rates of interest, he faced growing financial difficulties. In the end, he lost much of his property, and wound up spending the rest of his life in France. I have seen pictures of him in a resplendent uniform; I wonder what became of it.

While the railway seemed a promising project, no one grew rich from the enterprise. Earlier on, Moses Montefiore had also envisioned at one time the construction of a Jaffa-Jerusalem Railway, but he was too cautious an investor to pursue the project. The railway line became financially viable in the 1920s, far too late for Josef Bey Navon, who had already been forced to sell his shares.

Other notable Sephardi figures in the economic field were the Chelouche family, which arrived from Algeria in the 1840s. Of the three brothers who had set out on the journey, only one survived, but he and his progeny helped to create various industries, first in Jaffa and later in Tel Aviv. The Bejaranos from Ruschuk in Bulgaria came somewhat later; they were prominent in the establishment of food industries, above all the production of fruit juice. The Recanatis from Thessaloniki founded the Discount Bank, which became one of the biggest in the country and eventually had holdings in many segments of Israeli industry.

Menashe Eliachar was for many years president of the Jerusalem Chamber of Commerce and a member of countless other public bodies, as was his brother Elie. At the Eliachar home in Rehavia, British officials met Jewish leaders and socialites as well as Arab notables, including Ragheb Nashashibi, the mayor of Jerusalem, and even some of the Husseinis.

Not all the Sephardim went into business. The Aboulafias could be found in every walk of life. They probably produced more rabbis and scholars in the Middle Ages and modern times than any other single clan, and one of their ancestors had been the Sephardi chief rabbi of Jerusalem who also officiated in Damascus. The Valeros, a family of bankers and importers, also counted in its ranks physicians and advocates. The names Mani, Azulai, and Bardaki could be found among British-appointed judges during the Mandate. At the young Hebrew University Italian Jewish professors of Sephardi origin could be found named Franco, Racah, Toaff, Tedeschi, Cassuto, and Bacchi. Another Jewish academic from Italy, Sergio della Pergola, is today head of the Institute of Contemporary Jewry there.

During the 1930s, some of the more ambitious Sephardi leaders decided that their community's place was also in politics. They founded a number of organizations, such as the Council of the Sephardi Community in Jerusalem, the Association of Sephardi Youth, and the World Federation of Sephardi Jews. For a while, during the early years, there was a Sephardi party in the Knesset. But the party was small, and their negotiations to enter a coalition with other center and right-wing parties failed.

The endeavors to establish a political party on a purely ethnic basis were unsuccessful prior to the mass immigration from North Africa and Iraq. The Sephardi community consisted of a great variety of local groups who did not always see eye-to-eye—those from Haleb (Aleppo) and from Bukhara; from the Maghreb and from Turkey; those of Kurdish origin and others from Urfa; those who had come from Egypt and Yemen; as well as at least a dozen others. Some of the old, established families were wealthy by the standards of the time, but most were very poor. In brief, it was anything but a homogenous community.

The leadership of the Sephardim was not exactly democratically elected but self-appointed, and this brought about a generational revolt when the old notables came under pressure by a younger generation eager to move into the front rank. Furthermore, the base of this party was small and didn't show much initiative in wooing the new Sephardi immigrants from Bulgaria and Turkey who arrived after the state was founded. But even had they done so, it is doubtful whether such a party would have lasted. The ties that had bound them together—the Ladino language, a specific culture with its emphasis on family life and customs that had developed over the centuries—grew progressively weaker. In the first place, the Moroccans, Persians, Yemenites, Iraqis, Kurds, and Central Asians did not speak Ladino. Secondly, the young Sephardim intermarried with Ashkenazi families more than the earlier generation and they became fully integrated into Israeli society, holding jobs in virtually every government office and every profession. Furthermore, beginning with World War I, Sephardi families from Palestine and the neighboring countries migrated, first to France, and in later years mainly to the Americas.

True, there was another wave of mass immigration to Israel from North Africa in the 1950s and '60s, but what did the Sephardim from Jerusalem and Safed have in common with the Moroccan Jews, or even those who came from Iraq?

The term *Sephardi* has been often misused and some words of clarification are needed. *Sepharad* originally meant "Spain," and Sephardim were those who escaped from Spain during the Inquisition. But even the original meaning of the term is in doubt; when the prophet Obadiah mentioned "Sepharad" (the only time the word appears in the Bible), he almost certainly did not refer to the Iberian peninsula. When Jewish writers in the Middle Ages discussed Spain, they usually called it Espania or al Andalus. When the Jews were expelled from Spain and Portugal in the late fifteenth century, the majority went to the Ottoman Empire where they were on the whole well received. Others went to Holland, Italy, even Germany and Eastern Europe. Some of the Jews from North Africa and the Arab countries who arrived in Israel after the state had been established were obviously of Sephardi origin, as their names show, but many were not. Jews from Spain certainly did not escape to Yemen or Ethiopia or India, and even in nearby North Africa there had been a native Jewish population that was not Sephardi in origin. The very liberal and thus misleading use of the term *Sephardim* goes back to the days of the British Mandate, when for simplicity's sake all those who were not obviously Ashkenazi were categorized as Sephardi. Such practices are known elsewhere—in the United States and Britain during the 1970s all those who were not English or WASP were declared to be "colored" by overeager social workers of a radical persuasion.

The new immigrants from Morocco and Iraq, from where the majority came at the time, hardly ever mingled with the Sephardi Jews long resident in Jerusalem, let alone those from Italy or Bulgaria. Nor indeed had the émigrés from Morocco much in common with those from Babylon. The Sephardim proper not only spoke a different language, their folklore and music was also quite different. (Ladino, locally called *haquitiyah,* was spoken by a few Moroccan Jews in Tangier, but for most it was a foreign language.) The Moroccan Jewish cuisine specialized in dishes such as *djej bi looz* (chicken with almonds) or orange rice; the Sephardim were eating *huevos haminados* (hard-boiled eggs) and *sanbusak* (filled pastries).

Among Moroccan Jews there were saints and wonder workers, diseases were thought to be caused by demons, and fortune telling and the use of amulets were fairly wide spread. All these practices can also be found among North African Berbers and Muslims (the Marabut), but they were not common among the Sephardim.

As for Moroccan Jewish music, the *piyyutim* (songs) are similar to the Arab *sama';* both have their origin in medieval Andalusian tunes, though the words are different. Sephardi music developed over the centuries along different lines.

Iraqi Jews have their own culture, which they trace back to Babylonian days, and so have the Yemenites. These various groups may have their conflicts with the Ashkenazim (who are internally deeply divided), but conflicts per se do not make for a national and cultural identity. To put it more bluntly, for Moroccan Jews most of the other Sephardim are little more (and certainly no better) than honorary Ashkenazim. Some political leaders and ideologists use the word Mizrachim, meaning Eastern Jews, but this too is problematical for both historical and geographical reasons. North African Jewry is geographically located well to the west and south of the Ashkenazim of Central and Eastern Europe.

The old established Sephardi families of Jerusalem are gradually losing their specific identity. This is a development with many precedents: The majority of Sephardim in Italy have disappeared over the centuries in a process of cultural and social assimilation; the Sephardi families who emigrated to the Americas or Western Europe have become part of the local scene, and the same is true with regard to Latin America; the most prominent member of the Montefiore family in Britain is an Anglican bishop. Ladino is still spoken by some fifty thousand people in Israel, and there are attempts being made to preserve and collect their cultural heritage, in the same way as the Yiddish tradition is preserved in various places in the United States and Israel. In Ma'aleh Adumim, near Jerusalem, there is a center for the study and preservation of Ladino, and a Jerusalem high school is actually teaching the language. Israeli radio still broadcasts for an hour a day in Ladino. Several streets in Jerusalem are named after prominent Sephardim, including some of the twentieth century such as Elie (but not Menashe) Eliachar and Cassuto. Eliachar Square is between Sanhedria and Ammunition Hill on the north side of town. There is a Navon Street and a Navon Square. On the whole, Jerusalem municipality shows a bias in favor of cultural and religious figures rather than business people when honoring its former citizens. Thus there is a Rav Chelouche Street but no place in honor of the Chelouche entrepreneurs.

The Ladino religious schools, such as the one Menashe Eliachar went to in his youth, have disappeared, and so has the press and Ladino literature. It is doubtful whether it still can be considered a living language. The various Sephardi councils and cultural associations lead a marginal existence, and only a few musicologists and cookbook writers keep the culture alive.

Nor is family (or clan) cohesion any longer very pronounced. It probably never was as close as some chroniclers want us to believe. The legal wrangling over the possessions of the Farhi family lasted for decades and split the family down the middle. You'll find certain Eliachars have not been on speaking terms with other Eliachars for decades on end, and the same is true for the Aboulafias and other clans. Father and mother Eliachar had six children, two of whom, Menashe and Elie, wrote autobiographies not mentioning the others at any great length.

What about their politics? There is no clear and consistent pattern. While Labor Zionism was the leading force in Israel, some of the younger Ladinos joined this movement (including Yizhak Navon, who became president of Israel); in view of their "bourgeois" backgrounds, this was not an obvious choice. During later years, some of them found a home in the right-wing Likud. Even earlier, Irgun and the Stern Gang had a fair number of young Mizrachim, but they usually came from poverty-stricken neighborhoods, not the leading families. Few if any have joined the religious party (*Shas*). Religious extremism has traditionally been alien to them, so these groups hold little attraction for the Jerusalem Sephardim.

As for relations with Palestinians and Arabs in general, some Sephardim were prominent in the *Kedma Mizraha* association of the 1930s, which worked for Jewish-Arab rapprochement. One was Elie

Eliachar. Born and bred in Jerusalem, he was prominent in the life of the community and in his later years served as president of the World Sephardi Federation. He advocated negotiations with Palestinians from the beginning and favored an open Jerusalem, one that could serve as the capital of two independent states. In his recollections Eliachar mentions the fact that Moses Montefiore had offered funds to the Jerusalem Ashkenazim to teach Arabic in their religious schools, but they had refused. (This, to be fair, had occurred well before the Zionists came.) In the 1920s, Eliachar and his father went to see Menahem Ussishkin, the Russian Zionist leader, with proposals to solve the Arab-Jewish problem. Ussishkin is said to have roared, "You are speaking of an Arab problem. I know of no such thing. Our problem is the Jewish problem."

Elie Eliachar, who spoke fluent Arabic and had many Arab friends, fought all throughout his life for better relations with the Arabs. But he also knew that such peaceful coexistence could not be achieved from a position of weakness, and he was not willing, unlike his friend Jehuda Magnes, to give the Arabs veto power over Jewish immigration. In the end, Eliachar emerged as a lone voice among his Sephardi contemporaries who, while sympathizing with his desire for peace and good neighborly relations, thought these aims utopian.

From the next generation came Meron Benvenisti, born in 1934. He served as deputy mayor of Jerusalem under Teddy Kollek and is the author of a number of influential books on Jerusalem and Israeli-Palestinian relations. Meron's father, David, was from Thessaloniki. David Benvenisti was the author of various guidebooks to Jerusalem and Israel written for the Ramblers' Association and the Jewish National Fund. These texts are well informed and patriotic. He focuses on Jewish settlements and Jewish connections, but ignores the Palestinian Arabs (except, of course, in Jerusalem). Writing forty years later, his son, Meron, notes with sadness the senior Benvenisti's disregard for the inhabitants of the Arab villages, their way of life, and their culture.

According to his son, David Benvenisti's patronizing attitude was based on an idea of European superiority which in turn was born of the Zionist pretension regarding the progress which the Jews would bring to the backward East, and especially the Muslim peasant farmers who were "lazy, dirty, ignorant, and disease ridden." Much of Meron Benvenisti's views on Jerusalem, the sad plight of the Palestinian Arabs, and the nature of the endemic conflict are only too true, and his pessimism well founded. But I can also understand the seemingly reactionary views of his father. Let's put aside for a moment fashionable attitudes regarding Israel during the 1990s. The belief in the superiority of European civilization and, more specifically, the importance of its values, were not at the center of conservative and imperialist thought. It was also an attitude one can readily locate in the writings of Marx and Engels, Lenin and Trotsky. If Muslim Spain once had a civilization superior to that of other parts of the world, so had Europe during the nineteenth and early twentieth centuries.

The Arab villagers were not particularly lazy (as anyone familiar with early Zionist writers such as Moshe Smilanski can attest), but they were certainly poor, disease ridden, and not highly educated. The Zionist mission to bring "progress" to Arabs was misguided. The Zionists found it difficult to understand how an educated Arab such as Musa Alami could say that he preferred another century of backwardness to receiving the blessings of civilization from the Zionism. Meron Benvenisti has strongly urged fellow Israelis to take responsibility for injustices committed in the past, such as the dispossession of the Palestinians and ethnically discriminatory laws against Israeli Arabs. His has been a sane voice for peace even though he cannot have many illusions as to its resonance among Jews and Palestinian Arabs alike. But it is impossible to maintain that such views have been widely shared among the Sephardi community such as it still exists.

The Sephardim of Jerusalem are gradually disappearing as a distinct community. Some of the sons have followed in the footsteps of the fathers: Menashe Eliachar's companies were taken over by his son Oded. Avinoam Tocatly runs the huge insurance business begun by his father (an Ashkenazi orphan adopted by a Sephardi family). Joe Almalikh is among the leading figures in the search for oil in Israel. The president and CEO of SciTex, the pioneer of Israeli high-tech enterprises, was Oded Chelouche. The best-known Farhi of her generation is Nicole, who has a London-based fashion design business. Recently she opened a store in Manhattan that includes a chic restaurant and bar. She is competing with the likes of Giorgio Armani. Her ancestor, the banker Farhi of Damascus who became a "pasha," would have been proud of her.

The Sephardim are found not only in business. Avraham Aboulafia, born in Saragossa, was one of the great kabbalists of the Middle Ages, an intrepid traveler who went to Palestine to look for the River Sambatyon where, according to tradition, the ten tribes had dwelt. A century earlier, Meir Aboulafia had engaged in a long controversy about Maimonides' opinion on the subject of resurrection. Todros Aboulafia was another leading kabbalist, while Samuel ben Meir halevi Aboulafia was a leading financier, philanthropist, communal leader, and builder of the historical Toledo synagogue. Among their descendants today are professors of history (at Cambridge University) and of philosophy (at the University of Colorado), medical doctors, and experts in the aviation industry. Lauren Aboulafia, also of Denver, is a model. Many Aboulafias are in entertainment: Shirley Aboulafia has performed beautiful Christmas music, another is a movie director, yet another was an actress back in the 1930s. Some of the descendants of the Jerusalem notables can be found even on the fringes of the radical cultural scene in the United States: Lisa and Naomi Tocatly are among them (as for the titles of their songs, parental guidance is advised). Jenine Abarbanel of Fort Collins, Colorado, worked on the B-2 stealth bomber and, in her own words, is an unapologetic feminist and tree-hugging environmentalist who eventually wants to be an astronaut. For all one knows this could be a contemporary manifestation of the kabbalism of her famous ancestor, R. Isaac Abarbanel, who was also an opponent of dogmatism as far as his religion was concerned. For centuries the kabbalah was the prevailing religious fashion, not an alternative, oppositionist approach.

And so I return to my point. There is a Mizrachi problem, but this does not refer to the old Jerusalem Sephardi aristocracy. Nor does it apply to those who came from Iraq—their representation not only in business and politics but also in teaching and medicine is far greater than their numbers in the population would predict. It is mainly a problem of Moroccan Jewry as well as some other minor communities, and the question why this should be the case has been given insufficient attention, partly perhaps because it was considered a taboo subject.

CHAPTER 5

REHAVIA: KAUFMANN, KOEBNER, AND THE GERMAN JEWS

R ICHARD KOEBNER WAS PROFESSOR OF MODERN HISTORY at the Hebrew University when there were only a few hundred students enrolled. Richard Kaufmann was the most important town (and country) planner in Palestine during the 1920s and '30s. They had in common their first name, a shared country of origin in Germany, and that they belonged to the same generation: Kaufmann was thirty-three when he arrived in Palestine soon after the end of World War I; Koebner was fifty when he came in 1934. They were next-door neighbors in Rehavia, Koebner at 34 Abarbanel Street, Kaufmann in the adjacent house at number 32. Neither man appears in the telephone directory of 1946. The two neighbors must have met, but I have no idea whether they ever had a real conversation. There are now modern multifamily houses on these sites, some in a strange eclectic style. Kaufmann would not have approved. Abarbanel is now a one-way street, but there is little traffic. On one end of the street there is a playground, and number 24 has become a home for senior citizens. It is not an inexpensive neighborhood; a four-room apartment recently sold for $660,000. The German Jews and the university professors have disappeared, their place taken by well-to-do "Anglo-Saxons" of the national religious persuasion.

Why Koebner? Why Kaufmann? They are of interest not just because of the roles they played in the formation of the roots of a nation. They illustrate the fact that many German Jews found it more difficult than others to feel at home in the new country.

Rehavia was built by Kaufmann. Many streets in this quarter bear the euphonious names of Jewish poets and sages from medieval Spain and Italy; Metudela, Bartenura, Al Charisi, Alfasi; Abarbanel Street (also occasionally spelled Abrabanel) is to remind us of the distinguished Spanish Jew Judah Abarbanel, who figured prominently in Heinrich Heine's poems. He lived in the second part of the fifteenth century; born in Lisbon, he died in Venice and is buried in Padua. He was a man of many parts—statesman, banker, early Renaissance humanist, philosopher, and Bible exegist. He was a member of a leading Spanish Jewish family, the descendants of which can still be found in many parts of the world. Abarbanel Street is quite short—it takes less than five minutes to walk from one end to the other. But within two hundred meters of Koebner's residence there lived almost everyone who was anyone in Jerusalem's cultural and social life, which is why many of its residents make reappearances throughout my story.

This is not to suggest that Koebner belonged to the local high society—nothing would be further from the truth. He was a bachelor at the age of fifty, did not entertain at home, did not see many people other than colleagues and students, and, generally speaking, was a bit of a recluse whose whole life was devoted to study and teaching. Koebner lived on this street simply because it was the part of town where a professor was expected to live.

Koebner's bachelorhood came to an end during World War II. He had asked an agency to send him a woman to bring some order into his nonacademic affairs. Great was his surprise when Gertrud Elkus appeared at his door. He had known her in his hometown. She had, in fact, been the flame of his younger years. They drifted apart, and Gertrud (who had studied philosophy with Ernst Cassirer in Berlin) had married a physician.

There is yet another, even more complicated version, according to which Koebner had been a "friend of the family" back in Germany. Gertrud could not make up her mind whether to follow her husband to America or Koebner to Jerusalem. Since all these people have been dead for a long time, it would take a historian of Koebner's stature and persistence in getting at the historical truth to disentangle this complex affair, which was further complicated by the fact that Koebner's sister disliked Gertrud and tried to break up the relationship. In any case, Gertrud opted for Palestine in the end. The two got married several years later and lived happily ever after. Eventually they coauthored a book about aesthetics.

Koebner was born in 1885 in Breslau, a major city in what was then eastern Germany and is now part of Poland. His father was a physician. Another member of the family owned the best bookshop in town. Very little is known about his childhood; Koebner strongly believed that one's private life was no one else's business. He went to a local high school and later studied history in his hometown as well as in Berlin and Switzerland. He trained as a medievalist and his few publications were about early German urban history and rural settlement. In 1920 he became a lecturer in his hometown. He was ousted by the Nazis in 1933. He had published only one book about a minor figure of the Merovingian period and a handful of learned papers. Koebner's name was not well-known even in the profession. Outside Germany he acquired some fame only after writing the lead essay, "The Settlement and Colonization of Europe," for *The Cambridge Economic History of Europe.* It came out halfway through the war.

Why was Koebner invited when the Hebrew University decided to make a key appointment in the history department? Why select a medievalist to teach modern history? Could they not have done better than this little-known academic from a provincial university? Wasn't there an embarrassment of riches given the large number of major figures who had lost their jobs in Germany?

The brief answer is that there were not many candidates to choose from. There were few, if any, Jewish professors of modern history in Britain and the United States, and those who could be found had no great desire to move to a backwater such as Palestine. The German universities seemed to be a more promising hunting ground, but only at first sight. There were at the time seven Jewish full professors of history in Germany. Six of them had been converted, and the seventh was a specialist in Jewish history. The state of affairs with regard to the associate and assistant professors who had been expelled was not very different. It had been next to impossible for a Jew to get a full professorship before World War I, and they faced many obstacles even after the war. All together, some forty historians of Jewish descent (including archivists) were employed by German universities and other institutions of higher learning prior to 1933, but only three went to Palestine. Several waited too long, or could not get a visa to emigrate, and perished in the Holocaust.

Koebner was not a leader in his field, but some of his colleagues at the Hebrew University knew that he was a man of great erudition. The authorities on Mount Scopus decided to accept the risk and to invite this little-known academic. Among Koebner's publications there was not a single one dealing with Jewish history. But this had not been his field and so it was not held against him.

The difficulties facing him in the new country were enormous. He knew no Hebrew and he was at an age when acquiring a new language is not easy. Throughout all the years he taught at Hebrew University, he read (often stammering) from a text prepared in German. But he would have faced problems even if he had known the language much better; there were simply no equivalents in Hebrew for many of the terms he had to use. Koebner tried very hard to express himself in a language that never became his own, and his students appreciated his efforts. It was the source of much frustration; teaching large lecture classes cannot have given him much satisfaction in these circumstances. The fact that he had to teach eighteenth- and nineteenth-century history rather than his specialty, the Middle Ages, did not bother him much because he was almost equally at home in the more recent periods.

He couldn't do original research in Jerusalem because the archives and other sources he needed were in Europe. He became more and more interested in the origins of historical concepts, for instance the terms *despot* and *despotism,* about which he published a long essay for the Warburg Institute in London, and the word *imperialism,* about which he wrote a massive book together with a former pupil. If confronted with the postcolonialists and their use of the term *colonialism* (to use a freely invented subject), he would suggest that one should first go back to the Latin roots, the word *colere* (to till, cultivate, inhabit), then proceed to the Sanskrit, old Persian, and Slavonic—*kolo.* A *colonia* in ancient Rome was a settlement, usually a coast guard community of some three hundred citizens and their families, established for defensive purposes. A colony in the life sciences connotes a group of organisms that live and interact closely, like bees or ants.

But wasn't it true (the post-Zionists would argue) that the Zionists had called their early settlements "colonies"? Did it not mean that they were colonialists in the modern sense? True enough, Koebner would maintain, the Hebrew term for settlement, *moshava,* was the same as the term used to signify an imperial colony. This is the case for many languages, including German, which was the official language of the Zionist movement. In Germany, a trader dealing in *Kolonialwaren* was not necessarily an imperialist, nor was he limiting his choice to imports from overseas colonies. It was simply a more fancy term for "grocer." And a German *Laubenkolonie* had nothing to do with colonialism; it was a set of allotments, usually near a big city, in which devotees of horticulture, mostly working or lower middle class, grew a few flowers or vegetables on a very small space.

Such studies could be pursued at considerable length and there is no gainsaying that they were a good antidote to loose thinking and muddleheaded conclusions. Above all, Koebner warned against facile historical analogies. It is unlikely that he would have compared Israel in 2002 with Weimar Germany, as one of his successors did.

Koebner, like most German Jews of his generation, had been a German patriot, and the country's defeat in World War I had come as a blow. Yet after World War II, he refused to set foot on German soil again. He had broken with his German past. He admired Britain, but Britain was on a collision course with the Jewish community in Palestine after the White Paper of 1939 that virtually ended its promises made in the Balfour Declaration of 1917. This led to a campaign of anti-British terrorism that hurt Koebner, and that he bitterly opposed.

Although he was a Democrat, he also believed that to maintain peace and order in the world some major powers were needed, and Britain seemed to him predestined for this role. He was not in principle opposed to a Jewish state, but he feared that the price would be too high.

Thus it was not surprising that shortly after his retirement from the Hebrew University in 1953, he decided to settle in the Temple Fortune region of north London, where a cousin, his only relation, had made his home. He continued to give occasional lectures in England

and was invited to Princeton. But a sudden disease put an end to his life in 1958; Gertrud survived him by many years.

Richard Koebner, though he remained a stranger in Palestine, made a contribution to the cultural life of the country that had given him shelter. He helped to educate and act as a guide for a young generation of historians. He explained to them what historiography was all about, he taught historical method, and he steered them away from narrow-mindedness and provincialism. But his contribution was intangible, its fruits could be seen only many years after, whereas Richard Kaufmann quite literally changed within a few years the face of Jewish Palestine.

Kaufmann was born in Frankfurt am Main into a very assimilated Jewish family and, as with Koebner, little is known about his early years except what he studied and where. His teacher in Munich was Theodor Fischer, one of the great architects of his age. He began of his career during the years leading up to World War I, and had the misfortune to be stationed near Verdun, the most dangerous part of the German western front. But he survived and was later transferred to the Russian front. In his spare time he submitted a proposal for a major building project in a town near Charkov, and to his great surprise won the competition.

He must have been fairly well-known early on, for he had been warmly recommended to Arthur Ruppin who was then in overall charge of Jewish settlement in Palestine. Clearly Kaufmann was also a man of uncommon enterprise, for few planners and architects were willing, even after the ravages of the war, to leave civilized Europe and transfer their activities to the wild Near East. He was a Zionist, but equally important was the opportunity to plan and build a country almost from scratch. The challenge must have interested him giving more scope to realize his ideas than working in a continent which was largely built up and in which there was little room for new ventures.

And thus Kaufmann came to Palestine less than two years after World War I had ended, and since he came from a former enemy country this cannot have been easy; he was one of the first Jews from Germany and Austria to make the move. During the next three decades he planned and built one hundred twenty agricultural and ninety urban settlements (not to count some one hundred fifty individual buildings), among them kibbutzim, agricultural cooperatives, and urban quarters, mainly in Jerusalem but also in Haifa and Ramat Gan and the Dead Sea region.

Richard Kaufmann helped to introduce to Palestine the simplicity of the International style—flat roofs, clear horizontal lines, rounded corners—in contrast (and in succession) to the ornate neoclassicism of the late nineteenth century. But far more important was his pioneering idea of the garden city in Palestine, which had originated in England before the turn of the century and subsequently spread to other parts of the world.

The garden city was first developed by Ebenezer Howard, an English stenographer and typewriting expert, who advocated it as part of a whole concept of social reform. The garden city was a leading forerunner of environmentalism. According to his original ideas, there was to be common ownership of the land and a vegetarian lifestyle. There was also to be a social mix as far as the population was concerned (this never materialized as can be seen, for instance, in London's Hampstead Garden suburb). The more ambitious targets of social reform fell by the wayside, but garden cities came into being in Letchworth, Welvyn, and Stevenage in England, Hellerau near Dresden in Germany, and later on in Sweden, Finland, Japan and (much later) in France.

If the main motive in England was decentralization in the wake of the Industrial Revolution and the advent of a place away from the squalor and the slums congested cities, it was a reaction against the ugliness of the "new quarters" (outside the Old City of Jerusalem) that had come into being in Palestine during the second half of the nineteenth century. Above all there was the need to create homes for new immigrants. Kaufmann returned from a research trip to Europe in 1922 full of optimism that the job could be done despite all the difficulties. Much of his work was in the Valley of Jezreel, the heartland of the kibbutzim and moshavim from Nahalal to Ein Harod, but his work in Jerusalem is my main concern.

Kaufmann planned three of the main quarters in this city—Bet Hakerem in the west, Talpiot in the south, and Rehavia somewhere in between, as well as several smaller ones such as Mekor Haim and Bayit veGan. These are today the most desirable neighborhoods in Jerusalem with tens of thousands of residents. The basic idea was that each house should have a garden, that it should be set back some distance from the street, and that in places like Rehavia where not enough land could be bought there should at least be a certain distance between houses. The fact that there could be only relatively few private gardens in Rehavia appears a blessing in retrospect because of the lack of water for irrigation. Kaufmann's plans provided for the planting of trees and setting up children's playgrounds as well as other such amenities, which are self-evident today but were not considered essential in the 1920s.

Bet Hakerem and Talpiot were his first projects. The early residents of Bet Hakerem were mainly from the teachers' seminary that had opened there in 1913. Among the founders of Talpiot (the name is taken from the Song of Songs) were employees of Jerusalem banks, government officials, and a few public figures, or, to be precise, people who attained fame in later years. (The Nobel prize winner S. Y. Agnon lived in what is now 16 Klausner Street; his home is now a museum.)

Bet Hakerem and Talpiot were, at the time, outside the municipal boundaries of Jerusalem. The distance presented certain difficulties, especially for security—Talpiot had to be evacuated during the riots of 1929 and it was again endangered in 1936–38 and in 1947–48 as the road to town passed through Arab quarters—but it had the advantage that the residents were not subject to the stringent regulations of Jerusalem municipality; they were exempt, for instance, from the order that all new houses be built of Jerusalem stone.

These garden suburbs, as Kaufmann envisaged them, were to consist of one-family homes, but gradually this practice was discontinued and three- or four-story houses were built, in which several families lived. He had thought of these quarters as quiet neighborhoods with opportunities for taking leisurely walks free from the hustle and bustle of the city center. But with the expansion of the city and the immense growth of traffic, this is no longer true of Rehavia.

Among the architects and planners who came to Palestine from Central and Eastern Europe during the 1930s there were perhaps two dozen who had been associated with Bauhaus or other centers of modern building such as Le Corbusier's office in Paris. The most internationally famous was Erich Mendelsohn, who between 1933 and 1941 divided his time between London and Jerusalem. Mendelsohn bought the famous windmill at 5 Ramban Street in Rehavia and made it his office. This is a Jerusalem landmark, originally built in the 1870s when it stood in the middle of nowhere. He was very much in demand and received important commissions, such as the Hadassah Hospital on Mount Scopus, Weizmann's home in Rehovot, and both the Schocken Library and their home in Talbiyeh to name but a few. His ambition was to serve as the official chief architect of the country, but there was no such position.

Mendelsohn was critical of his colleagues from Europe who, he claimed, were slavishly copying a style that had developed in a different climate and different physical and cultural conditions. This was unwarranted criticism, for everyone agreed that the International style had to be adapted to local conditions. They were quite willing to learn from existing styles and modes of building, but there were, alas, few lessons to be learned from existing structures in Jerusalem, where there was an incredible mixture of styles. The most prominent and characteristic buildings were such architectural monstrosities as the Palace Hotel and the massive Turkish prisons. There was a Mediterranean style, to be sure, but the cupolas, arches, and arcades so typical of it did not attract Kaufmann, who believed in the principles of modern architecture.

Kaufmann had always concentrated on building houses that enabled the residents to tolerate the summer heat—this was after all, the period before air-conditioning—by designing smaller windows and in some cases two roofs, one atop the other with space in between. In the final analysis, there was not much difference between the houses Mendelssohn built and those constructed by his colleagues. Mendelssohn left for the United States and greener pastures in 1941; with the White Paper of 1939 and the outbreak of the war, the building market deteriorated. Kaufmann had grown deeper roots; he remained in Palestine.

During the 1920s, Kaufmann had been mainly engaged in planning settlements. During the subsequent two decades, he became more preoccupied with building houses. The reasons are obvious. By the early 1930s, most of the major planning had been done, and although many new settlements were still to come, a general pattern had been established. The next major wave of immigrants came only after the state of Israel had been born, and the influx was so enormous, the financial resources so limited, and time so pressing that there was little room in anyone's schedule for planning. Israel suffers the consequences to this day. Kaufmann and his contemporaries were not faced with a design problem. They were dealing with social and economic problems. Even talented architects like Kaufmann and Mendelssohn lacked the vision needed to build giant temporary absorption camps comprised of tents and barracks, the so-called ma'abarot.

In later years, when the "development towns" came into being, more intelligent planning would have been of enormous help, but by that time Kaufmann was no longer alive. There was very little money as well, and great pressure to do something quickly. No great laurels could be earned. Visitors to Israel in the twenty-first century are struck by what is perhaps the greatest collection of mid-twentieth-century architecture, and they are impressed by the intelligence and the sensitivity of planners like Kaufmann. They are equally impressed by the congestion that now tends to paralyze urban and inter-urban traffic and the dire need for a new generation of planners to build satellite towns to alleviate the pressures and to prevent worse problems in the future.

In different ways, Koebner and Kaufmann represent the fate of German Jewish immigrants of a certain age who came to Palestine. Kaufmann had volunteered to settle well before Hitler emerged in Germany. Koebner was compelled to leave his university. His work was very much rooted in the history of Germany, whereas Kaufmann could have practiced his profession almost anywhere in the world. German architects and planners who left Germany after the Nazi rise to power were among the very few professionals received with open arms abroad, in Turkey and the Soviet Union, in England, and even the United States—where they were especially welcome in Chicago.

For Koebner, mastery of the Hebrew language was essential, whereas for Kaufmann it was a minor issue. Those who came to Palestine as children or adolescents did not face these problems. Even those who had just finished law school elsewhere could find their niche in their new homeland; many leading positions in the Israeli legal system (including the Supreme Court) were held by men and women who had arrived in their twenties. Even in medicine, older doctors made their way successfully, but then no one expected them to make long speeches in flawless and elegant Hebrew at the sickbed of a patient. Those in trade and banking often found it difficult to get accustomed to Eastern European and Middle Eastern business customs (there was a saying at the time: How can you make a small fortune in Palestine? By arriving with a big one). But eventually many of them also had modest success. Many went into agriculture—temporarily—and somehow survived the experience.

The truly tragic cases were those who had taught in German schools and universities, German speaking rabbis, middle-aged lawyers with no international experience, not to mention German-language writers. Many of them led a miserable existence as peddlers and small grocers, unsuccessful insurance agents, and the like. For them, mastery of the language was crucial to success, but even if they had known the language, the openings were few and far between. It was, of course, not even a specific Palestinian-Israeli problem, but a problem of emigration and exile.

Koebner was extraordinarily lucky to find work in his profession at a time when equally distinguished German professors had to wash dishes in the United States until they found employment in a minor college, and some never even got that far. There was, for example, the sociologist Norbert Elias. Born and educated in Breslau, and only a little younger than Koebner, he published the highly original *The Civilizing Process* just before the start of World War II. Fate was not kind to him; the best jobs he could find during his exile in Britain were temporary fellowships and work as a teaching assistant at a minor university. He lived into his nineties, long enough to be recognized as one of the greats in his field.

It is not certain whether Koebner fully realized how lucky he had been, safely ensconced as he was on Abarbanel Street with shade trees in front of the house and many neighbors of similar background in the immediate neighborhood. He was too old to get accustomed to a wholly different environment, to feel culturally at home in Palestine. Koebner's world had ceased to exist when the Nazis came to power.

Kaufmann could not possibly have foreseen he had chosen one of the very few professions that would guarantee a full and satisfactory career amid the vicissitudes besetting German Jews in the first half of the century when he registered in Frankfurt University many years earlier. Nor could Koebner have anticipated that he had chosen one of the least likely ones to help him to find his place in the world in later years.

The story of the German Jews who went to Palestine, especially the story of their social and cultural impact, has yet to be written. Their political influence was small, but they or their offspring were quite prominent in local politics—at one time the mayors of Jerusalem, Tel Aviv, and Haifa were of German-Austrian origin. For a long time they dominated the legal system and the universities, and their influence on musical life (to give one example) was decisive, more or less till the arrival of the Russian Jews. The "Jeckes" or German Jews were not loved; they were thought erroneously to be pompous, stiff, cold, and lacking knowledge of and interest in things Jewish. They faced great difficulties during their early years in the country, and were the butt of countless jokes, and not always good-natured ones. It was many years later that something like a wave of nostalgia spread, and recognition of both their enormous contribution and regret that there had not been more of them.

Almost fifty years have passed since the death of Koebner and Kaufmann. The population of Israel is about thirty times what it was in the days when Kaufmann made his blueprints for Rehavia and Talpiot. The Hebrew University has about thirty times as many students as in the days when Koebner gave his inaugural lectures there. The number of cars seems to have increased a thousandfold, and Jerusalem has many more inhabitants than in the 1920s and '30s. Bet Hakerem and Talpiot are still expanding. Kaufmann would still recognize Rehavia, Talpiot, and Bet Hakerem and the Number 4 bus which Koebner took every day from the center of town to Mount Scopus, which is still running on more or less the same route. The character of Abarbanel Street where Koebner lived has hardly changed, and the old *Palestine Post* building on Havazelet Street, where Kaufmann had an office on the second floor, is still standing though sadly run down. The building survived a major bombing in 1948; this happened in the evening when no one was in Kaufmann's office, nor in mine, which was adjacent to his. I had seen him earlier that day leaving for home together with his constant companion, a bulldog.

There are a few reminders. There is a Richard Koebner Center of German History at the Hebrew University, and there have been articles, a dissertation, and exhibitions dedicated to Kaufmann's work. He was given the honorary title Builder of the Country. There is a little street in Jerusalem called Architect Street (Rehov Ha'adrikhal) with a sign in small letters: "In honor of Richard Kaufmann." His wife, Gurit (Karman), a physical education teacher, is remembered as the mother figure of Israeli folk dancing. But it is also true that during the last years of his life he received only few commissions. A new generation of Israeli architects was taking over from the pioneers. The pulse of history in Israel, even in Jerusalem, the most conservative of its cities, has been beating very quickly indeed, and this is now in almost every respect a different country and a different city.

CHAPTER 6

SCHOLEM AND THE
HEBREW UNIVERSITY

I WENT BACK TO 28 ABARBANEL STREET WITH MY WIFE SOME years ago, and a sad journey into the past it was. The house apparently had not been lived in for years, the gate opened with difficulty, the garden was neglected, and the blinds in the windows were down. An elderly lady in the house across the street saw us entering the property and asked whether she could be of help. She invited us to tea and said that occasional visitors came from abroad to see the house in which Gershom Scholem and his second wife, Fania, had once lived. But now—she shrugged her shoulders.

I remembered the days, more than thirty years earlier, when almost any time of day or evening a steady procession of mostly graduate students (Scholem's seminar took place in his home), and visitors could be seen walking up the outside staircase to Scholem's small apartment on the second floor, past the apartment which had once belonged to the three Cohn sisters. During World War II, Scholem's circle of friends, called *Pilegesh,* met at his place and talked over coffee and cake on Saturday afternoons. The conversations were always animated and there was the occasional competition, such as writing German poetry in the style of Heine, Rilke, or Stefan George.

Pilegesh is a Hebrew word that means "concubine," but there was no sexual implication as far as Scholem's group was concerned. The word was chosen simply because it was one of the only words you could spell using the first letters of the names of those who regularly stopped by the circle—the linguist Hans Jacob Polotzki, the mathematician Hans Lewy, the physicist Samuel Sambursky, et al.

I don't think there was any other person in Jerusalem, certainly not another academic, not even Martin Buber, who had so many visitors, and not only celebrated figures. There were those whom Scholem had known in Berlin in his younger years, there were friends and friends of friends. Scholem, a prickly conversationalist, liked company, and although he had no children of his own, he liked children and more than once asked me to bring along my daughters.

Until the 1950s Scholem was well-known mainly to people in Israel and those in his field of study, Jewish mysticism. As a young man he had accompanied the great writers Haim Nahman Bialik and Shmuel Agnon on their walks, but the politicians liked his company too. Many thought of him as an *ilui* (genius). Berl Katznelson, a founder of Mapai, the workers' party, would drop in for long talks, as would Israeli president Zalman Shazar (who had known him in Berlin), and even Ben-Gurion. There was a time when the leaders of the Jewish community in Palestine were avid readers and genuinely interested in both Israel's leading intellectuals and the intellectual problems of the day.

Then, in the 1950s, Scholem's fame spread in Europe and even among the New Left as a result of his friendship with Walter Benjamin (I never fully understood the Benjamin cult, which persists to this day, but if Scholem thought so highly of him, I bow to his judgment).

Then the Christian theologians came, and the religious philosophers, and the sociologists of religion, and the students of messianic movements, and the psychologists (mainly the Jungians, to whose meetings in Ascona he frequently went), and the literary critics—and in the end an intellectual tour of Jerusalem was not complete if you didn't have tea with Gershom Scholem. Many came who had no interest in Jewish mysticism; the sage of Abarbanel Street had the reputation of knowing everything, which was partly true.

Relations with his colleagues were sometimes a little strained; he was combative, he had a biting wit, and he had been involved in frequent quarrels concerning university affairs. He had devoted friends as well as bitter critics but virtually everyone respected him, even if a little grudgingly. The Hebrew University made him a professor when he was in his early forties, which was almost unheard of, and when he retired he was elected president of the Israeli Academy of the Humanities and Sciences.

Scholem was born into a very assimilated Jewish family in Berlin. He became an ardent Zionist while still at school, not because of any personal anti-Semitic experiences but simply because he had reached early on the conclusion that, much as he was steeped in German culture, Germany was not his country and he did not belong. Hence his interest in the Hebrew language and in Jewish history and thought. He was equally knowledgeable in the field of philosophy and mathematics; in fact he graduated *summa cum laude*. Among the Zionists, he was the most radical, not in the sense of territorial conquest, but of living up to one's ideals. This meant acquiring a mastery of the Hebrew language and immigrating to Palestine as soon as was possible. He managed to be released from army service in World War I by pretending to be mentally unbalanced. (Some of his enemies would later argue that he had not needed to try very hard to create such an impression.)

During the years after the war he met and became friends with many of the young people who would later play a leading role in Jewish studies. Some of them would become his colleagues in Jerusalem: Shlomo Goitein, an authority on Arab-Jewish relations in the Middle Ages; the philosopher Hugo Bergmann; the historian Yitzhak Fritz Baer; the philosopher Leo Strauss. In 1923, he was offered two jobs in Palestine, one to teach mathematics, the other to be head of the Hebrew section of the National Library. This was a largely fictitious job at the time, and there was no budget, but Scholem accepted it anyway. He arrived in Palestine in September 1923, and soon after he married his first wife Escha, whom he had known back in Germany.

When Scholem came to Jerusalem he settled first in Abyssinian Street, named after the Ethiopian churches located there; Rehavia, Abarbanel Street, and the Hebrew University that were to comprise the entire compass of his world in later years did not yet exist. But there were two buildings on Mount Scopus: the so-called National and University Library (originally located in downtown Jerusalem)—a great name for a small library—and the Institute for Biochemistry (Chaim Weizmann's field was chemistry, and he had found it easier to collect funds for this purpose than for any other).

It was around these two smallish buildings that the Hebrew University came into being. The idea of a Jewish university had been in the air for a long time, well before the first Zionist Congress ever met. There had been a petition on the part of Sicilian Jews as far back as 1466 to establish a Jewish university, and the idea also appears in Rousseau's *Émile*. In the 1880s, it was taken up in a series of articles by Hermann Schapira, a professor of mathematics at Heidelberg. But although many people agreed with him and several resolutions were passed, nothing happened until, in 1913, the Zionist Congress decided to establish a university in Jerusalem that would be the intellectual center of the Jewish people. Mr. J. L. Goldberg of Vilna made a donation of seventy-five hundred pounds and an Odessa Zionist committee contributed a smaller sum. This was enough to buy the estate of an Englishman named Sir John Gray Hill on Mount Scopus. It was a good choice: John Henry Newman, in his classic book *Idea of a University*, notes that among the many elements required to make a university is "first and foremost a pleasant site where there is a wholesome and temperate constitution of the air; composed with waters, springs, or wells, woods and pleasant fields, which being obtained, those commodities are enough to invite students to stay, and abide there." There are not many springs or pleasant fields on Mount Scopus, but the panorama is truly spectacular.

The matter rested when war came. It remained, however, a matter of great importance on the agenda of many Zionist leaders. In April 1918, even before the war had ended, and before the whole of Palestine had been liberated from the Turks, a foundation stone was formally laid by Weizmann in Jerusalem. (Allenby, the British military commander, told Weizmann that he thought it premature—a Turkish counteroffensive was possible and they might have to retreat from Jerusalem.) It took almost another seven years before the official opening ceremony took place in the presence of Lord Balfour (the former prime minister of Balfour Declaration fame, and also a philosopher), Field Marshal Lord Allenby, and British High Commissioner Sir Herbert Samuel, as well as many other notables such as Ahad Ha'am (Asher Ginzberg) and Chaim Bialik, the national poet.

Development was slow, and the need to collect money as well as the difficulties of doing it—the university never received financial support from the Mandatory government—were only part of the reason. Ronald Storrs, the governor of Jerusalem, had suggested the establishment of an English university in the city, an idea that did not appeal at all to the Zionists. There were basic differences of opinion with regard to what the character of the university should be. Some of the leading figures outside Palestine wanted the university to consist mainly of a few research institutes, predominantly in the physical sciences; the feeling was that it should not concentrate on teaching nor should it try to cover too many subjects. This was the background of the quarrel between Albert Einstein and Judah Magnes, the chancellor of the university from the beginning days up to 1935, when he became its president. Even though Einstein and Weizmann were scientists, their concept of a university was in many ways similar to the classic model: a place to acquire a liberal education and general knowledge that could be of no practical use, and certainly not of immediate, professional use.

Einstein complained that it was impossible to set up a university that could compete with leading institutions in Europe and America in a few short years; he warned of the danger that the Hebrew University would become a mere *Bauernuniversitaet* (a peasants' university). In general, Weizmann supported Einstein, partly because he thought that the emphasis should be on science rather than the humanities and also because he didn't want yet another rabbinical seminary on Mount Scopus. But he also wanted to retain the goodwill of Einstein, the most famous Jewish scientist of the century.

Einstein and Weizmann's fears were not unfounded, but Magnes and others were more realistic. Would leading scientists come to Jerusalem to do their research? The brief answer was negative. No one had any such intention, least of all Einstein. And what of the students who were knocking on the door of the new institution, who could not enroll in Polish and Romanian universities—and German universities after 1933? What about those Jews who wanted to study and obtain a degree? Those were good questions and, in 1928, they were answered with the establishment of the Faculty of Humanities. A small institute of Jewish studies had been on Mount Scopus from the beginning. Later, a Faculty of Science uniting biochemistry and biological studies was initiated. A prefaculty of medical studies was set up in 1937–1938, together with Hadassah Hospital, which was completed on the other side of the road on Mount Scopus at about this time. But for another ten years, until well after World War II, there were only postgraduate medical courses. Young people who wanted to study medicine had to go to Beirut or some European university, quite often in Switzerland.

In late 1938, when I registered as a student, the number of professors and instructors was no more than a few dozen and the number of students eight hundred sixty-four. By comparison, in the academic year 2003–04, of the 149,000 young Israelis enrolled in the country's seven universities, about 20,000 of them were at the Hebrew University. My career on Mount Scopus lasted a few weeks only, but since the place was so small, that was enough to get a general idea of what was going on. The one building I came to know reasonably well was the small library. On some mornings I was the only student there. The librarians were exceedingly helpful, though they seemed to have doubted whether the young man ordering a great mass of prewar Russian revolutionary periodicals (of which the library had an excellent collection) was a bona fide, serious student. I was happy to have escaped from Nazi Germany on the very eve of *Kristallnacht*, but studying appeared pointless for a number of reasons. It seemed obvious that war would break out in the near future, in which case my formal studies would come to an end, or at least be seriously interrupted. Above all, I was not yet eighteen. I did not know what I wanted to study.

Another six years would pass before I was to revisit the university with my wife. We were settled in the nearby Arab village of Issawiya. (Jerusalem rents were out of our reach.) At this time I spent mornings reading Russian history and a great many other subjects. The librarians were still the same, and some even remembered me.

In the 1930s the Hebrew university had absorbed students from Eastern Europe and Germany. Its academic standing was not of the highest, but it had the reputation of being a German rather than a Levantine university, as far as standards and general rules of behavior were concerned. This, needless to say, was a great compliment, for in the pre-Hitler days German universities had been considered the model to be emulated all over the world. The number of professors of German Jewish origin was actually small: Baer, Scholem (hardly a typical German professor), the mathematician Abraham Fraenkel, and Julius Guttmann in Jewish philosophy. They were helping to model the Hebrew university according to the standards they had been accustomed.

But there were many others, mainly from Eastern Europe, who had also studied in Germany or in Vienna and who had been influenced by the Central European tradition. Among them were Harry Torczyner, the great authority on Hebrew philology from Lviv (Lemberg), as well as L. A. Mayer, one of the world's leading authorities on Islamic art who hailed from Stanislawów, also then in Eastern Galicia. Both had studied in Germany or Austria, as had the archaeologist Benjamin Mazar, the classicist Victor Cherikover, and key figures in medicine such as Rachmilevitch and the physicist Israel Dostrovsky. Graduates of British, American, and Italian universities were the exception; it was difficult indeed to find anyone who had not earned a degree in Germany.

The story would not be complete without mentioning once more Dr. Judah Magnes. Born in the United States and trained as a rabbi, he ran the university in an autocratic way, but it is doubtful whether it could have been run in any other way. A tall man with an imposing presence, he was a fine speaker and never afraid of controversy. He had been a pacifist during World War I and his politics were left-wing. Magnes had his difficulties with Weizmann and Einstein, who frequently interfered, but after the early years were not of much help to the university, anyway—especially as far as fundraising was concerned, which was the most urgent task at the time. It is doubtful whether Magnes would have lasted against such opposition without the strong support of his friends in the United States, where most of the contributions came from.

The Hebrew University was on its way to becoming a perfectly respectable, though not a leading, university when World War II broke out. Many students joined the British army or the Jewish defense forces. Soon after their return, a new war broke out at home and they were again enlisted. During the War of Independence, the Hebrew University was cut off from the rest of Jerusalem, and after a Jewish attempt to send a convoy to Mount Scopus in which almost eighty people were ambushed and killed, among them leading Hebrew University figures, the teaching there ceased altogether.

For the next twenty years it was a university in exile. Makeshift quarters were found in Terra Santa, a former Franciscan monastery, and later on a new campus was built in Givat Ram, a western suburb of Jerusalem. The student body grew, and so did the faculty. But they were cut off from their books and laboratories. The humanities suffered less than the sciences, but it was an unhappy period for everyone, that is, until the war of 1967 when Mount Scopus (previously an enclave inside Jordanian territory) again became accessible.

Today at the Hebrew University's main campus on Mount Scopus, there are many dozens of new buildings, some impressive, others less so. The university has seven faculties and twice as many schools, including business administration, occupational therapy, and one for overseas students. There are fourteen hundred senior faculty members, which is about twice the number of students when I studied there. The Hebrew University endowment has grown enormously. Whereas in the 1920s, ten thousand pounds was a major addition to the budget, a sum about which the university committees would deliberate for weeks and months, those in charge of gaining financial support from abroad now set one billion dollars as a target. But it has been increasingly difficult to get donations, and there is almost constant talk about an acute and severe financial crisis. Tuition at the university was free during the early years. Later on fees were charged, and though the sums involved were small in comparison to private universities elsewhere, they were still beyond the reach of those from poor families.

The main income of Hebrew University (as of all other universities in Israel) comes from the government (about sixty percent), still more funds come in from the Jewish Agency, and a network of "friends" in many countries. But the government has other priorities—most notably defense—and there have been substantial cuts in allocation to higher education. As the general economic situation deteriorated after 2001, the financial situation of the universities became serious; professors over the age of fifty-eight were offered early retirement and were not replaced. Tuition is about twenty-five hundred dollars a year, and class size has increased. In 1998, there was a long students strike (the senior academic staff was on strike too), and there have been strikes, or threats of strike, almost every year thereafter.

The Hebrew University is no longer the only institution of higher education in the country; there are six others not counting the Open University. Enrollment is shrinking, and it is no longer the biggest or the best in various fields.

Bar-Ilan University has twenty-six thousand students (including students from several outside colleges) and Tel Aviv has slightly more. Even Ben-Gurion University in Beersheba has fifteen thousand students. In addition, there is Haifa University, founded in 1970 (about the same time as Ben-Gurion University) and spectacularly located on Mount Carmel. The Haifa Technion, founded a year before the Hebrew University, now has almost thirteen thousand students. The

Weizmann Institute of Science in Rehovot has some twenty-five hundred senior scientific staff engaged in research, more than any university. (The Haifa Technion, in comparison, has eight hundred sixty-four faculty members and they are virtually all engaged in teaching.) Then there is Open University as well as twenty-three community colleges from the Galilee and Safed to the south (Ashkelon), and twenty-six teachers seminaries have emerged during the last two decades. The intention was to direct those who wanted to study for a BA to the new colleges, whereas the universities should focus on those aiming at a higher degree. There is even a private university in Herzliya, but it covers only a few disciplines.

Standards of excellence, and of weakness, change in the academic world, and what was true ten years ago is not necessarily accurate now. But even so it can be said with confidence that those who wanted to study history or the contemporary Middle East in the 1970s or '80s were probably better advised to go to Tel Aviv than to Jerusalem. The Tel Aviv School of Economics is on par with similar schools worldwide. Bar-Ilan has the largest school of education and social work in the country. Beersheba was strong in mathematics; in medicine many of the best physicians and professors could be found in Tel Aviv University rather than Jerusalem where Hadassah Hospital once had a near monopoly.

A few Arab students enrolled in the Hebrew University even back in the 1930s. Today, between 12 and 15 percent of Haifa University's total student body is Arab, and other Arab students are studying in Jerusalem, Tel Aviv, and Beersheba, even though Arab universities have been founded in places such as Bir Zeit near Ramalla in Jerusalem, and in smaller Arab towns.

Women students were few and far between in the early days of the Hebrew University. Today, more than 60 percent of the students are female. About 70 percent of the students still come from outside

Jerusalem, but the university is becoming more and more an institution of that city and not of the Jewish people as originally envisaged.

Is there a division of labor among the universities? Yes, up to a point. It is clearly in the case with Bar-Ilan, which is a religious university, and of course Ben-Gurion University in Beersheba was founded to help to develop agriculture and industry in the Negev, the southern part of Israel which is largely desert. Thus Beersheba not surprisingly has an institute of desert research and, according to its original mandate, actively promotes hi-tech industry, agriculture, health services, and education in the region.

Seventy-eight years after it was opened, the Hebrew University is no longer a German university, and not only because German universities, however competent, are no longer the model for the rest of the world. The campus resembles in many respects American campuses or the newer universities in Britain. But the Hebrew University is more democratic than most universities in other countries, which does not always make for efficiency. The election of a dean or a rector, or deciding what courses should be taught may turn into a major political issue generating heated debate. It is said that the fights in academia have often been so bitter because the stakes involved are so small. This is true for universities in other parts of the world, but it applies perhaps even more strongly to those in Israel. There have been serious, ideological questions (for instance, should Jewish history be taught within the framework of general history, or separately), but these have been the exceptions.

Seen in retrospect, the question arises as to who was right in the heated debates of the 1920s. Weizmann and Einstein were justified in putting the emphasis on science, which today is the leading subject on virtually all the campuses. The president of the Hebrew University is Menachem Magidor, an expert in artificial intelligence; Jacob Ziv, the president of the Israeli Academy of Sciences and Humanities, is a leading figure in electrical engineering. Among the presidents of the other institutions of higher learning are Avishay Braverman, an economist, at Ben-Gurion University, ex-general Amos Horev at the Haifa Technion; Middle Eastern scholar and former ambassador to Washington Itamar Rabinovitch, at Tel Aviv; and Yehuda Hayuth, an expert in maritime transport, at Haifa University. Another former ambassador to Washington is vice president of the Hebrew University, and Tel Aviv has former ambassadors to Bonn and Paris in the same capacity. A professor of Judaic studies is unlikely to become president of an Israeli university unless he (or, someday, she) is a person of extraordinary gifts in other fields as well. Even Bar-Ilan University, heavily orientated towards Jewish studies, has the distinguished physicist Moshe Kaveh as its head.

The trend toward putting scientists into leadership positions (or, at least, the trend away from leaders who specialize in the humanities) exists in most countries, but it is of particular interest in Israel where the original idea was to set up a Jewish university. This very concept belongs to a bygone age. In the contemporary world there are universities in which Jewish studies are vigorously pursued. There is no Jewish physics or chemistry, just as there was no German physics (even though some misguided spirits at the time believed it), and the same is true for most other disciplines. It goes without saying that universities located in the Middle East ought to have a special interest in the local history, geography, and civilization, not to mention the anthropology and the archaeology of the region. But neither students of law nor of philosophy want or need to devote more than a small part of their time and effort to specific aspects of Jewish law or Jewish philosophy. Jewish and Hebrew literature and Jewish history are a different proposition. The great majority of students are opting for sociology, psychology, engineering, and computer science rather than specifically Jewish subjects. The choice of discipline depends largely on the job market.

In what way are today's students similar to and different from those fifty or sixty years ago and, again, from students in other parts of the world? Above all, they were in a hurry then, and they are in a hurry now. Those who arrived in Palestine during the 1930s or who returned from military service in 1945–1949 had no money and no one who could support them. Many had devoted the best years of their lives to the service of their country, and they wanted to graduate as quickly as possible. The same is true with regard to those who attend university now after spending two or three years in the army. For the great majority of them, there is no fooling around, no carefree student life, no fraternities and sororities, few if any sports. Political and social activities are minimal. A few people kick a ball around, but on the whole it is too hot in summer and too rainy in winter and, anyway, there is no time. Oxford may be rowing against Cambridge, Harvard competes against Yale, but if Jerusalem ever competes against Tel Aviv or Haifa such an event will attract little interest. No one has ever heard of athletic scholarships in Israel.

Students knew more about things in the 1930s and '40s, but at that time the student body was a small elite, only 1 or 2 percent of today's enrollment. An academic degree was unnecessary for many careers, so students could study wisely, and what interested them, without worrying too much about the practical uses of the courses they took. The students of that bygone period, born mostly in Europe, by virtue of geography and history and education abroad, mastered three or four or, if they came from Romania, even five languages. Up until the early 1950s, the majority of students were not native-born Israelis but had come from abroad. There are no statistics about professors, but I suspect that only in the 1970s and '80s was there any real change of guard, and those born and educated abroad became the minority.

Today, a degree is necessary for most jobs, so students gravitate to fields of study that will lead to employment—sciences and technology rather than the humanities. The knowledge of more than two languages is rare, except perhaps in the case of graduate students who continue their studies abroad. Another exception is Middle Eastern studies, where stringent standards prevail and where the knowledge of two Middle Eastern languages is mandatory. As for the professors, the average is high—there are senior lecturers who in other countries, notably the United States, would have gained a professorship years ago. At the very top, some have received offers from leading universities abroad. Many scientists have worked abroad, usually in the United States, with leading colleagues in their field at MIT, Caltech, and Bell Laboratories. Most physicians who specialize in one field or another worked for years in major American university hospitals. Leading Western academics are invited to come to Israel, though usually for short periods.

Even so, the Hebrew University, like the other institutions of higher learning in Israel, is competent but not outstanding. The Israeli universities can be compared with good universities in Europe and America, but not with the leading ones. They do not have the financial resources to compete, all other considerations quite apart. Critics of the contemporary university have pointed to the great changes—usually for the worse—that have taken place in recent decades as the result of their increase in size, the expansion of bureaucratic administration, and a growing quest for publicity, not to mention the challenges of the Information Age. The historical mission of the university was to educate—to make students smarter and teach them to *think*. Today there is a real danger that the modern university has become merely a training ground for specific professions—it teaches students to *do*. Is the university losing its soul? This is a troubling question for universities with endowments of many billions of dollars and for those whose existence was secured by massive and permanent state support. For the universities in Israel and other, less fortunate countries, the question of survival was, and is, paramount. It could well be that the truly important questions about the sense and purpose of life in general, or of the role of a university, occur only at a certain level of economic security, not among those stumbling from one financial crisis to the next.

For the last twenty years of his life, following his retirement from the university and from teaching, Gershom Scholem continued to lead a very busy life. He served as president of the Israel Academy, was in high demand at conferences all over the world, and was frequently interviewed by interlocutors in Israel and abroad. He wrote his autobiography, which unfortunately covers only his German years and his first steps in Palestine. He edited his correspondence with Walter Benjamin and others, and there was, of course, the steady stream of visitors to Abarbanel Street. He closely followed events in many fields but wrote relatively little.

I had been introduced to Scholem by my friend, the writer and historian of ideas George Lichtheim, who had translated Scholem's magnum opus, *Major Trends in Jewish Mysticism.* Richard Lichtheim, George's father, whom I also knew in Rehavia, had been one of the early German Zionists, for reasons very similar to Scholem's—the realization that much as the German Jews were steeped in German culture, they did not belong, and that assimilation had been not only undignified but eventually a failure. Lichtheim senior became a Zionist diplomat in Turkey during World War I, and in Geneva during World War II. He was one of the first who realized the full extent of the disaster that had befallen European Jewry, and his alarming reports to Jerusalem were disbelieved for almost two years.

George Lichtheim, with all his admiration for Scholem, did not share his fascination with Jewish thought. He was a skeptic, and his exchanges with the master are among the most interesting and provocative in Scholem's wide correspondence.

I had the first of several long conversations with Scholem when I worked on my *History of Zionism* in 1970, and I began by asking him what had made him a Zionist. Scholem thought for a moment and then said, "I was repelled by the most unfortunate craving of our people constantly to travel. And what is the situation now that there is a state? They travel more than ever before." Scholem was one of the most formidable polemicists I knew, but he was also aware that there were certain limits not to be exceeded—things one was entitled to say but not to put on paper. He liked to gossip and was given to little indiscretions, often amusing, sometimes less so ("Buber had a roving eye").

Scholem became involved in the famous debate about the German-Jewish dialogue (and symbiosis), which has had repercussions to this very day. It began in 1964 when Scholem was asked to contribute to a book in honor of Margarete Susman, a German Jewish essayist and poet who had belonged to what was known as the Association of German Citizens of Jewish Faith. Susman had been one of the protagonists of the German Jewish dialogue and what she considered the indestructible communality between the German and the Jewish spirit.

Scholem's polite reply to this invitation was uncompromising. There had never been a dialogue, he said. This was pure fiction. True, many Jews had been desperately looking for such a dialogue and a symbiosis during the preceding two hundred years, some in a dignified way, others groveling and in a spirit of subservience, but there never had been a true exchange between equals because there was no interest on the German side to listen and to talk. Even those sympathetically inclined had regarded the surrender of Jewish traditions as a precondition, for the Jewish community, as they saw it, was in a process of advanced disintegration. They were willing to accept individuals as equals but certainly not the Jewish community as a whole. Scholem wrote that there had been much Jewish cultural creativity in Germany, but it had led nowhere and certainly had not been accepted by the Germans. And how could one even consider renewing a dialogue after the Shoah? How to conduct a dialogue with the dead? Was this not tantamount to blasphemy?

It was a very powerful statement, and who could deny its essential truth? To read even now about the first and second generation of German Jewish intellectuals, the sons and daughters of the Enlightenment, Rachel Varnhagen and Henrietta Herz and their friends in Berlin and elsewhere most of whom became converts, is a painful experience. It is easy to understand the reaction of a later generation of young Jews (such as Scholem) who found the idea of total assimilation despicable. This was also at the bottom of Scholem's dispute with Hannah Arendt, the author of a biography of Rachel Varnhagen, in the wake of the Eichmann trial. Arendt was in some ways a latter day, more successful Rachel who did not have to convert since she lived at a time when being a non-Jewish Jew was no longer an embarrassment. Indeed, it had become fashionable. Scholem accused Arendt of being indifferent to Israel, of not loving it, which was true. Arendt replied that she loved individual people but could not possibly love a whole people, and the debate came to a natural end.

Could it not be argued just as well that if assimilation was undignified, it had been equally undignified that the Jews, in the Middle Ages, decided to stay in countries that did not want them, where the people did everything to make the Jewish experience intolerable? True enough, but where could they have gone?

And once the walls of the ghetto came down, was it not natural that they tried to deny or hide the things that made them different from their fellow citizens? If they had believed in the faith of their ancestors and then given up for opportunism, this would have been despicable. But if they no longer believed in the religious tradition, and wanted to distance themselves from their Jewish heritage, however esthetically displeasing to some, this was not a betrayal. True, they could have turned against all religion rather than converting to

Christianity, (or in the case of Moses Mendelssohn's daughter, Dorothea Schlegel, first to Protestantism and later to Catholicism). But agnosticism was not common at the time.

Only the Orthodox Jews were more or less immune to the temptations of the Enlightenment. The Jewish religion was simply not particularly attractive to young educated Jews. Judaism had resisted change, and so adherence to tradition was bound to be based more on ritual than on piety. Conversion was the ticket to European culture, as Heine had put it, and European culture was infinitely more attractive than the Jewish tradition. Of course, it was true, as Scholem had maintained, that even the most tolerant Germans had no interest in the Jews as such, for what contribution had they made before the eighteenth and nineteenth centuries to European culture?

But this was not a specific German problem; the reaction in Britain and France and Russia, in fact everywhere else, was the same. A "dialogue" existed in none of these countries. A great part, probably the majority, of educated Jews turned their back on their own religious tradition and left the community. There was no secular answer to the consequences of the Enlightenment except a *Trotzjudentum,* an attitude that rejects the surrender of their identity because it is undignified, even cowardly. This would lead either to Zionism or something like a Bundist ideology in countries where major Jewish communities still existed.

The weakness of Scholem's position was that he sometimes tended to equate assimilation with emancipation. The emancipation of the Jews from the heritage of the Middle Ages, from obscurantism and general backwardness was inevitable and desirable. Eventually Jews would find their place in this new world, some giving up Judaism altogether, others living in the state of Israel where a secular existence within a Jewish community was a possibility. In a world in which the borders between religions and cultures had become less rigid as the result of migration, demographic change, and changes in the zeitgeist, the position of the Jews who wanted to remain Jews became less problematic. Anti-Semitism certainly would not disappear, but it became just one of the issues of conflict among various ethnic groups and in most countries no longer the most acute and prominent one.

But what of the six or seven generations between the Enlightenment and the present brave new world? Scholem solved his Jewish problem by immigrating to Palestine and devoting his considerable energy, enthusiasm, and intellectual power to studying Jewish mysticism, a subject which had been wholly neglected for many centuries. He did not identify with it, nor was he a religious Jew. But he had found a subject of great fascination to keep him busy all his life.

There was a great upsurge of interest in mysticism in the second half of the twentieth century all over the Western world, and this explains in part the enormous interest in Scholem's work. Among observant Jews, opinions about any such preoccupation with the kabbalah were divided. Many religious sages of the eighteenth and nineteenth centuries thought that it was a dangerous subject, one that could lead to apostasy and even madness; they recommended that only married men over the age of forty should be permitted to deal with it. Nor were the academic experts quite happy for, as most of them saw it, the kabbalah was nonsense. However, as a very learned professor once conceded, while the study of nonsense was not an academic subject, the study of the history of nonsense was. (Incidentally, the attitude of the Sephardim towards the kabbalah and its concomitants from the book of Zohar to the prevalence of amulets had been far more liberal.)

Scholem was a wise and lucky man—he had solved his Jewish problem and founded a new science in the process. But not everyone could follow in his steps of becoming a student of Jewish mysticism. What were the others, the less fortunate contemporaries to do? The subsequent fate of some of Scholem's friends and of course those select members of *Pilegesh*, is interesting. Jakob Polotzki, the leading expert on Coptic literature, moved on to Copenhagen. George Lichtheim settled in London, where he committed suicide in 1972. The philosopher Hans Jonas could not find employment at the Hebrew University at the time. He taught first in Canada and later in the United States; when offered a major position in Jerusalem in the 1950s, he declined. Leo Strauss who, like Scholem, had been an early Zionist, also settled in America; he came to teach at the Hebrew University for a year, but he too refused an invitation to stay there. The Orientalist Shlomo Goitein, who had arrived in Jerusalem as a young man the same time Scholem came there, moved on to live and teach in Philadelphia and later retired to Princeton.

The fate of these and some other individuals does not necessarily reflect deep disappointment and bitter despair (though in some cases it does). It simply means that the situation of the 1920s, when Scholem had opted for life and work in Palestine, had changed and that in the second half of the twentieth century many more opportunities existed to follow one's inclinations and to find personal fulfillment. Abarbanel Street had at one time been a near ideal location for a Jewish thinker. But it has disappeared like ancient Yavneh or Spain of the Middle Ages or Berlin and Warsaw in the 1920s. The houses are still there, but the genius loci has disappeared.

CHAPTER 7

SHENHABI, THE
HOLOCAUST, AND
YAD VASHEM

I T MUST HAVE BEEN JUST BEFORE OR SOON AFTER THE END of World War II in Europe that I saw Mordechai Shenhabi, in Café Alaska on Jaffa Road, talking with great animation. Sitting at an adjacent table, I overheard part of their conversation but "memorial" and "Yad Vashem" did not mean anything to me. Nor did I know much about Shenhabi, even though I had met him a few times at political meetings that I had covered as a correspondent. He was a legendary figure. He was the first member of Hashomer Hatzair, the youth and kibbutz movement. He had arrived in Palestine on the *Ruslan,* the first ship from Europe after the end of World War I. (He landed on January 2, 1919, to be precise.) But he was not in the front rank of its leaders, nor was he the best known. His name seldom appeared in the newspapers. He was very active behind the scenes at small meetings and sitting on committees; he was a writer of letters and memoranda. He was a bit of a bohemian, and some thought he lacked perseverance and staying power. He had too many brilliant ideas and not enough time (or resources) to follow them up. Even today there is hardly anything about Shenhabi in books about the early years of Israel.

I learned more about him in later years. Mordechai Shenhabi (the original name of the family was Elfenbein) was born in Volozipek, a very small town in Galicia, on the Austrian-Russian border. Shortly after the outbreak of the war and the Russian advance into Galicia, the family escaped to Vienna. He attended Polish and Jewish schools in the Austrian capital and at an early age became active and prominent in the youth movement. He certainly took his Zionism seriously—he left school before graduation and went to work as a peasant in the countryside. Then, in late 1918, he made his way to Palestine via Odessa and Constantinople, not an easy enterprise for someone not yet nineteen in the postwar turbulence.

Shenhabi liked adventure and he was a man of quick decision, qualities he kept throughout his long life. After his arrival in Palestine, he worked as an agricultural laborer, first in Hulda, a collective settlement, and later in Galilee. He had an excellent knowledge of the language and faced no problems of assimilating to his new surroundings. In fact, after a year he was made a guide and advisor to more recent arrivals in the country.

He turned out to be an extraordinarily gifted youth leader, and his movement thought he would be better employed as an organizer in Europe than as an indifferent agricultural laborer. Shenhabi had become a kibbutznik, first at Bet Alfa and later Mishmar Ha'emeq, but during the 1920s and '30s he spent more than half his time on various missions to Europe, attending Zionist Congresses (he became an admirer of Chaim Weizmann) as well as summer camps of his beloved Hashomer Hatzair. From 1926–28 and then again in 1934–40 he was on extended missions through Poland and Germany.

There was something restless in his character; he was a wanderer between various places and people. There were women in his life, and they played an important role, but he never married, and to his great regret, this man so beloved by children and adolescents had no children of his own.

Shenhabi was a romantic and visionary, incredibly creative as far as new ideas were concerned. His weakness was that while most of his ideas were praiseworthy and indeed necessary, they often came too early, and by the time their turn had arrived Shenhabi was preoccupied with new projects.

He was a pioneer of kibbutz education at a time when few people even thought about the subject. He encouraged kibbutz industry at a time when everyone else was certain that kibbutzism should be exclusively agricultural. Some of the industries he helped to found exist to this day, such as Galam in Ma'anit, which produces industrial and edible starches. He envisaged the immigration of unaccompanied children to Palestine from Europe well before youth *aliya* was founded. He was no mean collector of contributions for the Jewish National Funds and his own movement, and after the Nazi rise to power he developed ingenious schemes, legal and illegal, to transfer Jewish money from Europe to Palestine. He had a special interest in the development of Jerusalem and established both a For Jerusalem Society and a Jerusalem bank well before the state came into being. He was not a religious believer but was instrumental in setting up a Bible building in Jerusalem. He befriended actors and artists and helped found a museum of applied art in Jerusalem.

But despite these many and various aspects of his life, Shenhabi should be mainly remembered for being the first to press for a memorial to the millions of Jews in Europe. He remained for years the main promoter of the project and was also the one who named the institution Yad Vashem, the Holocaust Memorial Authority.

As Shenhabi tells it, the idea occurred to him in a dream in August 1942, well before the full extent of the disaster was known. In the days that followed, the idea began to take concrete shape. He imagined a big memorial national park in the north of the country near the kibbutzim Dan and Dafne. In the middle of the park there was, in his mind's eye, a monumental building engraved with the names of all the victims. His vision for Yad Vashem included a research institute in Safed as well as several other buildings. Within a month, Shenhabi had elaborated the project in a four-page memorandum submitted to the Keren Kayemet (the National Fund for the purchase of land). A subsequent memorandum included drawings indicating how Shenhabi envisaged the site and the buildings.

In 1942, the enormity of events in Europe was not yet widely understood, in any case, Jews in Palestine were preoccupied with an immediate physical danger, for the country was threatened by Axis forces from south and north. Furthermore, the National Fund had little money; none was coming from abroad during the war, and whatever funds they had were needed for the purchase of land.

Yet for some reason the project was not rejected out of hand; in fact, it received additional impetus in November of 1942 when Palestinian civilians returning from Germany by way of a prisoner exchange brought to the Zionist leadership authentic information about the extent of the massacre in Europe.

But at the same time many objections were raised. Critics thought the project was too big and expensive, and that it ought to be tackled by another institution. Some raised points of principle: Was it not customary to erect monuments to remember victories and achievements rather than disasters? Ben-Gurion at a later date suggested that a memorial site of this kind should be in Jerusalem rather than in some distant place in the north of the country.

Nothing was done. Shenhabi was asked to keep secret the very existence of his memorandum, about Yad Vashem. It was only after the end of the war in Europe, on May 25,1945, that Shenhabi went public and an article about his project appeared in *Davar,* daily newspaper of the trade unions. Soon after, the National Council (*Va'ad Leumi*) accepted the Shenhabi resolution, and so did the Zionist congress in London. It was decided to establish a large executive committee (often the best method for burying a proposal), to bring in the Hebrew University and the chief rabbis, and to open a small office in Jerusalem with a branch in Tel Aviv. In 1947, the first Yad Vashem Congress at the Hebrew University considered the establishment of a research center concerning the mass murder of European Jewry.

A few months later, fighting broke out between Arabs and Jews, and it was not until 1950 that Shenhabi renewed his efforts with yet another memorandum. This one suggested the preparation of a list of all the victims and the idea of giving them retroactive Israeli citizenship. This idea became the Yad Vashem Act, finally passed by the Knesset in 1953—the lawyers had taken a long time to ponder the ramifications of retroactive citizenship and had found a great many obstacles. But in the meantime the idea of building a memorial to be financed, at least in part, by the Israeli government had gained ground.

While Shenhabi was not entirely squeezed out, the initiative for setting up Yad Vashem passed to a number of more prominent establishment figures, such as the minister of transport, David Remez, and the minister of education, Benzion Dinur. These were active politicians who could devote only part of their time to Yad Vashem. This helps to explain the further delays that occurred in carrying out the project. But to be fair, it would have taken years in any case—a consensus was needed on where the memorial should be located as well as its character and future activities. The architects' blueprints (among them some of the leading figures of their generation, such as Aryeh Elhanani and Aryeh Sharon) had to be considered. Finally, in 1957, some of the buildings on Mount Herzl were ready for occupation, and in April 1961, one of the main components, the memorial hall, was finished.

Today Yad Vashem is known to every Jew and many non-Jews worldwide. Located on Mount Zikaron (Remembrance Hill), it consists of two museums, several exhibition halls, many outdoor monuments, and a great repository of information about the Holocaust. About two million people visit Yad Vashem each year. In the Hall of Names, three million names have so far been registered. The Historical Museum presents the history of the destruction of European Jewry, and the Hall of Remembrance is a tent-like structure in which a memorial flame burns and where various ceremonies are held. There is a children's memorial, and an avenue and garden of the righteous among nations, honoring those non-Jews who risked their lives to help Jews during World War II. So far, some sixteen thousand such people have been commemorated, including eighteen diplomats. Each case is investigated in great detail by a committee founded in 1963 and headed by a judge of the Israeli Supreme Court. Originally, a tree was to be planted in honor of each of the righteous. This was discontinued for lack of space, and their names are now listed on a wall of honor in the garden.

Yad Vashem engages in education and research. There are special courses for teachers, an encyclopedia has been compiled detailing Jewish communities that were destroyed, conferences are arranged, books and periodicals are published dealing with various aspects of the Holocaust. As the number of survivors is quickly dwindling, a major effort has been made to collect written testimony as well as oral accounts. Modern technology is used. Yad Vashem's database and multimedia programs have been fully computerized. A new major structure has been built designed by leading architect Moshe Safdie—his magnificent entrance plaza creates a bridge between the everyday world and the sanctity of the memorial site and serves to prepare the visitor for the Yad Vashem experience.

Yad Vashem is not, of course, the only place commemorating the Jewish victims of Nazism. There are other smaller institutions in Israel, for instance the kibbutz museum devoted to the memory of the Warsaw ghetto fighters. In accordance with the law passed by the Knesset in 1953, the twenty-seventh of Nissan (usually in early May) is dedicated to the Shoah, and there are two minutes of silence when all traffic stops. Israeli school children are sent to visit Auschwitz. Radio and television programs, especially on Shoah Day, deal with the event.

All this is in line with the instructions of the Yad Vashem Law: to "collect, investigate, and publish all evidence regarding the Shoah and its heroic aspects and to inculcate its lesson upon our people."

The evidence has certainly been collected, investigated, and published, but the rest of the injunction of 1953 has been difficult to carry out. This has been the case since the very beginning. Interest in the Holocaust in Palestine and Israel, as in the rest of the world, was limited during the immediate postwar decades. Large parts of Europe were in ruins and the reconstruction of the continent was the most immediate priority. In Israel, these years were lost to the struggle for statehood, and once the state was established, the myriad issues raised by mass immigration, the enormous problems of absorption, the years of austerity (*tsena*), and mass unemployment. During these years, large sections of the population lived in tents and makeshift barracks. Those who had survived in Europe and immigrated to Israel were not particularly eager to tell their stories, and even if they had done so, the readiness to listen to them was less than great.

Yad Vashem was an obligatory stop for visiting VIPs even in the 1950s, but it was only after the Eichmann trial in 1961, after normalization and a certain prosperity prevailed in Israel, that the issue of the Holocaust became an issue of greater importance in public consciousness. The slow realization of the Holocaust's enormity also had psychological reasons—the extent of the disaster took time to register. Few books were written about the Shoah in Israel and elsewhere, and only one of them was widely read—*The Diary of Anne Frank,* which was essentially the emotional outpourings of an adolescent girl that only indirectly made comment on the tragedy. The fact that there was so little that was specifically Jewish in this book enhanced its appeal, of course, and made it possible for many others to identify with her.

The 1970s, '80s, and above all the '90s, marked the high tide of not only Israel's preoccupation with the Holocaust, but a concomitant awareness in the United States and Western Europe as well. In rest of the world, above all Asia and Africa, but also in Latin America and Eastern Europe, the murder of the Jews has never been an important issue. Knowledge of and interest in it hardly exists.

Many books about the Holocaust were published in Israel during these years. These took the form of personal accounts as well as historical descriptions. References to the Holocaust were frequent in public discourse. But how deep did it go? Essentially, the interest was limited to sections of the Ashkenazi population. Oriental Jews had hardly been affected by the mass murder: There had been some restrictions in North Africa under Vichy rule, but no killings, and the destruction of Greek Jewry (a wholly Sephardi group) was outside the purview of Middle Eastern and North African Jewry. Few of these Jews would go as far as Rabbi Ovadiah, one of their prominent spiritual leaders, who called the victims of the death camps "sinners," but there certainly was a great deal of indifference; the Holocaust was simply not part of their experience.

Even within the Ashkenazi sector there was strong resistance against the commemoration, certainly on the part of the ultraorthodox who regarded the killing as divine punishment for Jews who had strayed from the faith of their fathers and also for the misdeeds of the Zionists. This kind of interpretation was bound to strain the credulity of even the most faithful, because many Zionists, after all, had been saved whereas most of the ultraorthodox communities in Eastern

Europe had been destroyed. The question of why God had permitted the slaughter of his chosen people and especially those carrying out the commands of the religion was bound to bother both rabbis and their followers, and it continues to do so.

How to assess the work of Yad Vashem since its early days? It is easy to find debatable statements even in the law of 1953, which set the points for its subsequent developments. The word *holocaust,* to begin with, is unfortunate, for it means a sacrifice usually by burning, and this is not at all applicable to the fate of European Jewry during World War II. However, this is not a problem for Israel since the Hebrew term *Shoah* is far more appropriate and it has replaced, to a limited extent, the use of *holocaust* even in Europe and America.

The "heroic aspects" mentioned in the law were few and far between. But how could it have been otherwise? The great majority of Jews killed were elderly people, the very young, women without military training, and the sick. The small minority who could have resisted were isolated among a hostile or indifferent non-Jewish population and they had no arms except perhaps a knife and the occasional revolver. They were starved into submission and died of disease. If millions of able-bodied Russian prisoners of war died without resistance, how could one expect heroic actions from a civilian population? There were such cases of heroism not only in Warsaw ghetto, and they deserve to be remembered, but nothing much is to be gained by magnifying them.

And what "lessons of the Holocaust" are to be "inculcated upon our people"? What happened to the notion that chauvinism, racism, and the total contempt for human rights may have fatal consequences? It goes without saying, but the Holocaust was not envisaged and carried out by the Jews. Should the lesson be that one should resist murderous attack at an early stage? This again seems obvious, but what does it mean in practical terms? The issue of the "lessons" is difficult and complicated, and while there are no doubt certain lessons, there may be also false lessons such as the whole-world-arrayed-against-us syndrome, or the tendency to see Hitler and Eichmann in every perceived enemy of the Jews or of Israel.

Despite proclamations of shock and horror made by statesmen and public figures, the Holocaust has been denigrated almost since the beginning. It began with some British diplomats during the later stages of World War II who complained that the Jews were jumping the queue as far as the victims of the Nazi murder was concerned. After all, they argued, others suffered too, so why was it imperative that special assistance be given to the Jews? As late as 2000, the prominent American historian Arthur Schlesinger Jr., defending the Allied leadership against criticism, wrote in his autobiography that the only sensible policy for Roosevelt and the Allied leaders was to win the war as quickly as possible. But no one had suggested that the war should be won as slowly as possible; the issue at stake was whether, in 1944, an infinitesimally small effort should be made by the Allies to help surviving Jews so that at least some of them might live to Victory Europe Day.

This argument that specific Jewish concerns should not be prioritized prevailed in the Soviet Union and the Communist-dominated countries of Eastern Europe, where mentioning the murder of the Jews was virtually taboo until the downfall of communism. In the West there was the Holocaust denial industry on the extreme right, and the relativization of the Holocaust on the extreme left. But even many of those with no political axe to grind believed that too much publicity was given to the Holocaust. Why have a big museum on the Washington Mall? After all, the Holocaust was not part of the American experience, nor was it carried out by Americans on American soil. Why a Holocaust Day in Britain and a conference of heads of state in Stockholm? Why a huge memorial in the very center of Berlin which was certain to provoke antagonism?

Not all of these questions and comments were unjustified, nor were they always uttered by obtuse anti-Semites. What matters in any case was the underlying reluctance, the feeling that enough was enough and that there should be an end to the invocation of Auschwitz. There were many pleas in favor of amnesia, but this was an unnecessary endeavor, for amnesia was bound to become invasive soon enough in any case.

The interpretation of the Holocaust became mixed and controversial in later years as intellectual fashions changed among publicists, political scientists, and historians. Often an author would fasten on a small grain of historical truth and exaggerate it out of recognition (or even to the point of downright falsification) to serve his own pet theories. It began even before Hannah Arendt's complaints, in the wake of the Eichmann trial, that the Jews had not behaved heroically. It included books and articles claiming that Hitler was a weak dictator and was not really in control, that the mass murder happened more or less by accident, that the main concern of the Nazis was not really racial and ideological but economic-geopolitical (to make room for German settlers in the East), that Hitler hated Bolshevism far more than the Jews, and that he turned against the Jews only after it appeared that the war against Russia was lost. Those preoccupied with studying the Holocaust were criticized for not dealing with other groups that had also been persecuted.

On the other extreme there were those claiming that the Germans had always aimed at "eliminating the Jews" and that virtually all Germans were involved in the murder. And those regurgitating the Trotskyite line maintained that it was all a plot of the Israelis who used the Holocaust to justify their imperialist politics and the oppression of Palestinian Arabs especially following the war of 1967. Others argued that the allies had done everything in their power to save Jews and that every Jew who had wanted to emigrate before war broke out had been able to do so. No version was too outlandish and farfetched to find a band of fervent supporters. In fact, it was probably not by accident (as old Marxists would say) that some of the wildest fantasies became bestsellers not only in Germany, but also in other European countries.

All important historical events attract professional naysayers and lunatic fringes like a lamp attracts moths. An event so traumatic, so highly emotionally charged as the Holocaust, was bound to have the same effect. Some wanted to annoy the Jews in general; others to attack the Jewish establishment; some were convinced that the task of intellectuals was to be forever critical and the Holocaust had to be deconstructed; some wanted to peddle their political views; others wanted to make their mark by opposing an older generation of Holocaust historians. At the same time the elements of stupidity and ignorance, of boredom and contrariness should never be underrated— they all played their role in the motivation. And for obvious reasons, the provocative publications affecting not an event remote in history, but as painful and recent as the Holocaust, were bound to provoke both angry responses and a lot of publicity. And thus the anti-Holocaust industry generated protest and refutation, and instead of a dignified debate there was more often scandal and vituperation.

Those who followed the media for the first time in the 1980s and '90s could easily get the impression that the Holocaust was mainly about money, about class actions and greedy lawyers. It is true that without the loud and shrill denunciations made by professional Jewish spokesmen in New York, usually self-appointed, nothing much would have happened, neither on the part of German industry or banking. It is probable that no pictures would have been returned to their rightful owners by European museums. There is something to the question addressed by God to King Ahab, *"Ratzachta vegam yarashta?"* (Have you killed and also inherited?).

The price paid for this campaign was high, and it is not at all certain that it was worthwhile in the final analysis. The obscene fees of the lawyers will be what is mainly remembered, not the suffering of the victims. It seemed everyone felt entitled to add his or her "wisdom" to the existent interpretations of the Holocaust, and the Fagins became the central figures in the legal field. Yad Vashem exhibitions and learned studies could not possibly compete with the sensationalists and those bent on causing scandal.

In the history of warfare, the systematic robbing of corpses on the battlefield was a common practice even though punishable by law. And since the Holocaust was a giant battlefield, such practices became common, except that in our time there is no punishment, only substantial fees. Nor will anyone go to prison for using the victims for purposes of entertainment or propaganda, or for otherwise trivializing the Holocaust.

Thus the way the Holocaust is remembered and invoked more than fifty years after the event is often painful, especially to those who lost their families and survived by luck or accident. It is not so much the Holocaust deniers or belittlers who provoke indignation; those who hate Jews will always find a rationale for their feelings and there is no way to persuade them or to refute them on any rational level. Having had one set of their arguments refuted they will think of different ones. Underlying all this is a gut reaction that cannot be reached by way of argument. Nor should one get unduly excited about those, mainly in the academic world and not a few of them Jewish, who try to put the Holocaust in what they think is the "proper historical perspective," that is to say as just one occurrence in humanity's inhumanity towards fellow human beings.

After all, many hundreds of thousands of Armenians were killed or perished in World War I, and many Russian prisoners of war and Serbian civilians and gypsies were killed or starved to death in World

War II, as were some homosexuals and Jehovah's Witnesses, not to mention political enemies of the Nazis. The debates as to whether the Holocaust was unique are distasteful and wholly unnecessary. Every historical event is unique. Circumstances and motives are never the same; as Heraclitus said, you cannot step into the same river twice. Whether it was an unprecedented event is a different question. There have been instances of genocide from ancient history to Pol Pot, and Rwanda. But again, the historical circumstances were different in each case, and "comparative studies" are of limited relevance. They can also be misleading.

Perhaps one should show some forbearance even towards the forgers and the lunatics among the commentators about the Holocaust, and those who make their way in the world by exploiting the greatest tragedy in Jewish history, whether for personal gain or political advantage. Such people can always be found whatever the subject under discussion. But for those who were bereaved and who did suffer, it is a tragedy that the victims are not shown more respect, that their horrible fate is so often the subject of misuse to this very day.

There is but little doubt that those who want to relativize the Holocaust are bound to prevail as time passes by. The pain is no longer felt with the same acuteness. The awareness declines—and there is no way to halt this trend. Those inmates of the camps who survived and those who lost their closest relations and friends are dying out. With the years, other disasters are bound to occur and the recollections will of necessity pale, the Holocaust will appear no more of a tragedy than any of the wars or civil wars or natural disasters in history.

This can be witnessed even in Israel, partly because of the demographic change in the population—for large sections, the Holocaust was always a remote event. The ultraorthodox are opposed in any case to the way the victims are remembered by a secular society. But it is also a generational issue. Is it really a good idea to take the seventeen-year-old to

Poland, often without much preparation? Will he or she not regard the excursion as a way to have a good time, and are such youngsters at all capable of understanding? A leading Holocaust historian once noted that only those with a command of Yiddish can write authoritatively about the mass murder in Eastern Europe. This gross exaggeration does contain a tiny kernel of truth. I have realized that even sophisticated academics who were never exposed to Nazi rule, or at the very least another harsh dictatorship, find it exceedingly difficult to understand what it was like. This is not to say that they have no business studying, writing, and talking about the subject, but an extraordinary effort of empathy and imagination is needed on top of factual knowledge to provide more than a one-dimensional understanding.

Have the attempts to commemorate the Holocaust made by Yad Vashem and other institutions outside Israel been in vain? Probably not. The more publicity that is given to the Holocaust, the more antagonism is bound to occur. And not only among the neo-Nazis; it is equally resented by those who are simply indifferent, who think that the whole issue has been exaggerated, and that it should no longer figure so prominently in the public discourse. Yad Vashem and other such institutions cannot prolong and deepen remembrance beyond their natural span. But they can provide correct information where genuine interest exists, in the face of much ignorance and willful falsification.

I was twenty-one when the first authentic information about the mass murder of European Jewry was received in Palestine following the exchange of civilian detainees between Nazi Germany and the British in November 1942. Several dozens of them reached Israel and were interrogated about what they had witnessed in Nazi-occupied Europe. I was then living at a kibbutz, and our sources of information were meager—there was only the local newspaper and the occasional short-wave broadcast. I did receive, via the Red Cross, letters (twenty-five words maximum) from my parents right up to their deportation in June 1942. We knew the meaning of these events, young as we were and cut off from any special, detailed sources of information.

I wrote a long essay, or short story, at the time about the deportation of the Jews from my hometown. Many years later I found "The Jews' Transport" among my papers. I had not meant it to be published, so why did I write it? It was a cathartic act—I was trying to exorcise the guilt I felt about not having tried harder to get my parents out of Europe. Many years later I also retrieved letters sent to friends overseas in which, well before the end of the war, reference was made to Auschwitz and the destruction of European Jewry. If I, living in a small agricultural settlement far away from the centers of world politics and communication, knew about the Holocaust, how many others must have known?

After the end of the war other concerns prevailed, and not just in my own work and thinking. When Jews met and talked during those years, the Holocaust was seldom the main topic of conversation. What happened and who survived, and why, and what could have been done to save more people were questions that became very important many years later, but they were not the crucial ones at the time.

Perhaps the preoccupation with the real and actual problems that faced me and my contemporaries was only natural. The post-war period was full of dramatic and traumatic events. Perhaps it was an unconscious act of mental hygiene given the impossibility of being confronted day in and day out by the personal losses and the horrors that had taken place. I had read many of the books on the subject, but I did not visit Yad Vashem or other such institutions. My feeling was that I knew all I needed to know about the Holocaust. The historical museums and the exhibitions were for those who were not familiar with what had happened. My reasoning was probably correct, but it was certainly not the whole story. I also resisted too frequent and too intense a confrontation with the horrors in a public place; I wanted to be left alone with my grief. For similar reasons I have never visited Auschwitz or another death camp, whereas my children have been there. At a certain age they began to ask questions: why did other children have grandparents and extended families and they did not?

Another thirty years of preoccupation with wholly different topics were to pass until, in the 1970s, it occurred to me to find an answer to the questions as to who knew what about the murder, how soon the information was received, whether it was fully understood, and how people reacted. This culminated first in *The Terrible Secret* (1980), which led to the writing of a collective portrait of my own generation, those who had survived, and eventually to my work as the editor of *The Yale Holocaust Encyclopedia,* which appeared in 2001. I doubt whether thirty or forty years earlier I would have been up to the task intellectually or emotionally.

The abiding interest in the Holocaust is in many ways astonishing so many years after the event, but there is also growing indifference and indeed antagonism even in Israel. Last year on Yom Ha'shoah (Shoah Day), I happened to be in front of my hotel in Jerusalem when the sirens sounded for the two minute cessation of all activity in remembrance of the victims. The injunction was hardly observed: trucks continued to roll, many private cars and pedestrians did not stop, and some even got impatient with those who had stopped their vehicles and they honked their horns in annoyance and protest. Some of them were probably Palestinian Arabs and there is no reason why they should have observed the two-minute silence, but most were not. They were ultraorthodox or perhaps followers of Rabbi Ovadiah who may have thought that sinners should not be remembered.

It was then that I thought of Mordechai Shenhabi and what had become of his visions, and by one of these strange coincidences as I went a few steps farther my eyes fell on a small memorial. It said, in solemn, biblical Hebrew,

A memorial for Mordechai Shenhabi, of Mishmar Ha'emeq, who envisaged and strove without looking for praise to brighten up Jerusalem and make it more beautiful, to honor its past and present.

So Shenhabi, who had been made an honorary citizen of Jerusalem shortly before his death in kibbutz Mishmar Ha'emeq, is not entirely forgotten, even though the memorial has been placed at a most unlikely place—at the entrance of a small parking lot. Perhaps one day Jerusalem municipality will find a more fitting place for it.

CHAPTER 8

MUSA ALAMI AND THE ARAB-JEWISH CONFLICT

W HEN WORLD WAR II ENDED, MUSA ALAMI LIVED IN a stately home boasting some twenty rooms that his father had built in the section of Musrara close to Damascus Gate. (His phone number is listed as Musa Alami, lawyer, 4163).

On the ground floor was the entrance hall with a little recessed area where visitors left their shoes. This led to several interconnecting reception rooms with marble floors and walls painted with frescoes by Italian artists. It had clearly been built by a man of substance. Musa's father, Faidy, was not only a high official in the Turkish administration (and later, for a while, mayor of Jerusalem), he was also the head of one Palestine's leading families.

Musa Alami was born in 1897, the year of the first Zionist Congress, an event of which his family as well as most residents of Jerusalem—Arab, Christian, and Jewish—were unaware but which was to have a profound impact on their life and that of their descendants. The family originally lived in the El Wad quarter of the Old City but felt cramped and eventually moved to the house in

Musrara. Part of the year they spent in another house in Sharafat on the road to Bethlehem, a rocky area that had been transformed into a pine grove.

Musa Alami was to play an important role in the history of Palestine during several decades, right up to the end of his long life in 1984. He died in the city where he had been born. His story deserves telling, even if briefly.

Although he was the only male heir to one of the great fortunes in town, the fact that he would make a career in politics had not been preordained. When he was eight years old, Mr. Reynolds, the headmaster of Bishop Gobat school, sent him home with the suggestion that he become a blacksmith or carpenter since in view of his native stupidity there was little that education could do for him. After an interval as a carpenter's apprentice he ended up in the school of the American Colony and was subsequently educated privately and at the French École des Frères in Jaffa. There was another interruption in his education, this one caused by World War I, which he spent in the censorship office in Damascus. But at the end of the war he went to Cambridge to read law at Trinity Hall and was also admitted to the Inner Temple. He finished his studies with an honors degree some three years later, which shows that prognostications of teachers made at an early age should not always be taken as a final verdict.

After his return to Jerusalem, Musa Alami worked for the legal department of the British Mandatory government and eventually became the private secretary of General Wauchope, who was high commissioner for Palestine in the 1930s. Despite his high placement in the Mandatory government, he was uneasy about what he regarded the "generally pro-Zionist attitude" of the British. (The Zionists, of course, were convinced that the general attitude of the British was anti-Jewish.) Under the circumstances, he thought it his patriotic duty to help to counterbalance the Zionist influence. Alami would report later that there were intrigues against him in London, and his political enemies had succeeded in removing him from the influential position, even though he continued to work for the Mandatory government as a legal expert.

Surveying the state of affairs in Palestine in 1934, the standard of living for Palestinians was rising steadily, but so was political tension fueled by Arab fears of being swamped by a tidal wave of Jewish immigration: "The Arab press became more and more vitriolic in its attack upon both Zionism and British policy and the very air of the Holy Land breathed strife," according to Alami. But was there really a tidal wave? Due to the much higher birth rate of the Arabs, it appears that the Arab population of Palestine increased more than the Jewish except perhaps during 1935 when Jewish immigration was particularly high. However, what counts ultimately is not the facts but the perception, and there is no doubt that anti-Jewish feeling was rising even among people like Musa Alami who (in his own words) by temperament as much as by reasons of his official position stood aloof from the more violent manifestations of Arab feelings.

The story of Musa Alami is of interest even today for a variety of reasons, above all because it sheds light on Arab-Jewish relations. Alami relates that his parents had close Jewish friends and that he himself had a Jewish foster brother at birth. It was the custom at the time that if another male child was born in the same quarter at the same time, the mothers would nurse the other's son and the boys were considered foster brothers. Musa Alami's foster brother was the son of a Jewish grocer down the street.

Muslims, as Musa Alami remembers, lived in peace not only with Christians but associated with the Jews on terms of virtual equality. These Jews were not Zionists but old Sephardi families that had lived in the country for many centuries. They spoke Arabic, ate Arab food, enjoyed Arab music, and dressed like Arabs. Jews were very much in demand among Muslim leaders as personal assistants and because, having enjoyed a better education, they often wrote better Arabic than many Arabs. They were in demand as artisans and in other capacities as well.

But then the Zionists came. Musa Alami's first contact with the Ashkenazi immigrants was on a ship from Istanbul to Jaffa in 1919. These were a different kind of Jew—they had brought Zionist flags, intoned the Zionist anthem, and showed dislike and contempt not just for the Arabs on board but also the old-type Jews. The Zionists, he realized later in Jerusalem, were tough and aggressive, overbearing and truculent. Even his foster brother now evaded him. When he spotted Alami in the neighborhood, he dived down a side street instead of running to greet him

As a student in Cambridge, encounters with the new Jews were equally unpleasant. Invited by Jewish friends to a gathering of students, he was greeted with shouts of "*Shalom*" and inquiries as to when "you people in Palestine will finish with those dirty Arabs." This atmosphere of "complete, racial and religious intolerance" came to him as a shock. And what he witnessed later in Palestine, at a time when the first high commissioner and so many of the leading British officials were also Jews, only served to strengthen his conviction that the Palestinian Arabs were facing a mortal danger.

Musa Alami's meetings with Zionist leaders were still far off, but his opinion had already been formed. How correct are his recollections about the state of harmony which had once prevailed between Arabs and Jews and that was so rudely shattered by the Zionist invasion from Europe? It all depends how far back one goes. It is perfectly true that the Golden Age in Spain (1000–1141) was one of the great periods in Jewish history. And it is also true that under the Fatimids in Egypt and Palestine (969–1171) and at other times and places the Jews had done very well indeed. After that, the situation of the Jews in the Arab world deteriorated, but it was still better than in Christian Europe, and when the Jews were expelled from Spain in 1492, many of them made their way to the Ottoman Empire.

However, all this happened a long time ago, and it was precisely at the time of the emancipation of Jews in Europe during the nineteenth century that anti-Jewish persecutions began, mainly in parts of the Ottoman Empire inhabited by Arabs. There were no mass killings on the scale of the Ukraine pogroms after World War I, nor anything even remotely like the Nazi Holocaust. But the position of the Jews was that of *dhimmi,* the people of the book, meaning Christians and Jews who rejected the message of Muhammad. They were second-class citizens, ritually abused though not persecuted on the basis of a racial theory. They could live in peace as long as they did not become too prominent and did not, as one historian put it, enjoy themselves too ostentatiously. They were expected to maintain a low profile.

While there were often good neighbor relations, it is also true that Muslim society looked down contemptuously on the Jews. Most foreign residents in Jerusalem during the nineteenth century agree that the Jew was considered both mean and cowardly by the Arabs. Ann Finn, the wife of the British consul, reported that the very word *Jew* was usually accompanied by the words *ba'ad minak* (far be it from you). However, such enmity was part of the general xenophobia rampant in these parts of the world (and elsewhere), and it was probably less palpably felt in a cosmopolitan town like Jerusalem than in provincial centers such as Hebron and Nablus.

Most observers also report that anti-Jewish feeling among Christians (including Christian Arabs and in particular the Greek Orthodox) was stronger than among the Muslims and that most of the nineteenth-century blood libels against the Jews emanated originally from Christians rather than Muslims. If some of the less enlightened Jews referred to "dirty Arabs," in colloquial Arabic, references to Jews as dogs were equally frequent. As far as Musa Alami was concerned, what counted in the end was not the real state of relations between local Arabs and Jews but his perception, even if it was somewhat idealized and a little too rosy.

Musa Alami was aware of popular Palestinian feelings. In his autobiography, he describes the political scene in Jerusalem after the establishment of Israel in 1948. He writes,

"The new [Palestinian] leaders were a set of young men of some education, all of them in the traumatic condition induced by the consciousness of having suffered a resounding defeat at the hand of an enemy whom they had heartily despised."

In 1934, David Ben-Gurion and Moshe Sharett, leaders of the Jewish community in Palestine, requested a meeting with Musa Alami, not in his capacity as a senior government official but as a leading person in Arab political life, a supporter of the Grand Mufti Haj Amin, and the brother-in-law of Jamal Husseini, who was another central figure in the Arab world. We have only Ben-Gurion's account of these meetings, but Alami writes that these accounts were more or less correct. While Sharett (Shertok, as he then was) opened with soothing words comparing Palestine with a crowded hall in which there was always room for more people, Ben-Gurion was more forthright. He wanted to know whether the Palestinians would accept the creation of a Jewish state in return for Jewish support of a federation of independent Arab states with which the Jewish state would be associated, perhaps even incorporated.

This meeting took place in Sharett's Jerusalem home, and there was a second meeting at Alami's house in Sharafat. These conversations led to talks with other Arab leaders, but they were inconclusive even though Alami was favorably impressed by Ben-Gurion's frankness, and Ben-Gurion thought more highly of Alami than of other Arab leaders. Sharett believed that they might have led to an agreement if they had been more astutely handled, but he could have been over optimistic.

Musa Alami did not reject these advances outright, but as a government official he was not really in a position to speak with authority for the Arab community. For him the meetings were of interest, and he kept both the British and the other Arab leaders informed. But while he had an open mind, it is highly doubtful whether he regarded the conversations as anything more than exploratory in character. As his biographer later wrote, "He seems at this time to have regarded the Zionists rather as a Kenyan farmer regards elephants; dangerous creatures, always liable to destroy his property, and quite capable of being lethal, which he expects the government to keep under control, but against which he feels no personal enmity."

For the historian, these talks are illuminating footnotes. The Zionist leaders were no doubt correct in pursuing any and all possibility of reaching an agreement with the Arabs. But it is clear that these feelers were doomed. What the Jews could offer was obviously not sufficient even for a moderate, Western-educated Arab like Musa Alami. As he saw it, they wanted to bring in many hundreds of thousand of Jews from Europe, and this was bound to force out the Arabs. As Alami later wrote, "Why should Arabs have to suffer for Nazi crimes?" When Ben-Gurion suggested that the Zionists could provide immense help developing Palestine, Alami replied that he would prefer waiting one hundred years and leaving the land backward, as long as the Palestinians could do the job themselves. It was the obvious reply of an Arab patriot.

Alami was ousted from his government position as legal adviser by the British authorities and went into exile in Beirut, and then in Baghdad. Yet he continued to play an important role in negotiations with the British government in London in 1938–39. The preparation of the White Paper, which severely limited Jewish immigration into Palestine and envisaged the establishment of an Arab state with an Arab majority was largely his work. Alami complained that the Arab leaders, with their usual all-or-nothing mentality, did not recognize that the White Paper was a great achievement for the Arabs. He had a low opinion of the Palestinian Arab leaders whom he regarded as nonentities, except perhaps Haj Amin, the *mufti,* but he was too unyielding in his attitude and, in any case, had disqualified himself by working so closely with the Nazis during the war.

Alami's experiences in later years only reinforced his misgivings. As a patriot he felt it his duty to remain in politics. He again took part in negotiations with the British and others on the highest level, proposing the establishment of Palestinian propaganda offices abroad and the founding of an Arab development fund. But most of these plans came to naught because of the disunity within the Arab ranks and Alami's lone wolf style of work.

Thus arose the debacle of 1948, which coincided with the breakup of his marriage. He left the city not only because of the advancing Israelis but because he feared that some of his Arab enemies might use the opportunity to settle accounts with him. As a result of the war, the old family home in Musrara fell into Israeli hands, and the property of the Alamis in Jaffa and the Beisan Valley was lost. His second home in Sharafat was in Arab territory but almost on the demarcation line, not a good place to settle.

Outwardly Alami had changed little since his days at Cambridge. He was of medium height with a round face, a moustache, pronounced eyebrows, and a full head of hair, which had now turned grey. He smiled easily and often, even though the situation was quite sad. Alami retired to Jericho with frequent visits to Amman, his disillusion complete. The Palestinian leaders and the Arab League had proved to be useless. Help could not be expected from the Arab armies or from the great powers. But Alami, alone among the Palestinian leaders, preferred action to futile recriminations. He was a good fundraiser and succeeded in getting the money for building model villages for Arab refugees, in particular a farm-cum-school for war orphans. The land he was given a few miles north of the Dead Sea was not promising, but his persistency paid off. Water was found. His efforts attracted attention and support in various places. The farm prospered, and the produce of the villages was soon exported.

But again he became the victim of mindless Arab fanaticism. In 1958, in the wake of the overthrow of the Iraqi regime, there were riots in Jericho against British imperialism. Soon the rioters went on to destroy the work of Musa Alami, the "archtraitor." Alami rebuilt his farms, receiving help from the World Bank and the Ford Foundation. His dairy produces and poultry again found a market in Europe, Jordan, and even Israel (after the 1967 war the territory around Jericho was administered by the Israelis). Admirably, Musa Alami continued his work despite all the setbacks, despite the realization that his fellow Palestinians were so often their own worst enemies.

He died in June 1984, and the funeral took place in the Al-Aqsa Mosque in the city in which he was born. One of the mourners was overheard saying that he was the last of the Palestinians, and another added, "and one of the greatest." He was certainly not the last of the Palestinians, for at the time of his death Jerusalem had more Arab residents than at any previous period, but he was certainly the last and the most honest of his generation.

What became of the others after the disaster of 1948? Ragheb Nashashibi, another mayor of Jerusalem, became a Jordanian government minister, as did Hussein Khalidi. Mufti Haj Amin was exiled to Egypt, but since he did not approve of Nasser's regime, moved to Beirut. Jamal Husseini became a consultant to the Saudis. They all predeceased Alami.

Thus ended a whole era in the history of Arab Palestine. These leaders, virtually without exception, were notables and landowners belonging to the leading families—the Husseinis, Nashashibis, and

Khalidis in Jerusalem; the Tuqans and Abdul Hadis in Nablus; the Jaberis in Hebron; the Shawas in Gaza. They often fought each other for positions of influence, but at the same time they had much in common by way of background. Most of the Jerusalemites had gone to local schools and then trained at universities either in Beirut or Cairo. Most had studied law, but there were exceptions: Ragheb Nashashibi had trained as an engineer in Istanbul; Jamal Husseini, Hussein Khalidi, and Izzat Tannous had studied medicine. Yet others, such as Haj Amin al Husseini (the famous grand *mufti*) of Jerusalem, had studied at Al Azhar, the religious university in Cairo; so had his successor as *mufti* of Jerusalem, Sheikh Hussan al Din Jarallah.

Musa Alami was an exception among them. He spoke fluent English and French, and he knew and cared about what was happening in the rest of the world. There were a few Christians among them, such as Emile Ghouri, an editor of *al-Ahram,* the leading Egyptian newspaper, and Alfred Roch of Jaffa, but they did not belong to the inner circle of the leadership.

This had been the structure of power since time immemorial. The leading families almost all claimed to have descended from the Prophet Muhammad or, at least, as in the case of the Alamis, from Hassan, his grandson. The name Alami is probably Moroccan in origin; it is more frequently found there than in other parts of the Middle East. It could well be that the Alamis moved from the Maghreb to Palestine centuries ago. The name Nashashibi (another of the big families) originally meant "makers of arrows" and the many Husseinis and Khalidis also trace their families back to the early days of Islam.

The clans slowly transformed themselves into political parties. The Husseinis had their own party, and so did the Nashashibis. The latter was called Istiqlal. But these parties did not survive the defeat of 1948, and under Jordanian rule (1948–67), although some of the old politicians were co-opted, there was no room for party political activities. Thus a new generation of leaders began to emerge during the early 1960s, first outside Palestine and, after 1967, also inside the country.

This was what we think of as the generation of Yasser Arafat (who belonged to a minor branch of the Husseinis and who died in 2004) and those who came after him. The traditional families were still represented in the new leadership—for example, Zuhadi Nashashibi became finance minister of the Palestinian authority in the 1990s, and the main spokesman and negotiator of the Arab cause in Jerusalem was for many years Feisal Husseini, a grand-nephew of the famous *mufti* and son of an Arab military hero of the 1948 war.

But many members of these families have emigrated. The Nashashibis can also be found in local politics in California. The most prominent Khalidis of the present generation are American academics. Sheikh Sa'ad al Din Alami, a relation of Musa, was *mufti* of Jerusalem in the 1980s, a position that had greatly declined in importance. Other members of the Alami clan owned a sizeable cigarette factory in East Jerusalem. Adnan Husseini is at present director general of the Waqf, the Muslin council administering most holy places in the Old City and other land in this neighborhood. The best known of the Nuseibehs, another very old Jerusalem family, is Sari, president of Al-Quds University, the Arab university in Jerusalem.

But just as the demographic composition of Arab Jerusalem has changed over the last generation, so has the leadership in society, politics, and the economy. About half of the present inhabitants of Jerusalem hail from Hebron and the neighborhood. They dominate the markets as well as other sectors of the local economy, and they are strongly represented in the religious institutions. They are more traditional and conservative than the former elite, and support for the Muslim Brotherhood and its military wing, Hamas, is probably stronger among them than sympathies for Fatah.

But the changes are also palpable among the supporters of the Palestinian Liberation Organization and Fatah. Most of the new leaders did not come from the erstwhile landowning class, but from the middle class and those who had made money from trading. The new leadership was represented by men like Arafat himself: Abu Ala (Ahmed Qurei, born in Abu Dis near Jerusalem); Mahmoud Abbas (Abu Mazen), prime minister of the Palestinian Authority in 2003; and Faruq Kaddumi (Abu Luttof), who came from a wealthy family near Nablus, but had grown up in Haifa. These were the founders of Fatah: Arafat, who was born in Egypt, had studied engineering there; Abu Mazen, who had studied economics in Damascus and Moscow; Yasser Abed Rabbo, minister of culture and information, a native of Jaffa with a master's degree in economics and political science from the American University in Cairo; Saib Erekat, born in Jerusalem, studied in San Francisco and Bradford (England), earning a degree in conflict resolution and peace studies, then working as a journalist in his native city; Nabil Sha'ath, who had an American doctorate in economics and had taught at the University of Pennsylvania.

The generation of the founders of the PLO and Fatah were succeeded by another younger generation that included Marwan Barghouti, Mohammed Dahlan, and Hatim Abdul Qader who came from well-known families and had joined Fatah in their boyhood or as very young men. Some of them had been arrested by the Israeli authorities and, after their release, became security officials and local warlords, more powerful than their civilian colleagues.

The story of Barghouti, one of the most prominent members of this generation, is typical. A compact man, mustachioed, with a round face, he was born in 1959 in Ramallah into a well-known local family that also produced several prominent lawyers, physicians, and merchants. Barghouti first attracted attention as a student leader at Bir Zeit University and was among the chief organizers of the first intifada in 1987. Subsequently he was arrested by the Israeli authorities and expelled from the West Bank, whereupon he moved to the PLO headquarters in Tunis. He returned to Palestine with Arafat after the Oslo Accords, to which he gave hesitant and halfhearted approval. Arafat later appointed him head of the Tanzim paramilitary force, the most powerful of a dozen military and police agencies active under him and the one most actively involved in launching the second intifada in October 2000. He was caught by the Israelis in Ramallah in 2002 and sent for trial, which caused them more problems than they had bargained for.

Although the original elections from which the Palestinian National Authority emerged had been democratic, political parties did not develop in the Arab-controlled territories, other than the fundamentalist Hamas, which had boycotted the elections. Arafat had originally envisaged a secular Palestinian state, but under the pressure of Islamic fundamentalism, political life, such as it was, became more Islamic in character. Christian Arabs had played an important role in the early stage of the development of a Palestinian political consciousness, but none had belonged to the inner circle, and this did not change after 1948. Even among the terrorists there was a division according to religion, with Christian militants gravitating more to the radical Popular Front of the Liberation of Palestine (PFLP), which was secular, like the Communist Party. But as the communists shed their internationalist Marxist ballast and became gradually more nationalist and even religious, some of its leading members, as well as those of the PFLP, joined Arafat and gained high positions in the new Palestinian Authority.

Corruption spread in the territories under the new order of Palestinian control. The old leadership had been wealthy; although voicing nationalist anti-Zionist slogans, they had not been averse to selling land secretly to the Jews. But the younger elites were not that wealthy and, in any case, were greedier. Few of them were truly incorruptible. The so-called corruption report issued by the Palestinian parliament in 1997 revealed that three hundred million dollars had disappeared from the treasury of the Palestinian Authority and that kickbacks and nepotism had been the rule rather than the exception. The report probably scratched only the surface. It is a fact that a whole stratum of *nouveaux riches* emerged while state employees were grossly underpaid and wide sections of the population existed at starvation level. These abuses were more difficult to hide in a small country than in a big one, and led to not only tensions but even internal violence.

The word *corruption* has been too widely and indiscriminately used; the Middle East, like Russia, is not heir to the same traditions and standards of honesty in public affairs as Scandinavia and Switzerland, and even there corruption is not entirely absent. (It certainly has been rampant, even on the highest level, in Israel.) A case has been made, not entirely without justification, that in many parts of the world some corruption is vital for the economy to function smoothly. But it is equally true that once corruption exceeds a certain limit, it becomes a danger to the body politic of society, weakening national cohesion and the moral fiber.

The younger generation of Palestinian leaders has no feelings of reverence or admiration for those who preceded them. They barely figure nowadays in the schoolbooks and their anniversaries are not celebrated. Their parental homes have not become national shrines. The Nashashibis had their own imposing quarter above Sheikh Jerah. Jamal Husseini and Haj Amin also lived in this neighborhood. One of the main roads bears the name of Ragheb Nashashibi, and Orient House, the controversial headquarters of the Palestinians, was owned by Feisal Husseini.

I do not know what became of the ancestral home of the Alamis in Musrara (or Musriri, as the Arabs call it) with its divans and fine carpets.

Meah Shearim
November 2003

Meah Shearim
November 2003

MARKET MAHANEI YEHUDA
November 2003

JAFFA STREET
November 2003

OLD CITY FROM MOUNT SCOPUS
November 2003

MUSRARA
November 2003

Site of the Temple

The Shrine of the
Holy Sepulchre

THE HOLY SEPULCHRE

THE JEWISH QUARTER
IN JERUSALEM

Circa 1810
Courtesy Israel Museum

Ibn Gabirol Street, Rehavia
November 2003

BELGIAN CONSULATE, SALAMEH SQUARE, TALBIYEH
November 2003

10 BRENNER STREET, TALBIYEH
November 2003

KIBBUTZ RAMAT RAHEL HOTEL
November, 2003

It was sold before 1948 to a convent, but I am not certain that it still stands. Sharafat, where the Alami summer residence was, belonged to Jordan until the Six-Day War in 1967. The village was used as an occasional base for attacks against Israel, and one night in 1951 an Israeli unit destroyed the house of the *mukhtar,* or village headman. There were casualties, including women and children, one small link in a long chain of violence. After 1967, the whole area was occupied by Israel, and a big Jerusalem suburb named Gilo with more than twenty thousand inhabitants was built south of the village on the road to Bethlehem. A bus from Gilo to Jerusalem passes the village, and when the second intifada was launched, stones were thrown; peace for the inhabitants of this little place and their Jewish neighbors does not seem at hand.

Thus most of the traces relating to Musa Alami have vanished. And he deserved better from his people.

CHAPTER 9

GABRIEL STERN AND THE
BINATIONAL STATE

URING WORLD WAR II ON MOST WEEKDAYS A MAN IN
his early thirties carrying a heavy leather attaché case could
be seen hurrying along Jaffa Road, then turning to the
right at Zion Square and entering a bookshop named *He'atid* (the
Future). This was one of the city's leading bookshops, consisting of
two levels with three departments: new books, used books, and a
lending library. The man was of less than medium height, wore glass-
es, walked with a slight stoop, and was always somewhat disheveled.
His name was Gabriel Stern. He was a native of Altendorn, a little
town in the Rhineland, who had begun to study Arabic in his native
country and continued his studies at the Hebrew University. He had
a ready smile, but those who knew him a little better also knew that
he was a sad and lonely man with no family and hardly any friends,
male or female. He devoted his life to Jewish-Arab cooperation and
for a while played a role of some importance in these circles. Today,
many years after his death, his name is no longer remembered even
among the specialists.

The heavy leather attaché case mentioned is of some importance because it contained the correspondence of an association called *Ihud* (Union) and all the articles to be published in *Be'ayot* (or *Beayot Hazman*), its journal. *Ihud* was a very loose organization concerned with Jewish-Arab rapprochement. It did not have the resources to rent an office, hence the leather attaché case and the frequent visits to the bookshop, the owners of which were sympathizers. The bookshop was an interesting meeting place. The British high commissioner for Palestine would drop in on occasion, unannounced for fear of terrorist attack; Ben-Gurion browsed among the Loeb Classics of Greek and Latin texts; Avny Bey Abdul Hadi, one of the Arab leaders, was a patron, as were the local intellectuals (including a young man called Walid Khalidi who later became one of the main spokesmen of the Arab cause in America). Visiting politicians and military officers from the British army in the Middle East were frequent customers, as were Poles and the Free French.

Stern was a likeable man who had few enemies in the world despite his political views, which were considered extreme if not eccentric by most Jews. During the war he was once beaten up by Zionist activists for his refusal to join the army (he was a confirmed pacifist), but even the attackers soon realized that this most unmilitary man was not born to be a soldier and could not possibly make a significant contribution to the war effort.

I do not know whether Stern received a salary; if so, it must have been a meager sum for his employers were chronically short of money. But he had no other visible sources of income, and though a man of frugal habits, even idealists have to pay rent and eat. His job as secretary and coordinator was exceedingly difficult because he was dealing with a group of prima donnas with big egos and busy schedules. Arranging a meeting among them was next to impossible. Even coming to an agreement regarding an open letter or manifesto was very difficult. There was Judah Magnes, a long-term resident of Jerusalem and president of the Hebrew University, exceedingly busy at all times. There was also Martin Buber, the famous philosopher (more famous, alas, in Europe and America than in Palestine); Hugo Bergmann, also a philosopher and head of the National and University Library; and other very distinguished and prickly academics.

There were a very few doers among them (though it might be an exaggeration to call them men of the world). Such as there were included Chaim Margaliot Kalvarisky and Aharon (Aronchik) Cohen. But Stern could not really expect much help from these "practical people." Kalvarisky was then at the end of his long life and would drop in only rarely. I still remember him shuffling along Hassolel Street, always slightly furtively, usually hinting that he had been in touch with some promising Arab individual or group with whom a dialogue should be opened. He was of Russian origin but had studied agriculture in France and came to Palestine in the 1890s where he represented some of the interests of the Rothschilds and also engaged in the purchase of land. Kalvarisky was firmly convinced that good relations with the Arabs were essential. But early on he had learned a lesson that was alien, and even repulsive, to his political friends from central Europe, namely that living in the Near East (or the Levant, as others would put it) meant that one had to play according to local rules. In other words, *baksheesh* was not a dirty word and morally reprehensible but part of a way of life, a tradition which went back many millennia. Kalvarisky understood that a little money given to the right person or group at times went a long way, and more money went even farther.

Aharon Cohen was a totally different type. He was not, I believe, an official member of the circle but merely a close ally, the head of the Arab department of Hashomer Hatzair or kibbutz Arzi or Mapam as it was later called, the left-wing Zionist group (eventually a political party). He was a member of a kibbutz in the Jezreel Valley. He did not believe in working with the *effendis,* the rich and powerful ruling class in Arab society, but was deeply convinced that only Arab-Jewish working class solidarity and class struggle could provide a solid base for peace and cooperation. He was a Marxist-Leninist true believer Eastern European style, a red-haired autodidact with a very short fuse. He had taught himself Arabic and was a tireless worker for his cause. Once I went with him to see a leading Palestinian official in the British Public Information office and after exchanging the usual pleasantries, Aronchik introduced himself as "Ana Watani." *Watan* means "the homeland," but also "the nation." He wanted to stress his roots in the country. The official was clearly amused—what strange people these Jews were, a Bessarabian from Britchany who had persuaded himself that he really was part of the rebirth of Arabia—Lawrence of Arabia as a member of a kibbutz.

I later lost track of the members of this circle. Magnes died in 1948, soon after the establishment of the state, and Kalvarisky had passed away the year before. Aronchik the enthusiast ran into trouble. He was arrested in the 1960s and sent to prison for having passed on secret information to Soviet intelligence. I am sure he meant no harm, and I doubt he had anything of great strategic significance to convey. He simply belonged to the generation of Bessarabian Jews (often from small towns) who were traditionally orientated towards Russia and thought the Soviet Union could do no wrong. Perhaps he even believed he could help to change Soviet attitudes towards Israel. He was no traitor, simply a foolish man. After his release from prison, he published a big book about Israel and the Arab world, which was also translated into English with a brief preface by Martin Buber. (One gets the impression that Buber never read the book, for his comments have no bearing on its contents and are not relevant to it.)

The idea of Arab-Jewish rapprochement and the political attempts to bring this about go back to the early 1920s. The original inspiration came from Arthur Ruppin, a German Jew, who had lived in Palestine since before World War I and was the central figure planning Zionist settlement in the country. Ruppin thought that the country belonged to both Arabs and Jews, and he feared that unless a major effort was made to reach an agreement between the two nations there would be permanent conflict. The Jewish community would by necessity become militarized because it would have to defend its presence. Ruppin also thought that the Zionists had to look for friends in the Arab world outside Palestine. But he did not want to establish yet another political pressure group, let alone a political party (as some of his more radical colleagues did). He thought *Brit Shalom* (Covenant of Peace), as his group was named, should function as a study committee, collecting facts, analyzing them, and making recommendations rather than proposing a constitution for Palestine or engaging in other forms of policymaking.

But Ruppin's ideas did not prevail, and *Brit Shalom* went on publishing various memoranda which had little effect other than provoking the ire of the Zionist leadership that initially had been willing to help them financially and in other ways. Ruppin was the first to drop out of this group, finally despaired of reaching agreement with the Arabs.

Brit Shalom did not aim at a mass following—it was in the main a group of notables. Some of them had been born in the country, others had been there a long time, still others were recent arrivals. Almost all were academics at the Hebrew University, and German-speaking natives of Vienna, Prague, and Berlin. There were several Orientalists among them, who were convinced that Islam and Pan-Arabism were rising forces. There were a few English Jews, part- or full-time residents of Palestine, such as Edwin Samuel, head of the Palestinian radio station, and Norman Bentwich, the first attorney general of Mandatory Palestine. Above all, there was Magnes who, while not formally a member of *Brit Shalom,* was the most important single active force behind the scenes.

Born in 1877 to immigrant Californian parents, Jehuda Leib Magnes became a Reform rabbi who later became a conservative. He was very active in Jewish communal life, had an excellent knowledge of Eastern European and German Jewry, and, having studied in Germany, he had perfect German. He was a man of strong convictions who felt himself more at ease in opposition than in going with the mainstream. He was against America's entry into World War I and welcomed the Bolshevik revolution in Russia. With all this, he was well connected and kept many friends in high places among American Jewry. Friend and foe alike acknowledged his sincerity and the courage with which this inveterate dissenter fought for his convictions. He went to Palestine in 1922. He was the first chancellor and later the first president of the Hebrew University.

His views on the "Arab question" were abhorrent to the Zionist leadership, who thought him at best naïve and irresponsible. But when I asked David Ben-Gurion, many years later, who among the American Jewish leaders he thought most highly, he replied without hesitation, "Magnes." I asked him how this could be, since he had always been an ideological adversary. "Yes, but he was almost the only one who came to live in Palestine."

Brit Shalom was never a monolithic bloc. Whereas Magnes believed that the main goal of Zionism should be to found a cultural center for Jews in Palestine, this was not the policy of Hashomer Hatzair, the kibbutz movement, which was also very active in Jewish Arab rapprochement. Hans Kohn, one of the early protagonists of *Brit Shalom,* subsequently left Palestine and became a professor at Smith College in Massachusetts. He turned against Zionism because, as he saw it, it was no longer in the tradition of humanist nationalism. But humanist nationalism was on the retreat everywhere in the world and

Zionism, as Kohn's friend Hugo Bergmann put it, had probably been its last flicker. Others left the group because on the contrary they despaired of ever reaching an agreement with the Arabs, who were not willing to grant the Jews parity and equality, rejecting the idea of a binational state. At best they were willing to grant the Jews minority status such as they had in various European states. Ruppin, not a politician but a man of common sense, wrote in his diary that he feared there was no room for an understanding and the Jewish community in Palestine would live with Arab hostility as far as one could look ahead.

Brit Shalom ceased its activities in 1933, even though inconclusive talks with Arab leaders continued throughout the decade. Later on, another group of Jewish notables was founded called *Kedma Mizraha*. It consisted of more or less the same kind of people who belonged to *Brit Shalom,* with the addition of a sprinkling of old-time Sephardi residents of Jerusalem. But during the Arab revolt of 1936–39, there was not much room for new initiatives. Not until March 1939 was the League for Jewish Arab Rapprochement founded, and eventually, in 1942, during the relative quiet of World War II, yet another attempt by Magnes and his friends to launch some new initiatives in the field of Arab Jewish cooperation was created. They called it *Ihud.*

Ihud had found an Arab group, though a marginal one, that was willing to support a binational state in a self-governing and undivided Palestine. This was Falastin al Jedida (New Palestine) headed by Fawzi al Husseini, a member of a leading Jerusalem clan. But collaboration did not last long, for Husseini, considered a traitor by the Arab establishment, was killed by terrorists in November 1946, two weeks after he had signed a manifesto expressing support for the *Ihud,* but not the Zionist, leadership. As Jamal Husseini said, "Our cousin has stumbled and received his just punishment."

Magnes submitted the group's plans for the future to the various international commissions that visited Palestine between 1946 and

1947 in order to decide the future of the country. But the gulf had widened both between Jews and Arabs and also within the Jewish community of Palestine. Whereas Magnes was ready to limit Jewish immigration to appease the Arabs, most other members of his circle thought that this was impossible in the wake of the Holocaust and the urgent need to resettle European refugees. And thus with Kalvarisky's and Magnes's deaths, activities of *Ihud* came virtually to an end, even though some of its publications continued to appear as late as the 1960s.

It is easy in retrospect to ridicule the idea of a binational state as hopelessly unrealistic. But these blueprints were made in the 1920s and '30s, a time when the only binational states were civilized countries like Switzerland, Belgium, and Canada, places where binationalism worked reasonably well. In India, occasional communal riots took place, but the colonial power was holding the country together, suppressing separatist trends. The same was true for other Asian and African countries.

The Soviet Union seemed to be another country where various peoples peacefully coexisted. As Hannah Arendt, a sympathizer of *Brit Shalom* (but not a Zionist), wrote in 1945, one should give very serious attention to the Soviet nationalities policy as something to be emulated. What *Brit Shalom* should have addressed was the question of whether binationalism and democracy were compatible in the contemporary world. For unlike Switzerland, where binationalism had grown organically over the centuries, Palestine was not located in the center of Europe, or in North America; it was heir to different traditions and political cultures.

Today binationalism is dead. The only people who still advocate it are a few Jewish and Arab intellectuals, but even they do so without much conviction. Paradoxically, the only other proponents of binationalism are found on the Israeli far right; by hanging on to the territories, the country is becoming de facto binational. Following the historical experience (not to say disasters) of the last fifty years, including India and Cyprus, Sri Lanka and Afghanistan, the former Soviet Union, Yugoslavia, and so many other countries all over the world, it is difficult to muster any optimism about binationalism in this age of rising nationalism. Even in advanced, democratic societies the binational consensus is in danger of breaking up.

Seen in retrospect, the failure of *Brit Shalom* was not in its analysis of the political situation and the political prospects, which its members saw perhaps more clearly than many of their opponents. True, it was a group of politically inexperienced intellectuals—most of them were deeply apolitical people—whose humanist ideals were admirable but who chronically lacked influence. They were the salt of the earth trying to swim against a strong and very dangerous current of history. They did recognize that a permanent conflict with the Palestinians and the Arabs would cause serious problems, not just in foreign policy but also internally. What would be the character of a state more or less permanently under siege? Their decisive weakness was their inability to offer realistic proposals to solve the conflict along with the fact that they simply had no partners among the Arabs. The Palestinians were not willing to accept the Zionists except as a minority in their midst, and this was not a prospect that filled *Brit Shalom's* hearts with joy given the fate of national minorities in the Arab world and elsewhere.

Thus with the foundation of the state, the story of *Brit Shalom* and its successor organizations came to an end; a few dissertations were written in later years but there was no real interest in the subject. Then, in 2000, *The Jewish State: The Struggle for Israel's Soul,* written by Yoram Hazony, was published with great fanfare. The cost of the huge advertisements in the Israeli and American press must have been almost equal to the establishment of another settlement on the West Bank. This book claimed that *Brit Shalom* and its successors had been responsible not just for post-Zionism but generally speaking for Israel's spiritual decline, the undermining of Israeli morale, the demise of Zionism, and even eventually the end of the Jewish state. A group of German Jewish intellectuals, headed by Buber, had acted as a fifth column from the very beginning, poisoning the body politic and the soul of the Jewish community.

It was a Homeric struggle between the forces of good and evil, and the main culprit was Martin Buber, the wunderkind of German-Austrian Zionism who grew up in Lviv, in Eastern Galicia. Buber had been a proponent of cultural Zionism since the beginning; he was the rediscoverer of Hasidism as far as Germany was concerned and the author of the "Three Speeches on Judaism," an influential document that helped to stir considerable interest in the subject among a generation of young Jews who by and large no longer cared greatly about it.

Buber worked in the tradition of European neo-Romanticism, and there was a strong element in his thought of the ivory tower, of a preoccupation with the self, of a spirituality divorced from realities. What did he mean in practical terms when he wrote that "we want Palestine not for the Jews but for mankind and for the realization of Judaism"? It is hard to know. Buber was not greatly interested in the real world. Such a division between Jews and the spirit of Judaism was unintelligible to most of his readers and listeners. The Jewish religious tradition differentiates between Jerusalem from above and Jerusalem from below, the latter being the real Jerusalem; Buber was mainly preoccupied with the former. Buber's philosophy and theology are often mystical and aimed at the individual rather than the group, and certainly not the nation. But this emphasis on the I and the Thou doesn't make him an enemy of the Jewish national idea or the Jewish state. Buber was, after all, instrumental in bringing about a return to Judaism (and eventually to Israel) of hundreds and perhaps thousands of people who otherwise might have gone elsewhere. It was an unusual achievement for an anti-Zionist, as Hazony labels him. These "German Intellectuals," as Hazony calls them, came to Palestine with only one aim: to fight against the coming of a Jewish state. Their Trojan Horse was the Hebrew University in Jerusalem.

Nor can Yoram Hazony forgive the second generation of Hebrew University professors, such as the historian Jakob Talmon whose main work was about the French Revolution and totalitarianism. This Hazony misconstrued as an attack against Zionism rather than against utopianism and messianism in modern politics. He also imputed the idea of equating the Jewish state with totalitarianism. Talmon was an admirer of the British conservatives, and his book was essentially a critique of Marxism, but this did not register with his critic.

Hazony is equally suspicious of the medievalist Joshua Prawer, who wrote his main work about the Crusaders. Surely, Hazony thought, this was an implied attack on Zionism, which was also considered by Arabs as a foreign implant bound to fail in the end. The fact that Prawer was a professional historian, and as such genuinely interested in the topic, was clearly too simplistic for a believer in conspiracies like Yoram Hazony.

Why did Gershom Scholem, the great scholar of Jewish mysticism and the kabbalah, write one of his main works about Sabbetai Zevi, the seventeenth-century impostor who promised to lead the Jews back to Palestine but failed to do so? Surely this was yet another attempt to undermine Zionism and give it a bad name; he should have written about some positive Jewish hero. Nathan Rotenstreich, rector of the Hebrew University, was a neo-Kantian philosopher and thus heavily preoccupied with questions of ethics. But this too is suspicious because it was bound to lead Rotenstreich into a critique of the immoral policies of the current Israeli government. With the same logic the author could have found fault with Leo Mayer of the Hebrew University for devoting his life to the study of Islamic rather than Jewish art. There is no end to the paranoid possibilities.

What is the truth behind these alleged conspiracies of the elders of German Jewry? Most of them were true academics without much interest in politics. The Hebrew University was called by its critics the "last German university" because of its conservative, hierarchical character in both essence and form. At the same time, many of them thought it their duty as citizens and intellectuals to voice critical opinions. Some intellectuals have always, justly or unjustly, played the role of the conscience of the nation. This is particularly true for the left, most obviously in Britain, France, and the United States, but their impact has usually been modest. In any case, the desire to get involved in politics was less pronounced in Palestine, all things considered, than it was in most other countries.

Their ideas as described by Hazony are a caricature, but where he goes even more astray is in his exaggeration of their political influence, which was minimal. Martin Buber, allegedly the great antagonist of David Ben-Gurion, was virtually unknown outside intellectual circles, and even many of those who knew his name had only the vaguest idea of what he stood for. Hugo Bergmann, who was close to Buber and saw him virtually every week during several decades, wrote in his diary in 1953 that "we had sent Buber to the world and he had been so successful giving a new meaning to the dialogue between Jews and Christians, but the young people in Israel he never reached because they had come from a very different cultural climate."

I attended one of Buber's first public lectures in Jerusalem (he had arrived in 1938), an address to the Hebrew University's students' union. The translator of the Old Testament knew Hebrew, of course, but it was not a living language for him. He had wanted to give his talk in German, but this had been rejected by the university authorities. (They had not been able to make up their minds for years whether to make Buber a professor of Jewish studies or philosophy or theology; eventually he became professor of sociology.) The audience's reaction was far from enthusiastic. What he had to say was so distant from Palestinian realities that it seemed not to matter.

This was also the reason why the members of the German Jewish kibbutz movement, who had been strongly influenced by him in their country of origin, turned their backs on him during later years: his message was no longer relevant. Buber remained largely isolated during his life in Palestine and Israel, and he had very little influence even within the university. There is a Buber School of Jewish Studies in Germany and also in the United States, but not in Israel. In fact, his treatment was a little shameful considering that he was, after all, a scholar of world renown. Some belated amends were made on the occasion of his eighty-fifth birthday.

What is true of Buber applies equally to Hugo Bergmann, Gershom Scholem, Ernst Simon, and the other members of the circle. Scholem became world-famous for his studies on the kabbalah, but he was not a political activist, merely a loyal citizen of the state of Israel. If the elders of German Jewry were such charismatic and destructive personalities, there should have been some tangible sign of this among the student body. There were a few communists among them, but believers in historical materialism had no use for the mystic Buber. Some of them later in life became Zionists, such as the historian Shmuel Ettinger and Gabriel Baer, the latter an erstwhile Trotskyite. There were at least as many followers of the extreme right, such as "Yair" (Avraham Stern of Stern gang fame), and Geula Cohen who became a devoted disciple and friend of Scholem and Hugo Bergmann, which did not in the least affect the ardor of her nationalist convictions.

The "German professors" bear no responsibility for the fall of Ben-Gurion as Hazony seems to think, or for the discrediting his concept of Israel as a Jewish state. They are even less responsible for the inanities of the postmodern post-Zionists who appeared on the scene years after the older professors had passed away. If Ben-Gurion's political career ended in failure and sadness, this was the result of his rigidity and his antics towards the end of his life. The post-Zionists received their inspiration not from Buber, Scholem, or Magnes (whom they'd never heard of) but from Homi Bhabha, Gayatri Spivak, Edward Said, Felix Guattari, and other current Indian-Arab-French gurus of the postcolonial school of thinking. It was probably inevitable that the inanities of the post-Zionists would provoke an answer by the nationalist right. In Yoram Hazony and his thoughts about the fifth column, they have found a worthy opponent

But on one point Hazony was right: toward the 1960s at the latest, those mentioned in his book had become very skeptical about Zionism, or, to be precise, about the character of the state that had emerged from it. This can be seen perhaps most clearly in the diaries of Hugo Bergmann, his letters to Robert Weltsch, and other friends. Bergmann was one of the oldest members of the "Prague circle" (which also included Max Brod, Franz Kafka, and Franz Werfel). Before World War I, he had been very active promoting a cultural Zionism of sorts, partly under the influence of Martin Buber. Bergmann had been the first of them to settle in Palestine. Having served as an officer in the Austrian-Hungarian army (like Robert Weltsch), he came to Jerusalem in 1921, was the first director of the National Library, later the Hebrew University Library, and, still later, he became professor of philosophy, serving as the rector of the university for many years. I knew Weltsch much better than Bergmann. Weltsch had been the great editor of *Juedische Rundschau,* the mouthpiece of the German Zionists, in Berlin during the 1920s and up until the autumn of 1938; he went to Jerusalem but settled in London after the end of World War II. Weltsch tended towards pessimism in his political judgments, and it was not surprising that he should reach the conclusion that Israel was not the state he had dreamed about.

The only one of this circle to leave Palestine permanently and turn against Zionism openly was Hans Kohn. He too had served in the Austrian army during World War I; he had been a prisoner of war in Siberia, and after 1918, he had witnessed the excesses of nationalism in Eastern Europe. This made him a critic of political nationalism in general and of Jewish political nationalism in particular. He came to Palestine in the 1920s but never found his place there. He immigrated to the United States where he became one of the founding fathers of the study of nationalism, a subject on which he wrote many books.

Hugo Bergmann, on the contrary, with all his criticism of the way the state of Israel and Israeli society had developed, had become well integrated. In fact, he was one of the central figures of the intellectual establishment, a member of countless committees, academic and otherwise. He was at home in Rehavia (he lived at 51 Ramban Street) but it is also true that on occasion he wrote nostalgically in his diaries about the early days in Jerusalem. He regularly went to pray in synagogues of various ethnic groups, but also attended workers' seminars and ecumenical organizations and he had a weakness for theosophy. Hardly a day passed without him giving a lecture somewhere in the country—later also on the radio and on television in a brains trust. He had countless friends and many admirers. But with all this, he and other members of his circle became disappointed with the kind of Zionism as practiced in Israel. This was not the society they had dreamed of in their younger years.

Now, sixty years after the days of Magnes and Gabriel Stern, there are more groups devoted to the cause of Jewish-Arab rapprochement and cooperation than ever before. The most prominent is Peace Now, which was founded in 1978 by some three hundred forty-eight reserve officers. It is devoted to a peaceful and just end to the conflict. It believes that security, human dignity, and a promising future can come only through peace. Over the years it has organized many demonstrations in the streets of Israel, issued manifestoes, and held conferences. Some of its members are in the Israeli parliament. *Gush Shalom* was created by the indefatigable Uri Avneri, who began his political career as a member of *Irgun. Du Kium* (Coexistence) promoted coexistence in the Negev, trying to replace the atmosphere of tension and suspicion with cooperation and understanding (a similar group worked in Galilee). Interns for Peace, established in 1976, wants to train community development peace workers in Israel as well as in the Palestinian territories. The Israel-Palestine Center for Research and Information is a joint Israeli-Palestinian think tank devoted to developing practical solutions for the conflict. *Bat Shalom* is a feminist peace organization working towards a more just and democratic society shaped equally by men and women. *Batzelem* has been protesting energetically against violations of human rights by Israeli authorities in the occupied territories. *Oz Veshalom* unites some religious Zionists opposed to the Israeli occupation of the West Bank. *Yesh Gvul* is a group of army men refusing to serve in the occupied territories.

Foundations give money to support the activities of these and other such organizations. They have websites, and intensive exchanges are going on. *Neve Shalom (Qahat al Salam)*, founded in the early 1970s, is a cooperative village near Latrun half way between Jerusalem and Tel Aviv that provides bilingual education for Jewish and Palestinian Arab children. It also houses the Center for Spiritual Pluralism and the House of Silence for reflection, meditation, and prayer. There are various academic and non-academic centers for conflict resolution and the encouragement of contacts between Arab and Jewish families. Many of these activities were supported by liberals in the United States, and some are in fact based in America. But the biggest and most active were founded by Israeli initiative.

Alas, not all of these groups are what they appear to be. The *Salam Review* based in the United States made its contribution to the peace effort by calling the then Vice President Al Gore "Al Whore"; they obviously resent his pro-Israeli stance, but such verbal assaults were unlikely to contribute to peace in the Middle East. Simona Sharoni, author of *Gender and the Israeli-Palestinian Conflict*, reports that the policies aimed at Palestinian and Israeli women deal specifically with Palestinian women who are affiliated with factions of the PLO that have "a progressive socialist platform, namely the Democratic Front for the Liberation of Palestine, the Popular Front for the Liberation of Palestine, and the communist party." Whether George Habash's extreme nationalist followers ever had a progressive and socialist platform is a moot point, but I doubt whether they would have called their platform socialist and progressive in this day and age.

With the intifada of 2000–01 and the terrorist attacks inside Israel, the peace movement, which had not been united before, split further and its internal dissent became more pronounced. Peace Now, which consisted of left-wing and liberal Zionists, concentrated on the peace issue, supported Barak's offers to the Arabs, and felt deeply disappointed that these had been answered by armed attacks. *Gush Shalom* consisted of non- and anti-Zionists, but its early initiatives, such as the demand that Jerusalem should be the capital of both peoples, won support well outside its ranks. With the outbreak of the second intifada it became more radical, but it was also torn by internal dissension. (Earlier it had been critical of the Oslo peace process and in its posters had depicted Barak as a murderer of Arab babies.) It appeared under the banner of pacifism but also displayed a lot of Kalashnikov submachine guns in his posters.

Gush Shalom tried to unite the extreme left, but its chief guru, Uri Avneri, was anything but a Marxist by political orientation. The strength of *Gush Shalom* was in its dynamic publicity. Its weakness was its ideological vagueness—it advocated a just solution of the Arab refugee question without making it clear what justice would mean in this context. The fact that it used postmodernist language in its propaganda ("the Palestinian narrative," "the Zionist narrative," etc.) did not help to broaden its appeal.

With so much good will and enthusiasm, and, in contrast to the 1930s, so many resources, why has there been so little response? Or, to be precise, why has there been so little political effect? There is no simple, easy answer. The growth of Islamist terrorism, especially suicide terrorism, and the radical opposition to the existence of a Jewish state in any shape or form by organizations such as Hamas and Islamic Jihad, played a crucial role. There has been a slow impact on Israeli public opinion, as seen in support for the peace process, and also the initiatives of former prime minister Ehud Barak, willing to make concessions that were unthinkable even a few years earlier. That these concessions were not sufficient for the other side is less important than the fact that Barak was able to break certain taboos (even if it cost him his political career).

The attempts to reach a better understanding with the Arabs in the occupied territories were probably doomed anyway. Given the constant confrontation between occupier and occupied, there could be no significant progress, no understanding between equals and neighbors. The only solution to this conflict is political. The only solution is to move out of the territories, or at least most of them. But even if Israel did this, there still was the question of the refugees and of Jerusalem, about which no agreement seems possible.

The Arab countries have not absorbed the refugees of the 1948 war, but rather kept them in camps in miserable conditions, partly because they did not want them but also as a political weapon to use against Israel. In Europe, Asia, and elsewhere around the world, tens of millions of refugees had been absorbed. But the situation in the Middle East is different and eventually came to constitute the main bone of contention on the road to peace. Israel is an overpopulated country. The return of great numbers of the descendants of Palestinian refugees would do more than just create economic and social problems. It would in all probability lead to more war.

The situation of the Israeli Arabs is different, of course, but here too the main initiative should have come from the state. It goes without saying that those striving for closer collaboration, if not for friendship, among the peoples are fighting an uphill struggle. National minorities feel discriminated against and persecuted in virtually every country, and it should not come as a surprise that those looking for Arab partners for their peace initiatives do not find many, given the political tensions, insufficient attention on the part of successive governments, and the general atmosphere of a highly charged nationalism with a strong and growing religious-fanatic admixture.

What became of the protagonists of Jewish Arab rapprochement of that faraway time? Gabriel Stern, who at one time held together all the loose ends, began to work for a daily Hebrew newspaper *Al Hamishmar* in 1949. He remained interested in Jewish-Arab relations but also became an expert on the Christian presence in Jerusalem and the holy sites. He died in Jerusalem in 1983; the newspaper folded recently. Much of the Hebrew press of the period has faded away, replaced by television and the Internet. Many of the members of *Brit Shalom* lived to ripe old ages. Among the last to pass away were Gershom Scholem, Ernst Simon, and Robert Weltsch. Weltsch, like Hugo Bergmann, was in his nineties when he died in an old-age home in Jerusalem; Buber was eighty-seven when he died in 1965. They are sadly missed, above all at the Hebrew University, which has produced or attracted men and women of many accomplishments but none of a stature equal to that of the old-timers.

Hassolel Street has changed its name. For reasons unknown to me, it is now Rehov Hahavazelet. He'atid, the bookshop, is gone. The ownership and the character of the shop changed several times; today it is occupied by a stationer and a fast-food restaurant. Ruppin Road is one of the main streets leading out of Jerusalem in the direction of Tel Aviv, and Martin Buber Street is a little-known thoroughfare leading from the Hebrew University eastward to an Arab neighborhood. (There is a Buber street in Berlin and also a Buber school; there are Martin Buber streets in Bremen, Cologne, Kassel, Darmstadt, and other German cities but not in Vienna where he was born.) Magnes Square is a tiny but charming place in the middle of Rehavia, and there is also a Magnes Street on the Hebrew University campus in Givat Ram. Kalvarisky is forgotten except by a few historians dealing with Jewish-Arab relations. As for my friend, the tireless Gabriel Stern, he is no longer remembered even by the staff of the Jerusalem association of journalists, which says that it has no record of him. And the center of the activities aiming at better relations between Jews and Arabs, more an uphill struggle than ever, has moved away from Jerusalem to Tel Aviv and Haifa.

CHAPTER 10

RECOLLECTIONS
OF TALBIYEH

WHEN I FIRST CAME TO JERUSALEM IN 1938, TALBIYEH WAS one of the most attractive parts of the town and therefore altogether out of reach. But when I returned in 1945, I somehow managed to live on the borders of the quarter, usually on the wrong side of the tracks. For some time I stayed at the corner of Arlosoroff and Obadja mi Bartenura streets. There is a surfeit of history in Jerusalem and almost every street name is a further historical provocation. Chaim Arlosoroff was the boy wonder of the Zionist movement in Germany. He was killed in late 1933 at the beach of Tel Aviv in circumstances that remain a mystery to this day. Had he lived, he might well have become prime minister or foreign minister of Israel. All we know about Bartenura is derived from three letters. He was born in Italy around 1450 but came to Palestine, settling in Jerusalem. He became the spiritual head of the Jewish community, which was so poor that, being a considerable scholar, he also had to act as grave digger.

After about one hundred yards, Bartenura becomes Brenner Street, which shall appear in our narrative later on, for at Number 10 the relations of Edward Said lived. Yosef Brenner was an iconoclastic left-wing Hebrew writer and critic who lived in poverty. He was killed in Jaffa during the Arab riots of 1921. Said was also a critic, but as a past president of the Modern Language Association he must certainly be considered to be very much in the mainstream. He wrote in his autobiography about living in this neighborhood as a schoolboy; I was a bit older when I lived there.

No one knows the origin of the name Talbiyeh; earlier it was called Nikoforia after a monk who lived in the vicinity. The quarter was developed during the 1920s and '30s in the area between Terra Santa in the south and the Hansen Leper Hospital, which was founded by Germans in the 1880s. It was probably the only building in that neighborhood at the time. Like many buildings of that period in Jerusalem, the hospital was designed by German architect Conrad Schick, whose work can be seen to this day on the Street of the Prophets and its environs. Today the (new) Jerusalem Theater is the main landmark in the vicinity, but the Israeli president's residence and the Van Leer Institute, where the Israeli Academy of Science is housed, are also located in Talbiyeh.

The founders of Talbiyeh were a group of Christian Arabs who bought the land from the Greek Orthodox patriarchate. Talbiyeh is dotted with comfortable houses (few are more than two or three stories high) built in various architectural styles, with gardens and massive iron gates, inscriptions in various languages, broad staircases and ornaments, arches and sunken patios. Above all, Talbiyeh offers excellent views of the Old City and of Bethlehem to the south. Jews acquired land and built houses there from the beginning. Nowadays, houses in this quarter sell for two to three million dollars.

Talbiyeh has not changed very much over the years except for the new buildings. The official name is now the Hebrew word *Komemiut,* but no one uses it, just as the central square of the quarter, officially named Wingate Square, is still called Salame Square as it was in the old days. On this square, the Hana Salame building (now the Belgian consulate) is without doubt the most remarkable structure. Salame was a wealthy Christian Arab merchant who made his money mainly by supplying food to the British forces in the Middle East during World War II; his brother Constantine was also building there. An interesting exhibition a few years ago ("To Live in Jerusalem" curated by David Krojanker, the indefatigable historian of Jerusalem architecture) showed an astonishing similarity between the interiors of these houses and those of their Jewish neighbors. For instance, the building a few steps away from Hana Salame belonged to a well-known local lawyer, American-born Shalom Horowitz. The style is European, or International, or Bauhaus as it was then called, except perhaps for the dining room, where there were pictures on the walls. There were also some Oriental style buildings—one, a villa called Harun al Rashid of Arabian Nights fame, could well have been situated in tenth-century Baghdad.

Farther down, next to the Horowitz place, lived Harry Viteles, also an American Jew, who had for many years been a representative of the Joint Distribution Committee in Palestine and who wrote a multivolume history of cooperation in the country. He was about forty years older than me, but we became friends. My wife and I were frequent visitors to his apartment, and I owe him, among many other things, for my first pair of decent trousers at a time when textiles were expensive and rationed. They had belonged to the archaeologist Nelson Glueck who had left some of his belongings with Harry when he ended his excavations. They were made of seersucker, a material I had never seen before.

Again a few steps farther down, at 6 Balfour Street, Salman Schocken, the German Jewish department store magnate, publisher, and book collector, had a substantial library built in 1935 that contained many exceedingly rare manuscripts. Schocken's home, one of the most impressive in Talbiyeh, was around the corner on a side street (now Smolenskin Street). Schocken had known Mendelsohn in Germany, where the architect had designed some of the leading Schocken department stores (the one in Stuttgart can be found in most histories of modern architecture). Mendelsohn, one of the most famous architects of the time, lived in Palestine for a few years during the late 1930s when he built many private and public houses and later went to the United States as Schocken did.

Mendelsohn loved Talbiyeh, and at the southern end of Balfour Street he built a windmill, a landmark to this very day that served as both his office and apartment. He liked the light of Talbiyeh, especially in the late afternoon, which he thought was the light Rembrandt had tried to depict; he named one of the balconies in the Schocken Library "Rembrandt." The Schocken villa was (and probably still is) one of the most valuable buildings in Talbiyeh. Soon after the war, it became the headquarters of General Evelyn Barker, the commander in chief of British troops in Palestine who suggested that one should hit the Palestinian Jews (who caused him much annoyance at the time) where it hurt them the most—in their pocket. But the pockets of the Palestinian Jews at the time were not deep and Barker's strategy was ineffectual. After the British had left, Salman Schocken tried to sell his villa for two hundred thousand pounds. The state of Israel wanted to use it as the official residence of the president. But Yitzhak Ben-Zvi (the second president, after Weizmann) and his wife found the house too ostentatious and not in keeping with their modest lifestyle. It eventually became the Rubin Academy of Music.

Next to the Schocken villa now is the official residence of the Israeli prime minister. This house was built between 1936–38 by Edward Aghion, a wealthy Greek Jew from Alexandria. Many other prominent Jewish citizens of Jerusalem lived in Talbiyeh, including some of the better-off intellectuals, such as Martin Buber. Buber belonged to the League of Arab-Jewish Rapprochement (which changed its name to *Ihud*). The league published a monthly called *Beayot* (Problems), for which I occasionally wrote. As the result, I came to know most of the leading members of the group, including Hugo Bergmann and Ernst Simon, who lived within a few hundred yards of Buber. There were no clear borders between Talbiyeh (a mixed neighborhood), Rehavia (which was entirely Jewish), and Katamon (predominantly Arab).

Talbiyeh was a truly international place. The Salames and Bisharas lived next to Armenians such as Matossian and Dr. Klabian. The Salame buildings were designed by Zoltan Hermet, a Hungarian Jewish architect. The Jasmin House Hotel in Talbiyeh was run by Jasmin Kana'an, an Arab woman whose mother was German. ("Mixed" marriages were not that uncommon in the quarter.) The small Antonio Monastery was designed by an Italian, and Hana's brother Constantine Salame owned a villa designed by a Frenchman. There was a Montserrat Institute belonging to the Spanish where the Bible was translated into Catalan. There were at least half a dozen consulates on Balfour Street, the main road in Talbiyeh. The Jewish *mukhtar* (headman) of Talbiyeh was the publisher Ruben Maas, an early arrival from Germany.

Relations between Jews and Arabs were friendly or at least normal even at the time of great tension such as the riots of 1936–38 and again in 1946–47. During the war, illustrious exiles from Europe and elsewhere lived in Talbiyeh, including King Peter of Yugoslavia and Emperor Haile Selassie of Ethiopia.

The Salames had many Jewish business associates and even a few Jewish friends, and the same is true for most of the other wealthy Christian Arab families. There was not much socializing, but there was mutual help. There was little tension except perhaps if an Arab landlord wanted to get rid of a Jewish tenant, as happened in the case of the Said family and Martin Buber. Arabs and Jews shopped in the same stores, often in the German Colony in the valley toward the railway station. The Arab grocers gave credit to their less affluent Jewish customers (I was one of them). When a member of an Arab family fell ill, chances were that he would consult Hermann Zondek, who lived in Ben Maimon Street, between Balfour and Terra Santa, or if it was a female member of the family, she would go to Hermann's brother Bernhard. Both had patients from all over the Middle East, including some very prominent ones.

Zondek had been hesitant to come to Jerusalem. He had left Germany in 1933 and spent a year in England. His experiences during his first visit to the city had not been encouraging. When he asked to see a hospital, he was shown what he thought was a little synagogue with a dozen elderly men praying. His friends advised him not to immigrate to such a backward country, but he ignored their advice, settled in Jerusalem, and lived to see the emergence of a modern medical system.

In cosmopolitan Talbiyeh, Jews and Arabs lived in peace and harmony until the riots broke out in early December 1947. Edward Said was a schoolboy then, and I was a young journalist, but we walked the same streets, went to the same cinemas (the Arab Rex and the Jewish Regent). We had to show our special passes when entering the British security zones that had been established in 1946 following the King David bombing in Talbiyeh, the German Colony, and some other parts of western Jerusalem. Said remembered that Talbiyeh and the neighboring districts were exclusively populated by Palestinians. Elsewhere he writes that Jerusalem, unlike Cairo, had a homogeneous population made up mainly of Palestinians.

This reminded me of the (probably apocryphal) stories about Herzl, who during his visit to Palestine in 1898 managed to not see the Arab inhabitants of the country. I consulted reference works. In

1947, according to the statistics of the Mandatory power, Jerusalem had a population of one hundred fifty-seven thousand, of whom ninety-seven thousand were Jews; the rest (sixty thousand) were mainly Arabs, but also included many thousands of Greeks and Armenians, as well as monks and nuns from all over the world. There had, in fact, been a Jewish plurality in Jerusalem since the middle of the nineteenth century.

The demographic estimates for the early years of the nineteenth century differ wildly—between three thousand to nine thousand Jews out of a total of twenty thousand inhabitants. There were good reasons for boycotting a census, for it meant exposing oneself to taxation. On the other hand, not being counted meant that financial support from Europe for the poor Jewish community would decrease. The Jewish population of Jerusalem grew steadily during the 1850s and '60s, partly because of the migration from other Palestinian Jewish communities such as Safed and Tiberias, but mainly because of the arrival of newcomers from Europe. Steamships from Europe were calling at Jaffa and Haifa from about 1860 on, and as a result the number of both pilgrims and immigrants increased. There was a temporary decline because of cholera and smallpox, but by 1880 the Jews constituted at least half of the total population of the city. Later on, when Edward Said went to school in Jerusalem, the city had a Jewish mayor, Daniel Auster, the uncle of the American novelist Paul Auster.

However, the Jerusalem remembered by Said was not cosmopolitan. It was almost purely Arab. Said reported that "our society was destroyed in 1948." If he was referring to the presence of the wealthy Christian Arab families in Talbiyeh, he was right. But if he meant Arab Jerusalem he was mistaken for the number of Arabs living in Jerusalem is now three or four times larger than it was in 1947.

The peaceful coexistence of 1947 did come to an end suddenly. I well remember the days in early December 1947 when my landlord in the German Colony, Mr. Faraj, a sergeant in the local police force, told me that though some of his best friends were Jews, there had to be a war, but that after the war, everything would be fine again. Both assumptions seemed to me doubtful.

Unfortunately, Sergeant Faraj's fatalistic views prevailed. It started with several (probably spontaneous) attacks against Jewish buses. In the beginning only stones were thrown. But a few hours later shots were fired. During the days after December 2, several Jewish areas came under fire and the Jewish residents had to escape. The Jewish commercial center outside the Old City was burned down and pillaged by the *Shabab* (the young Arab militants organized in the *Najada,* the *Futuwah,* and other groups), many Jewish families lost their livelihood. Close to where I lived, a colleague, an Anglo-Jewish journalist named Stern, was killed. After a few days of murder, arson, and pillage, we too became refugees, having to evacuate quickly from the German Colony, leaving some of our belongings behind. It was not an easy time—we had a month-old baby, and had to sleep for weeks on the floor of crowded apartments belonging to friends until we were allocated a three-room apartment we had to share with two other families.

In later years, Said and others have expressed the opinion that an admission of guilt by the Zionists for what they did to the Palestinians in 1947–48 would be an absolute precondition for a reconciliation between the two nations. If this could help the peace process, I would be all in favor of such an apology. The Barak government on various occasions in fact expressed regret in the Israeli parliament about the suffering of the Palestinian people, especially the refugees living in miserable conditions. But how could it apologize for the Arab uprising in December 1947 following the U.N. partition plan, and the invasion of the Arab armies in 1948 that started it all? It could be argued that the Palestinian Arabs had no alternative to taking up arms against a plan that threatened their vital national interests. The recourse to arms may seem justified, even inevitable, but it always involves risks, since no one knows how it will end. Hitler launched a war in 1939, and in the end many millions of Germans, expelled from Poland, Czechoslovakia, East Prussia, and other places, most of them no doubt innocent of war crimes, paid the price.

I have often asked myself what would have happened if the Arab attacks in December 1947 and the months after had not taken place— if the Palestinians had, however reluctantly, accepted the U.N. decision to partition Palestine. Counterfactual history has no certainties, but chances are that the Palestinians would have gotten a state in 1948 and that Jerusalem would have been a separate entity under international supervision. It seems unthinkable that the Israelis would have violated the U.N. resolution and expanded the territory allotted to them, forcing the Palestinians to flee from the territories seized by them. In that case, the Jewish state would never have been recognized on May 15, 1948, when the British left.

Would a small Jewish state have been viable? Would a Palestinian Arab state have been able to exist? We do not know whether a binational state could have survived, or whether it would have led to conditions similar to India, Cyprus, Sri Lanka, Northern Ireland, Quebec, Croatia, Bosnia, or wherever else such experiments were made. All we know for certain is that the Palestinian Arabs were not willing to accept the binational solution either: Palestine was Arab and had to remain Arab, just as Jerusalem was Arab and had to remain Arab. On the basis of these assumptions, Mr. Faraj was right and so was Said, and the tragedy was inevitable.

Finding a solution for the future of Jerusalem is said to be the most difficult part of the peace process, though it has never been clear to me why it should be so. I have great sympathy for those who demand that the city must never be divided again as it was from 1948 to 1967, even though it has been a divided city for years. As for the ultraorthodox

Jews, many of them do not recognize the state of Israel, and state borders mean nothing to them as long as they can pray at the Wailing Wall.

There is the mythical Zion and the reality of Jerusalem, and the reality except for a decade or two has been often sordid. When I first came to Jerusalem, I did not like the city. By and large it was a dirty, noisy, and dilapidated place. In essence, it was the Turkish provincial town it had been for centuries. The Old City was one big bazaar with the hucksters trying to sell their quasi-religious amulets and holy water from the Jordan River. Jaffa Road, the main street, was a mixture of a Eastern Poland and deepest Anatolia; Mea Shearim, where the ultra-orthodox lived, reminded me of a medieval ghetto; and the Oriental Jewish markets and residential quarters were, at best, fashioned out of a fascinating ugliness.

These impressions could be dismissed as the prejudices of an arrogant young man from Europe alienated from the sources of his religion and Jewish traditions. But the Zionist leaders beginning with Herzl reacted in a similar way. They were appalled by what they saw, and while paying lip service to the place of Jerusalem in Jewish tradition and while keeping the political institutions there, they all chose to live in Tel Aviv.

While looking through a Russian archive recently, I came across letters written by Alexander Borisovich Lakier, an ancestor of mine. Lakier's father had been a German Jew but he carefully hid the fact and established himself in Russian society; Lakier was Russian Orthodox. Alexander Borisovich was a landless Russian nobleman and a leading travel writer of his time, who had visited Jerusalem in 1859. (His impressions of the United States were published a few years ago under the title *A Russian Looks at America*.) But this man who had found something noteworthy and interesting all over the globe, from the Reading Room of the British Museum to the private garden of the president of Harvard College, had nothing good to say about Jerusalem and kept his impressions to himself except in letters to his family.

Jerusalem had the good fortune to have a mayor of genius for almost thirty years after 1965. Under Teddy Kollek, a great deal was done to clean up and beautify the city. But since Kollek, the city has been going downhill, even though considerable funds have been invested. The growth of the ultraorthodox population, bent to turn Jerusalem into one big ghetto, have greatly contributed to this development. At the same time, Jerusalem with its narrow lanes has become a giant traffic jam at most hours of the day and even at night. There is a considerable amount of pollution even though there is hardly any industry. It is not an exaggeration regarding the Israeli wanderlust that many Tel Avivians know their way around Paris and London better than Jerusalem. The Arab percentage of the population is slowly growing while there is a steady Jewish exodus of the secular population because the Orthodox are waging a relentless campaign to remodel the city in their image. And since the Orthodox have large families, the demographic clock is ticking away, their number and political influence are constantly growing.

At the same time, paradoxically, young Orthodox families are also leaving the city because the rents are too high. And so Jerusalem is coming down in the world after the great clean-up under Teddy Kollek, a city for visitors and pilgrims but not (with the exception of a few oases still including Talbiyeh and the German Colony) a particularly enjoyable place to live. And it remains a riddle why this problematic holy city should remain the main bone of contention on the road to peace.

Whether Edward Said had a legal right to that house in Talbiyeh I do not know. He certainly had every right to fight for the Palestinian cause even if he had been born in Outer Mongolia, had never so much as visited Jerusalem, and had never attended school there. As Ehud

Barak said when he was prime minister, had he been born an Arab, he might well have become a terrorist. This statement caused indignation among some circles in Israel, but it is the truth. Whether an advocate of the Palestinian cause living in relative luxury and security in New York had the moral right to oppose the peace process, to fight, so to speak, to the last Palestinian from a safe distance is another question entirely.

Nor is it that difficult to understand the radicalism of the late Edward Said. Did it rise out of the deep moral commitment he so frequently invoked, or was it Said's Christian origins? Once upon a time this did not greatly matter, but with the rise of Muslim fundamentalism, the situation of non-Muslim Arabs has become precarious. They are under psychological pressure to show that they are as patriotic as their Muslim compatriots. As Ali Abu Sakar, the head of the Jordan's "anti-normalization" with Israel campaign, said, "I am a Muslim, and the Jewish people are our enemy." There was no reference to being an Arab or to Zionism. One Christian Arab leader solved this problem by moving to Iraq and converting to Islam, but for those who are secularists, this may not be a way out of the dilemma. Nor is it a specifically Arab predicament. The Jews in the Russian terrorist movement prior to World War I had to prove their attachment to the cause by being more extreme and more foolhardy than the others. The same is true for the role of women in many groups. Another example is Semyon Frank, the Russian philosopher who died an émigré. He reached the conclusion that a full identification with his native country was possible only if he also embraced the state religion, and so he and his family converted to Russian Orthodox. The same goes for Boris Pasternak, and it would be easy to adduce other examples from other countries.

To blame Said for not having embraced the tenets of Zionism is, of course, ridiculous. His case against Israel was as logical and legitimate as that of the German refugees who were expelled from Eastern Europe after World War II or the many millions of Indians and Pakistanis who had to flee when the subcontinent was divided. What weakened his position were the blatant contradictions in his public posture and self-righteousness. Showered with honors, acclaim, and publicity, one of the most influential intellectual figures in the United States, this avatar of political correctness, presented himself as a persecuted outsider, leading a marginal and vulnerable existence. He made himself out to be a lonely, courageous voice in the wilderness. Said's polemical style was shrill, ad hominem, and deliberately injurious. But when he was paid back in his own coin he tended to become weepy, like a boxer good in the attack but incapable of taking punishment. Criticism of Said, as he saw it, was never justified, but a priori vicious, based on poisonous lies spread by Zionists and Orientalists out to destroy his good name and reputation as a humanist.

He upbraided the Palestinian leadership for selling out to the Zionists and, above all, for not building a democratic and incorrupt state. But why should the Palestinian state be different in character from the other Arab countries? He grimly attacked Arafat for having broken bread with Barak in the latter's home, but if the Israeli prime minister had refused to socialize with the Palestinian leader, he would have been called a racist, or worse. Said attacked the late King Hussein of Jordan (not Saddam, not Qaddafi) as the most repressive and reactionary ruler in the Middle East, and his attitudes to other moderates in the Arab world was similar. One is hard-pressed to find in his writings a single word of criticism, let alone condemnation, of the truly repressive Arab regimes from Iraq to Libya. He did sign an appeal of Arab intellectuals (most of them émigrés) opposing an international conference of Holocaust deniers in Beirut, but later withdrew his signature. He did criticize anti-Semitic remarks made in the presence of the Pope by the Syrian leader Hafez al-Assad, but this apparently stemmed from his concern that this did not make a favorable impression abroad.

Said adopted the cause and the arguments of Arab nationalism, and no one can blame him for the stand he took. But at the same time he claimed to be a man of the left, simultaneously nationalist and internationalist, in excellent standing with progressives everywhere. One of Mr. Said's friends whom, he said, he admired greatly, has proclaimed that the Israeli left is much worse than the right, and another, the Christian Arab Clovis Maksoud, has written that Arab intellectuals should have nothing to do with the new Israeli historians of the post-Zionist school because all they want is to refurbish Zionism.

Said, a secular intellectual, wrote books defending Islam against its detractors and cordially approved of a scurrilous attack against the poisonous Jewish religion and its horrible impact over three thousand years. He bitterly denounced the Western intellectuals who fought against Stalinism and its sympathizers during the 1950s in the framework of the Congress for Cultural Freedom, because the congress was financed in large part by the CIA.

Edward Said, with all his great success in the United States, wisely decided not to transfer his activities to the Arab world, just as some militant American Zionists have preferred to stay in their homeland. It is doubtful whether there was room for him in the Arab East. He reminded one of Frantz Fanon, author of fire-eating books about the psychological benefits of violence whom the Algerian militants nevertheless did not regard as one of their own. Had he lived (he died in 1961 at the age of thirty-six), independent Algeria would have imprisoned or shot him. Said is greatly admired on American campuses and by progressive Jewish intellectuals, but in the Palestinian territories his books were banned. In a book review some twenty years ago, I compared him with some of the New York radical Jewish intellectuals of the 1930s, and I see no reason to modify this appraisal. He played Trotsky ("no war and no peace") in the age of the weapons of mass destruction. Just as the young Said did not see the Jews around him in

Talbiyeh or in Jerusalem in 1947, he did not see the realities on the ground in Palestine-Israel.

No one can know for sure whether the peace process ever had a chance. It is quite unrealistic to assume, as many Israelis do, that Arab hostility in Palestine and throughout the Middle East will give way in the foreseeable future to feelings of friendship. It is unrealistic also to believe that terrorism will cease. The maximum the Israelis are willing to offer is too far from the minimum expectations of the Palestinians. It could well be that an accord reached will not hold. But we will never know if we don't at least try. And the alternative is grim. There is little time left for negotiations; a disaster could occur in the Middle East a thousand times worse than all the past wars together. Those trying to undermine the attempt to defuse a potentially very dangerous situation under whatever pretext and for whatever reason bear a heavy responsibility.

And what became of the large, stately house 10 at Brenner Street, the ancestral home of Said's family where Martin Buber also lived and where this excursion started? The same house was occupied by the International Christian Embassy. The signs were in English, Hebrew, and Russian. Yet another attempt to convert the Jews? Inside you learn that the organization's mission was to help the Jews to resettle Israel. There is nothing in their literature about Christ and conversion. This embassy was founded by nondenominational Christian friends of Israel in 1980 at a time when several countries withdrew their diplomatic representatives from Jerusalem. Recently, the embassy moved farther down to the German Colony, and the house is empty, for rent or sale. Some property developers want to add on a story or two to the building, even though it is on the list of protected sites.

And among a few old-timer's memories of the old Talbiyeh linger on.

CHAPTER 11

MEA SHEARIM AND THE BLACK HATS

A T THE ENTRANCE TO MEA SHEARIM, POSTERS ANNOUNCE, "This is a residential area not a tourist site." Other posters request (or demand) that visitors be dressed modestly—women in long dresses, their blouses should be buttoned up, and their arms and shoulders covered at the very minimum. Nor should there be mixed groups of men and women. Little boys and girls look angrily at strangers who dare to invade this neighborhood. One finds curiosity and sometimes hate in their looks. The young men walk quickly (one seldom sees them strolling leisurely) to synagogues or religious seminars, carrying their prayer books in little plastic bags, one of their few concessions to modernity.

Mea Shearim, situated in northern Jerusalem, is certainly among the ugliest tourist attractions in Jerusalem if not the whole country with its dilapidated houses, dark gateways, windowless facades, the general absence of gardens and trees, the garbage in the streets and laundry hanging from clotheslines, the little shops selling religious devotional objects, and of course the omnipresent Yiddish- and

Hebrew-language posters plastered on the walls of the houses used by competing religious sects to defame each other. The Talmud says that God gave ten measures of beauty to the world and that nine of them went to Jerusalem. Mea Shearim was shortchanged in the beauty department. It would be unjust to blame God. Having said this, a tourist attraction it still is, and a growing one at that.

Several hundred, perhaps one thousand, Orthodox Jewish families lived there when I first came to Jerusalem. The name Mea Shearim means one hundred gates, but there are only six gates in the area. Originally, Mea Shearim was not a homogenous residential district. Secular Jews lived there, and a number of substantial buildings could be seen which were not in Jewish hands at all such as the Italian Hospital, the St. Louis Hospital, and of course the few churches in the area. The Ministry of Education is now located nearby, and has been a source of friction and clashes because some of the female employees go to work in immodest attire, at least according to the rigid standards of the local residents (they may have worn jeans rather than long skirts). Mea Shearim is riddled with little prayer houses (*shtibelach*) and a few *yeshivas,* but I could find only one of them in the telephone directory of 1940, the Hebron *yeshiva.* The others probably did not need phones because their whole world extended only a few hundred yards in each direction. If someone shouted loudly enough, he could probably reach everyone he wanted to communicate with.

The Hebron *yeshiva* was famous among religious Jews, but it was by no means extremist. Among those who attended it was Chaim Herzog, later a major in an elite British regiment and after that president of Israel. Among the students in later years there was Menahem Elon, subsequently a Supreme Court justice, and Aryeh Deri, the most gifted politician produced by Moroccan Jewry, a wunderkind whose career was interrupted by an unfortunate affair concerning misappropriated money, which landed him in prison. Today the Hebron *yeshiva* appears in the directory with four different addresses and more telephone numbers. There are five more pages of *yeshivas* listed, and even if some of them are high schools and not full-fledged *yeshivas,* there are more than two hundred of them.

Mea Shearim was one of the first Jewish quarters established outside the Old City in 1874. It was built by Conrad Schick, who was the most prominent and prolific architect in Jerusalem at the time (he was also a bit of an archaeologist). Schick first made money in Palestine assembling cuckoo clocks when they were in fashion. He was a man of many parts and became one of the most beloved citizens of Jerusalem; a street is even named after him.

In the beginning, Mea Shearim was a secular neighborhood with shops selling better quality merchandise than could be found in the Old City; some saw it as an emergent "Paris of the Orient." But the dream of Paris was not to last, and over the subsequent three decades Orthodox Eastern European philanthropists gave money for the building of housing estates for the very Orthodox population of the Old City. Bate Ungarn consisted of some one hundred twenty housing units, and the other projects were a similar size or smaller. Most of these two-story houses exist to this day, though some were damaged when this area was in the front line during the 1948 siege of Jerusalem.

Among the inhabitants of Mea Shearim during the 1930s and '40s were the *Neturei Karta* (the Guardians of the City), the most extreme not so much with regard to religious observation but certainly with regard to their rejection of everything Zionist. The very Orthodox, to be sure, had never subscribed to Zionist ideology, but they had somehow reached an accommodation with the Zionists even before World War II, receiving subsidies from the Zionists and participating in the electoral process of the Palestinian Jewish institutions and later to the municipality and the state of Israel. A radical wing headed by two young firebrands named Amram Bloi and Aharon Katzenelbogen split away in protest and engaged in demonstrations, sometimes violent. During the War of Independence, they hoisted the white flag of surrender, preferring Jordanian rule to that of the Zionists. I remember meeting Amram Bloi in a sweets shop on Jaffa Road, of all places, during the siege of 1948. The saleslady refused to serve him because he had, as a matter of principle, neither an identity card nor a ration book (just about everything was rationed at the time). He started shouting, cursing Zionism and the secular Jews. But we were the only customers in the shop and since there was no chocolate, Zionist or non-Zionist, in the first place, his demonstration was ineffective.

Neturei Karta and similar such sects were tiny. They were a curiosity rather than a socio-political movement, and no one took them very seriously. These little groups were of interest mainly to journalists because of the outrageous headlines they made possible. They were also of marginal interest to students of anthropology. But they were anything but a significant political factor. The whole ultraorthodox community was small, limited to a few streets between the Perelman houses in the south and the Neitim complex in the north. Each of today's major *yeshivas,* such as *Mir* (3 Bet Israel Street) or *Ponevezh* (originally founded in Lithuania, since 1944 located in Bne Braq), have more members today than the whole extremist community did at the time. True, many *yeshivas* exaggerate the number of their students in order to receive greater state subsidies; they include dropouts, occasional visitors, and perhaps even nonexistent individuals. Statistics about the size of *yeshivas* should therefore be taken with great caution, but even so there is little doubt that the overall number of those learning in these institutions is far greater than ever before.

It is not justified to talk about these groups as a "community." They often presented a united front against the secular world, but they are split into dozens of sects. These sects have little in common with one another and there are bitter quarrels among them, sometimes on ideological-theological lines, but at least equally often because of disputes among their religious leaders and rivalries that go back to the history of the various sects in Lithuania, Poland, Galicia, and Hungary. To give one example, Satmar (from Satul Mare in Romania) and the Habad (Liubavicher) are both influential sects belonging to the Hasidic trend, but the former is violently anti-Zionist whereas the latter is militantly Zionist. There are bitter quarrels even within sects, usually about the succession of the *rebbe,* who plays a central part in the Hasidic world. He is not only spiritual guru but also the guide and ultimate authority on virtually everything. There are even deep conflicts within leading families, such as the Abu Hatzeira clan (of Moroccan origin) and the family of Ovadiah Yosef, the leading figure in the Sephardi community.

According to the religious philosophy of some of these Orthodox sects such people are put on earth to enjoy themselves, but in Mea Shearim it is difficult to find manifestations of joy. It was always a sad, poor, and depressing neighborhood, the prevailing colors black, dark grey, and dark brown. The children, with their sidelocks, look pale and sickly; few men look straight ahead (let alone around them) as they walk; the women, following the instructions of the rabbis, dress so as to attract as little attention and interest as possible. The language of conversation is Yiddish, not Hebrew; the sacred language is not to be profaned by daily usage. But it is neither the classic Yiddish of Eastern Europe nor the juicy language of daily usage of the *shtetl;* it is a half-dead bastard language sounding equally foreign to speakers of German and Hebrew. The neighboring Bucharian quarter is just as poor, but it is certainly more colorful and exotic, and less depressing. As always there are a few exceptions. The Belz sect built a magnificent synagogue with Indian teak panels, Chinese granite floors, and enormous chandeliers that could well be the largest and most splendid in the world. It can accommodate thousands. According to press reports, patrons who donated one million dollars or more got front row orchestra seats.

How much has Mea Shearim grown and how much more important has it become? As I stand on the junction of Mea Shearim and Strauss (Yeheskel) Streets and take in the neighborhood, my first impression is that many shops have changed hands. There is a sign in English, "The Comer," marking a place where one can purchase ice cream, baguettes, and natural fruit juices. There is a flower shop, a takeout food store, a women's and children's clothing store, even a photo shop. Several shops sell religious objects, including goblets, candlesticks, and embroidered challah covers. An Ashkenazi *shofar* can be purchased for thirty dollars, a Sephardi *shofar* for a little more.

Neturei Karta hardly exist anymore. It split in the 1970s after the death of the two founders and has now become a satellite of the Satmar. The remnants are headed by New York-born Rabbi S. R. Hirsch who has been appointed a minister in Arafat's Palestinian authority. (There is no evidence that he has ever participated in the activities of this body, but they have also established contacts with the Nation of Islam leader Louis Farrakhan.) The members refuse to pay taxes, both municipal and state, and, of course, they do not vote, serve in the army, or have any other contact with Israeli authorities. Their financial support comes from a handful of dealers, mainly of diamonds and precious metals and also property in London and the U.S. You may well ask how can they collect transfers in banks and post offices and the money orders sent by well-wishers in London and America without means of identification. The men send their wives, who will produce an Israeli identity card when needed.

If *Neturei Karta* are near extinction, Mea Shearim has expanded in every direction. Something like the Neturei Kartaization of the whole neighborhood, indeed of much of Jerusalem, has taken place. Most of the area north of Jaffa Road is now black-hat country, with the exception only of the quarters in which Oriental Jews reside. Relations between the ultraorthodox and the Oriental Jews are not cordial. The latter find it often difficult to get along with the habits of the Eastern European *shtetl* transplanted to the Middle East: they call the Orthodox men "zebras," referring to the black-and-white-striped robes of some of the sects (grey/black on weekdays, yellow/brown on the Sabbath). Only cognoscenti can identify the sects according to their clothing—the Vishnits Hasidim tie a knot in the right side of the cloth band on their hats, whereas the Belts Hasidim tie it on the left. Only the "Lithuanians," who do not belong to the Hasidim, can easily be identified; some of these groups are clean shaven, their black hats have a crease and look relatively modern. The hats are an essential part of the *haredi* uniform. The hats cost hundreds of dollars and according to time-honored custom are bought by the bride for her future husband.

Many other parts of Jerusalem are now dominated by Orthodox and ultraorthodox. This includes *Kiryat Moshe* (which houses Merkaz Harav, one of the bigger *yeshivas*) and *Bayit veGan,* both established in the late '20s, and then there is *Givat mordechai,* which was built in the 1950s. Orthodox neighborhoods in Mekor Baruch and Romema and large parts of Ramot are closed to traffic on shabbat. This is true also for areas of Yefe Nof, one of the older suburbs, and Har Nof, where Orthodox newcomers from America and Western Europe live as well as the Shas aristocracy from Rabbi Ovadiah to Aryeh Deri.

This is not a full list, and the expansion is by no means surprising, considering that there are now between about three hundred to three hundred fifty thousand *haredim* in Israel, perhaps half of them living in Jerusalem.

Haredim is the name now commonly used. It appears in the Bible, and literally means fear and trembling (in the sense of God-fearing). While the population of Jewish Jerusalem has grown fourfold since

1948, the number of Orthodox has grown thirtyfold. In1948 there were perhaps a few hundred students in the Israeli *yeshivas.* In 1996, the Ministry of Religious Affairs listed one hundred fifty-four thousand, and by 2002 their number had grown to more than two hundred thousand, about half of them in national religious schools, the others in schools of the Mea Shearim type.

There are countless *yeshivas* now in existence, black hat (ultraorthodox) and knitted caps (*kipa sruga,* the distinguishing mark of the religious-nationalist trend), some anti-Zionist, others militantly Zionist, some housed in new, solid, massive buildings, others small in rundown old houses. *Somayakh,* which has American support, is modern; its website has more than a billion bytes of Torah literature and reportedly gets three hundred thousand hits daily. But many others are more traditional such as Mir, Vishnitz, Toldot Aharon, and many others. Some are *yeshivas hesder,* whose students serve in the army, but for the truly Orthodox, the great majority, this is an abomination. The *Yeshivat Hakotel* has three fitness rooms and even a computer room. Such institutions are considered blasphemous by the ultraorthodox; there were no fitness and computer rooms in the *yeshivas* of White Russia and Hungary, they argue, so why have them now? Even worse are the modern *yeshivas* for girls, a concept wholly unacceptable to the extremists, but they are usually outside Mea Shearim.

What is the reason for this enormous growth during the last two decades? In part it has to do, no doubt, with the general resurgence of fundamentalist religion all over the world. Some of the *yeshivas* of Eastern Europe managed to escape at the very last moment (such as members of the Mir yeshiva by way of Shanghai), but most of the Orthodox heartland was lost as the result of the Nazi mass murder. Some of the survivors made their way to Palestine-Israel; others settled in the United States. Furthermore, Jerusalem has attracted most of the Orthodox immigrants from the West in recent decades. The birth rate of the ultraorthodox is very high, and this too helps to explain the growth of Mea Shearim. The number of secular young people who, following a religious experience, returned to Judaism and moved into Mea Shearim has been relatively small (counted in thousands rather than hundreds of thousands). On the other hand, there are also defectors leaving the ultraorthodox camp. Less is written because it is not trumpeted from the rooftops and the media seldom report it.

The ultraorthodox have received considerable strength from their alliance with Moroccan Jewry. The Yiddish-speaking Lithuanian Orthodox are wholly different in their mentality, customs, and attire from the North African Jews. Their attitude towards the Moroccans was, and remains, at best one of condescension. They feel themselves greatly superior to them as far as religious knowledge and the observation of the religious duties is concerned. They are reluctant even to eat or drink in the houses of the Sephardim, who, they think, are not strictly kosher, and "mixed marriages" are uncommon too. They reject the cult of saints among the North African Jews as well as their belief in magic and amulets.

Yet for all this, the Moroccans were only too eager to attend the *yeshivas* of the Lithuanians and, generally speaking, to cooperate with them. The decisive factor was probably that Moroccan Jewry (except its upper class, which did not come to Israel) was very traditional in its outlook. It was put off by the secular Israelis who wanted them to become absorbed spiritually and physically in Israeli society. However strange the manners and customs of the Eastern European Ashkenazi ultraorthodox, their way of life was perhaps less alien to Moroccan Jewry than that of secular society. They had common interests with the ultraorthodox, for instance setting up and maintaining their own school system.

All this does not mean that the Ashkenazi ultraorthodox could firmly count on their Oriental brothers; sooner or later, the Oriental Jews would look for their emancipation from Lithuanian tutelage. The establishment of their own political party (Shas) distinct from both the anti-Zionist ultraorthodox and the religious nationalist camp was the first step. More recently, the Sephardi rabbis have stressed the need to restore the former glory of both their ritual and their interpretations of Judaism. They argue that after the destruction of the Temple they were the first to return to Palestine (the official title of the Sephardi chief rabbi is "First in Zion"), that they not only have seniority but that they are the true spiritual descendants of Maimonides and Rabbi Joseph Caro, the chief interpreters of Jewish religious practice. Therefore, their ritual, their text of prayer, their ritual slaughter, and their other practices should prevail in the land of Israel, not those of the Ashkenazim.

Their demographic growth (they have an impressive average of 7.6 children per family) gave the ultraorthodox a political strength they never had before. As a result of the fragmentation of the Israeli party system they were able to tip the political scale. It depended on them whether Likud or the opposing camp would get to power. A former generation of rabbis had strictly kept out of politics, but with their exponential growth, the leaders of the ultraorthodox stepped into politics with gusto. At the same time this growth has created major social, economic, and political problems.

Almost half of the Jerusalem *haredim* live below the poverty line, which does not come as a surprise considering that only 28 percent of the males are gainfully employed. True believers, devoting their life to the study of the Torah, were never very rich, but as long as the number of *yeshiva* attendants was relatively small and more of them were part of the workforce, the problem was not insoluble. A talented young student (and the selection was harsher in the olden days) would be found a wife from the daughters of a well-to-do sympathizer of the sect, a merchant perhaps, and the parents of the bride would buy them an apartment and take care of the material needs of the couple—for life if needed. With the explosion in the number of young *haredim* and the tendency to continue studies up to the age of forty or even beyond, there has been a radical change in the situation. There are not remotely enough wealthy fathers-in-law to keep the young couples afloat.

How to finance the life of the *haredi* offspring? Some donations come from a variety of wealthy merchants from London, Brooklyn, and even Australia. Many wives of *yeshiva* students go out to work, but without professional training, their earnings are low and account overall for less than 20 percent of the income of an ultraorthodox family. Nor are there enough suitable jobs for them. Leading rabbis have banned not only television but also access to the Internet. (The Liubavich are an exception in this respect, regarding the Internet as a godsend to spread their message.)

By and large, the state of Israel has come to replace the wealthy father-in-law. The Israeli government—that is to say, the Israeli taxpayer—subsidizes the *yeshivas* and those learning there in a variety of ways, directly by allocations from the budget of education and religious affairs, as well as unemployment benefits, pensions, disability, and child allowances. In addition to these direct money transfers there are the indirect subsidies. The students of ultraorthodox *yeshivas* do not serve in the army and do not pay income tax. According to demographic studies, the size of the ultraorthodox population is doubling every twenty years, or even sooner (the number of children born to these families was 6 percent of the Israeli total in the middle 1980s; a decade later it was 11 percent).

These demographic trends have far-reaching consequences. Despite all the state support, the ultraorthodox community is still poor and will remain poor. The *haredi* families do not starve and are not homeless, but their living conditions are still dismal. In view of their steady growth, the state will not be able to afford the financial assistance unless taxes are increased on everyone else or allocations are reduced for defense, education, and health. Economists believe that these transfers to the *haredim* will ruin the state social security budget in the not-too-distant future and affect in particular the communities in which many *haredim* live. The ultraorthodox parties are in a position to exert great political pressure to get more money, but the secular taxpayers are unwilling to shoulder an even greater burden on behalf of those unwilling to work. This resistance is aggravated by the fact that the beneficiaries of the taxes paid by the non-Orthodox are people who regard their lifestyle sinful and little better than criminal.

The *yeshivas* and the ultraorthodox movement are relatively recent phenomena. The *yeshivas* only came into being in the nineteenth century. The idea that a sizeable number of young and middle-aged men should devote their lives to the study of the Torah was unknown in earlier Jewish history. There was no one to support this way of life.

It could well be that the enormous growth of the ultraorthodox community will be their undoing. Even on the present scale they will be unable to maintain their way of life unless a far higher percentage of their men and women go out to work. But their leaders see this as undesirable, because at the workplace they will come in contact with people and influences considered highly dangerous. For the same reason they are opposed to military service: life in the army is permissive and impure, soldiers associate with people from different backgrounds and are thus subject to the countless temptations of the secular world. The world of the ultraorthodox can be maintained only in strict isolation. But how can this occur in the modern world? Even now, as the wives of those attending the *yeshivas* go out to work, there is the danger of contact with an impure world, and this is leading to a number of undesirable consequences. Tensions within the family are based in part on the jealousy of the husbands but also the greater assertiveness of the female breadwinners who in ultraorthodox families are traditionally subordinate to men.

Another consequence of the expansion of the ultraorthodox way of life is the spread of corruption and personal enrichment on the part of the leadership. As long as there was little money to go around there was not much opportunity for theft, but with the influx of big sums both from the government and other sources there was a far wider scope for fraud. Abu Hatzeira, Aryen Deri, and other leading figures of the Oriental ultraorthodox ended up in prison. So did Avraham Shapiro, a leader of Agudat Israel (and a minister in the Israeli government at one time). True, with increased prosperity there was also more fraud among the secular, but this is not a mitigating circumstance for those who pride themselves on having higher moral standards.

The ultraorthodox are almost always willing to forgive the transgressors in their own ranks. If one of their leaders betrays their trust, surely he must have good reasons to do so. In a similar way, the ultraorthodox of Eastern Europe forgave those leaders (such as the rabbis of Satmar, Belts, Ger, and others) who escaped at the last moment from Europe in the face of the Nazi onslaught instead of sharing the fate of their communities. The rabbi, it was thought, knew better than anyone else. What he did was a priori correct and by escaping he was no doubt fulfilling a mission imposed on him by God. As for the ultraorthodox among the Oriental Jews, it was always taken for granted that the leaders were entitled to a much better living than their followers. Standards of public honesty were different, and the fraud scandals were interpreted as secular intrigues designed to besmirch the reputation of God-fearing North African Jews.

When Aryeh Deri had to go to prison, having been sentenced by a judge who was not Ashkenazi, his followers threatened the country with civil war. In this case, as in some others, the religious motivation was reinforced by ethnic complaints. But the general assumption was that the legal norms of a secular state did not apply to religious leaders. Rabbis were above the secular law.

There are monasteries and convents in Christianity and Buddhism, practicing even greater isolation from the outside world than the *haredim* in Israel and they undergo greater sacrifices in their private lives, such as celibacy. Life in the community, be it the *yeshiva* or the *kolel* (the organizational framework of the religious community), provides a sense of togetherness, of security, perhaps even of warmth like in the Eastern European *shtetl* one hundred fifty years earlier. The great majority of today's ultraorthodox were born into traditional families. The number of those who joined them from a secular background is not very great but it is still interesting to know what attracted them. It probably has to do with the quest for certainties and the willingness to believe. In some cases, the escape into Orthodox religion may be rooted in the wish to find solutions to deep personal problems. In other cases it might be a response to the feeling of being lost in a confusing and chaotic modern world. This has driven some in Israel, as well as in other countries, into the orbit of the New Age movement and all kinds of sects of Far Eastern and other esoteric origins. And it was only natural that some of those in search of a message for how to live their lives would rediscover traditional Jewish religion in its most extreme form. What repelled and antagonized the secular— the heavy emphasis on ritual and the countless commandments and taboos, the central position of the rabbi as the ultimate guide, arbiter, and font of wisdom—might have been precisely the qualities that attracted others in search of strict order and an authority telling them what to do and how to do it.

For the great majority of those born into the ultraorthodox community, the situation was different. They had never known a different way of life. They had had no contact with the outside world except in times of emergency when essential services were needed. The forces of continuity and inertia were probably decisive factors. To be sure, there was genuine religiosity, but many secular people believe that the *yeshivas* have survived (and will survive) largely because of the deferment from army service. They say that if young men and women in Israel did not have to serve in the army, the *yeshivas* would vanish within a generation or two.

But military service will not disappear and the *yeshivas* will not vanish. In the meantime something like a *Kulturkampf* is under way with the anger of the secular mounting at *haredi* encroachments. Thousands of Jerusalemites, especially young people, have moved out of the city—they see it becoming a bastion of Jewish "Khomein-ism." The ultraorthodox, on the other hand, complain about Jewish anti-Semitism, the frequent and growing references to them as parasites and bloodsuckers, as black ants in their disgusting, anachronistic, and ridiculous garb. It is true that the language of secular, especially the intelligentsia, has been increasingly violent. As Tommy Lapid, head of the anti-religious party *Shinui* (Change) and later minister of justice, put it: "They are after all faithfully acting out the role assigned to them by anti-Semitic literature. They exploit the non-Jew, trade in his blood, and laugh at him behind his back. Only this time the goy is us."

There have been calls to destroy Mea Shearim, to crush the ultra-orthodox even if only metaphorically. Secular violence so far has been virtually absent, whereas *haredi* violence has manifested itself in attacks against traffic on the Sabbath, the burning of non-Orthodox synagogues, and similar actions.

The attacks by the secular population have not been directed only against the anti-Zionist ultraorthodox element. There has been equal bitterness about the wearers of the knitted skullcaps, meaning the "national religious," active especially in the occupied territories. Once upon a time, these groups were political allies of the Labor party with no particular foreign political agenda of their own; in fact, they gravitated toward moderation and peaceful coexistence with the Arabs. But then a new generation came to the fore, and following the Six-Day War, the outcome of which they regarded a heavenly miracle, they moved to the extreme right. It was from among the graduates of certain of their *yeshivas* that the militant underground arose, eager to reconquer Temple Mount (the murderer of Yitzhak Rabin was among them). They maintained that it was a mortal sin to give up even a single inch of historical Palestine and that those who favor a territorial compromise are traitors. The land belongs to God, and God gave it to the people of Israel. The ideology they developed was by no means in the tradition of Orthodox Judaism; they consider the possession of land as important as, if not more importance than, the fulfillment of religious obligations. Whereas Rabbi Eliezer Shach, the ideological guide of the ultraorthodox, threatened that if the *yeshiva* students were ever compelled to do military service (or other such duty) they would leave the country, the national religious willingly served in the army.

In view of their aggressive doctrine and practice they have been denounced by the secular population as a messianic junta, a bunch of armed gangsters who came out of some dark corner of Judaism and through their provocative actions are involving the state in endless bloody warfare. The argument of the ideological settlers is that the Jews have as much right to be in Hebron, or any other place on the West Bank, as they do in Tel Aviv and Haifa. If they were to give up their rights in Jerusalem, and on the West Bank, they would find it difficult to justify their presence in the country altogether. The small Jewish community in Hebron, and in other outlaying places in the territories occupied in 1967, is no more than the frontline in the war against the Palestinians. Seen in this perspective, Tel Aviv is defended in Hebron and other settlements.

But this is a military, not a theological, argument, and from a strategic point of view the settlements certainly do not make sense. Substantial units of the Israeli army are needed to defend them as well as the roads leading to them, which only serves to weaken Israeli security, not strengthen it.

The verbal attacks against the ultraorthodox and the national religious have been bitter and abusive, but the provocation was great. In earlier times there had been tolerance on the part of the secular. They did not share the beliefs of Mea Shearim, but they felt piety and respect towards the Orthodox, who had voluntarily chosen a life of poverty. They were, albeit in an extreme form, the heirs of a tradition that had prevailed in the Jewish communities over many centuries up to the Enlightenment and the emancipation of the Jews.

However, with all this it is still true that Zionism had come into being in deliberate opposition against the ghetto, the way of life in the Eastern European *shtetl,* the lack of dignity, the (sometimes self-imposed) misery, a life wholly dominated by the dead hand of the past. Zionism was not anti-religious. For the most part, it was simply indifferent to religion. But it wanted nothing to do with the perpetuation of the miserable life of the ghetto and its lack of freedom. This manifested itself in the rejection of Yiddish and the revival of Hebrew. As long as the *haredim* were a tiny minority in Palestine who wanted to be left alone, they were not bothered and continued the life of Ponevezh and Slobodka in Lithuania transplanted to the hills of Judea. (Slobodka's famous *yeshiva* was transferred first to Hebron, and after the massacre of the Jewish population there, to Jerusalem.) If they ignored the state of Israel and refused to accept its authority, the state ignored them.

But as their numbers grew, so did their political weight and their demands, as did hostility and anger toward them. It is certainly true that some of the attacks against the ultraorthodox are abusive, but are they incorrect?

The list of secular complaints is very long. The demand of the *haredim* to be excused from military service means that others have to shoulder a heavier burden. The *haredi* spokesmen maintain that the lives of the *yeshiva* students are more valuable than the lives of those defending them, and that those who have been killed in action were sinners. As Rabbi Ovadiah sees it, the victims of the Holocaust also were sinners; this is based on the doctrine of *gilgul neshamot,* the transmigration of souls (reincarnation), which goes back to Gnostic sects, and reappears in the kabbalah. It is a dangerous, almost postmodernist doctrine, because seen in this light, Ovadiah and his flock could easily be reincarnations of sinners.

In any case, service in the army is evil by definition. The Orthodox rabbis refused to bury those who had fallen in military actions in Jewish cemeteries if they are not Jews according to the *halacha,* the religious law. Secular citizens are angry not just at the fact that they have to defend and finance the life of the ultraorthodox and their institutions (and the fraud practiced inside these institutions), but also because of their deliberate provocations, such as defying the state mourning on Shoah Day, or the occasional burning of Israeli flags and other emblems of the state on the Lag Ba'Omer (a happy holiday celebrated with picnics and fireworks), and other occasions. Ultraorthodox institutions, unlike Palestinian Arab schools, have a dispensation from hoisting the Israeli flag. The *haredim* were showing intolerance not only toward religions that in Palestine and Jerusalem are equally holy but also toward other Jewish religious trends such as the Conservative and Reform, and there have been physical attacks against their practitioners. They successfully prevented the introduction of civil marriage in Israel and other laws and regulations that are the norm in most developed, secular countries. Their definition of who is a Jew (and who is recognized as a convert) had been accepted under pressure by successive Israeli governments. This definition is not just a matter of theological significance. It has essential practical implications in daily life, for it deprives those not considered Jews of many rights and benefits enjoyed by those recognized as Jews by the rabbis. They close down roads on the Sabbath and attack vehicles, including ambulances, and they have tried very hard to shut down entertainment throughout Israel.

The long list means that the *haredim* and their national religious fellow travelers essentially wanted a clerical rather than a democratic state, a state dominated by the *halacha,* just as the conservative Saudis as well as radical Muslims like the Taliban or the Persian mullahs want a state ruled by the *sharia.* Actually, the *haredim* would probably prefer not to have a state at all, but since this is impossible, it has to be a state in the image of the *Shulkhan Arukh,* the compilation of regulations composed by Rabbi Joseph Caro in Safed in the sixteenth century and modified by various other rabbis since. This is not acceptable to the majority of Israelis, and it is opposed to the basic tenets of Herzl and the Jewish state. Herzl wrote that "in our future state the generals will be confined to the barracks and the rabbis to the synagogues." But the rabbis of Mea Shearim, aided by the Orthodox leaders outside their camp, have no wish to accept the Herzlian vision and hence the cultural and political wars that spread in the 1980s and '90s.

If secular people called the *haredim* "parasites," the latter freely use epithets such as "clowns," "villains," and "criminals," and suggest that the leaders of the secular be hanged like Haman in the book of Esther. True, Rabbi Ovadiah Yosef, who made this suggestion, also compared his fellow Ashkenazi chief rabbi Shlomo Goren to the sons of the wicked Haman. He had been chief rabbi of Cairo, and in his language there are strong traces of the language of the Cairo markets. As for the rabbis of the national religious camp, they are perhaps a little more permissive in their interpretation of the *halacha,* but seldom dare to oppose the *haredi* spiritual leaders on essential points. Furthermore, they are more radical as far as their nationalist demands are concerned (which had become part of their religious doctrine); few of them out-right denounced the murder of Prime Minister Rabin. Some had implicitly justified it.

This in briefest outline has been the history of Mea Shearim. The secular majority has made many concessions, but there is a limit beyond which they were not willing to go, for it means giving up the democratic character of the state and essential human rights. Such conflicts are not unique in the modern world. They stem not so much from misunderstanding as from a conflict between a modern society and one based on a tradition that could not be changed or reformed. They stem from a spirit of intolerance.

What makes it even more difficult to accept for non-Orthodox Israelis is the fact that the major bones of contentions are not even found in the Bible, but are based on interpretation of the Bible by Maimonides, by Rabbi Caro and Rabbi Isserles of Cracow who, as even the *haredim* had to concede, had not been saints but mere mortals. Whereas the Catholic church has given up the doctrine of papal infallibility, the *haredim* are not willing to make such concessions. Traditional rules cannot be changed, and in any case, anything that is new is wrong and bad.

Tensions are growing and the question is often asked how all this is going to end. A deputy mayor of Jerusalem once suggested that only separation could prevent a worsening of the culture wars. But how far could separation go? Some secular and a few *haredim* have proposed the establishment of two states, one for the *haredim,* the other for the secular. But these are fantasies, for no one would pay for an ultraorthodox state. The medieval church had its monasteries, but the monks had no children and many of them were gainfully employed. Nor would it solve the problem of the religious nationalists who want the whole of Jerusalem. For the *haredim,* the question of political sovereignty is unimportant at least as long as Messiah has not come.

As I walk one day on Sukkoth along Mea Shearim Street from Sabbath Square and turn to the center of the quarter, I wonder at how little it has changed. Of course the *yeshivas* are larger and they are much greater in number. There must be at least fifty synagogues in this quarter and more *yeshivas.* Still there are the same shops selling phylacteries, skullcaps, black hats, religious books, ritual lamps, and tablecloths. Street vendors offer the *lulabs* (palm branches) and *ethrogs* (citrus fruits) essential for the celebration of the Feast of Tabernacles, as well as amulets, *shofars, mezuzahs,* pictures of religious sages of bygone days, and tapes of Jewish music; someone irreverently has compared it to the Christmas markets in European towns. There still is a great deal of smoking in Mea Shearim—I don't know how. The children are kept away from the secular temptations. Many of them have never been to Jaffa Road, the main Jerusalem thoroughfare which is less than half a mile away.

Secular books and newspapers are still out of bounds in the neighborhood, but they have two daily papers, *Hamodia* and *Yated Ne'eman* (a relative newcomer representing the followers of the late Rav Shach). There are also a few widely read weeklies, some catering to *haredi* women. These newspapers report in great detail speeches made by their representatives in parliament and also some edifying religious texts. The Olympic Games, a frivolous enterprise, are not mentioned, but there will be attacks against the sinful lifestyle of the secular. On the other hand, they do not cover events inside the ultraorthodox camp either, and the readers will look in vain for descriptions of life and living conditions among the *haredim.* To learn about this you have to spend an hour or two in the religious bath houses (assuming you are a man) or on the Mea Shearim market where the *haredim* can buy all the essentials far from the secular world. Buildings are still plastered with posters calling for a demonstration against secular abominations or denouncing rival sects. No other part of Jerusalem has so many billboards advertising specially priced housing projects for the *haredim,* obituaries in black frames, and above all political appeals: "If you want to commit suicide, join the *Nahal* [a branch of the Israeli army]." This is a denunciation of the national religious groups, which in contrast to the *haredim,* serve in the army. "Modesty patrols" tour the streets of Mea Shearim as they do some Muslim capitals.

Thus nothing seems to have changed. The monotonous singsong of children repeating a text after their teacher is clearly heard in the streets. The older ones continue to discuss with their teachers such time-honored questions as to whether the consumption of beans at Passover is permitted—the Ashkenazim are strictly opposed, the Sephardim think differently. Another important topic is the issue of cross-dressing: Why should women not wear jeans or trousers in general? There seems to be a clear ban in Deuteronomy, but what does the decisive phrase "*kli gever*" (the utensils of a man) really mean? Does it refer to clothes or to phylacteries or perhaps to weapons?

Cross-dressing is certainly permitted on Purim, so the ban is not absolute, and the sages have explained that much depends on fashions of time and place. There are heated debates as to how exactly a *sukkah* should be built for the holiday of the Tabernacles, and precisely what form it should take. A high priest, according to hallowed tradition, should marry a virgin. But what if the virgin "lost her virginity" while climbing a tree? Is it important whether she was three years old or less at the time, and does it matter that she was climbing up or down the tree? These and other issues can be discussed for a long time even though there have not been high priests in Israel for some time now.

Yet there have been changes, small and not so small. Despite political pressure and violent protests, more places of entertainment, shops, and coffee houses are now open on the Sabbath in Jerusalem than ten or twenty years ago. There are even gay bars not far from Mea Shearim. Despite the rigorous instructions of the rabbis, *haredi* women succeed in circumventing them; they do not walk about in shorts, but some of them are elegantly dressed by any standard. More *haredim,* male and female, go out to work, and there are special computer training courses for people from these circles (the Haredi Center for Technological Studies). Others have studied accounting and social work.

Could it be that the *haredi* dispute with the world is more about symbols rather than realities? How long will the *haredim* be able to maintain their lifestyle amidst the corrosive influences of the modern world? Some will certainly resist the temptations of the world surrounding them and pursue their traditional lifestyle, but a great many are bound to stray from the fold of the righteous. No one can say with any assurance whether this process will be gradual and partial or whether there will be a radical break. The rabbis in Israel, in contrast to other countries, have been very rigid about making concessions to the outside world. True, they have reluctantly agreed to enter Israeli politics, even though they reject the state. They know they have to play the political game in order to ensure their survival as a community.

Mea Shearim has lasted for more than one hundred years. Orthodox religion will persist. But it is safe to say that as a way of life, Mea Shearim it will not last another hundred years.

CHAPTER 12

MUSRARA AND THE PANTHERS FROM MOROCCO

THE PERSON I SHALL CALL JACQUES BENHABIB WAS BORN in Meknes, Morocco, in 1952. His family immigrated to Israel when he was four. His cousin Eli, almost exactly ten years younger, saw the light of the world in Katamon, a part of Jerusalem. Eli's parents arrived in Israel (by way of France, as did most Moroccan Jews) on the same ship as Jacques's father and mother.

Both families were housed at first in the tents of a Ma'abara, a transition camp at the outskirts of Haifa. The men could only hope to do seasonal, unskilled labor. Both Jacques's and Eli's mothers found work as maids in Haifa. They had been poor in Morocco too, but family and synagogue provided both cohesion and psychological support. The synagogue also served as a communal center. The rabbi was a guide not only in spiritual matters.

Many Moroccan Jewish communities and families were dispersed when they came to Israel. The newcomers did not know the language, and when they had complaints and demands they could not express them. The established residents, the Ashkenazi majority, told these newcomers that the beginning was always difficult and that when they had come conditions had been even harsher—they had literally starved, they had lived in tents for years, there had been malaria and hardly any medical services. There had been no one to take care of their elementary needs, no safety net at all.

But the newcomers were not convinced. Frequently, they came up against an attitude of contempt, as savages even. There had been violent clashes between Moroccan Jews and the Israeli police as early as 1958 when the Wadi Salib riots broke out in Haifa. There was some willingness to help among the Israelis, but efforts to help were in the main impersonal and paternalistic. Israelis were absorbed in their own problems, and the general situation in the region was far from stable. These were the years immediately after the Suez conflict of 1956. Nasser and the Syrians were still threatening Israel; the economic prosperity was nowhere in sight.

While many new immigrants were sent to development towns in the south, the Benhabibs moved to Jerusalem and lived in the quarter located between the Old City and the Russian compound, which had been predominantly Arab before 1948. The Arabs called this area Musriri, the Jews called it Musrara. The official name was Morasha, but it was not widely used. Katamon, where Jacques's parents settled, was a middle-class Arab area. A well-known Greek monastery named St. Simon can be found there (hence the name: *kata-mon* means "beyond the monastery"), as well as a few nice hotels. Jews and foreign residents also lived there.

There were many substantial houses built by wealthy Arabs in Musrara such as the one owned by Musa Alami's father. There were also some convents and churches, but on the whole Musrara was not a very desirable neighborhood; it had been on the decline even before 1948 and became a slum thereafter. The fact that it was a border area, where occasional battles broke out, was probably the reason no one developed it.

Jacques's career in school was not impressive. His schoolmates were mostly Moroccan, and the teachers found it difficult to maintain discipline. Jacques was frequently absent, and it did not come as a great surprise that at the age of fourteen he had his first run-in with the police. It was a petty affair, a theft of a few packs of cigarettes in the local supermarket, but the street gang to which he belonged made pilfering a matter of honor and by the time Jacques should have gone into the army, he had a police record, which made him ineligible for military service. Certain streets in Katamon became the main centers of crime in Jerusalem, with armed juvenile gangs raping, robbing, and selling drugs.

Jacques could have gone to one of the professional schools that trained young men in various trades, but his eagerness to learn was not great. Unemployment benefits were sufficient as long as he lived at home. Most of his free time was spent playing football in the open spaces of Musrara, seeing movies in the cinemas in the more affluent parts of Jerusalem, and hanging out with his friends.

It was out of this group of bored and unemployed young men that the Black Panthers were born in the early 1970s. A handful of young men met every day in the Musrara streets or at Café Ta'amon. Some social workers had suggested that they start political and social initiatives rather than forever complain and expect help from the state. At the same time, they had been joined by three militants who could advise them on how to best attract attention. They were from Matzpen, a small politically savvy Trotskyite group.

The history of Trotskyism in Israel is a fascinating study in frustration, failure, fractiousness, and perennial hope. Their basic orientation was, of course, towards the working class, but the Jewish working class was Zionist, and rejected them. So they transferred their hopes to the Arab proletariat, but that relatively small group did not welcome them either. So they put their hopes on all kinds of discontented groups who had no use for Marxist theory but who accepted their help. The Trotskyites thought that these groups would provide something that had always eluded them—political mass. (This strategy was also tried in other countries under the banner of rainbow coalitions or other such names.) The young revolutionary Moroccan Jews from Mishmarot Street, Stern Street (in Kiryat Yovel), and Katamon Chet seemed obvious allies.

Jacques was nineteen at the time, and although he was not a member of the small inner circle, he knew most of the Panthers and took part in their demonstrations. These were his friends and contemporaries, and he shared many of their convictions. He resented the Ashkenazi establishment, and felt that the Moroccans were not given a fair deal. He also believed that peaceful demonstration alone would not bring about radical change. In a way they were revolutionaries, for they introduced a political style hitherto unknown in Israel. When the police did not give them a permit to demonstrate in early March 1971, they went ahead anyway. Starting at Davidka Square, hundreds of young men (and a few young women) proceeded along Jaffa Road to the Russian compound and city hall. There were some ten such demonstrations, usually violent. There was great noise and fury, tires were burned, shop windows smashed, a few Molotov cocktails thrown. The police intervened, blows were exchanged, and the most militant among the protesters arrested (but never for any length of time).

The group's American and French advisers, who had participated in the student demonstrations of 1968 and after, offered advice: Establish an ideological program that demands an end to ethnic discrimination, as well as peace, bread, and work. Demand that the inhuman housing conditions be improved at once. Demand free schooling at all levels, and establish a minimum wage. The Panthers—more precisely, those who wrote their manifestoes and newspapers—demanded the observation of human rights and the democratization of Israeli society.

Some of the demands were quite specific: they wanted a twelve-month school year and a twelve-hour school day. (This seemed highly unlikely. No child would accept a year without holidays or a school day lasting from eight in the morning to eight at night.) There was also the demand for peace with the Palestinian people and an end to the war. They argued that the warfaring mentality was bound to erode Israeli democracy. But there was no evidence that the majority of young people demonstrating in the center of Jerusalem was any more inclined towards peace with the Palestinians than the rest of the Jewish population.

Without public relations the Panthers would go nowhere. Fortunately, journalists were eager to give them publicity in both Israel and abroad. Their language was a little bombastic: they would burn themselves, they would destroy the establishment, there would be demonstrations like never before. This was the stuff of good headlines. The Knesset listened to their complaints, and a special committee was set up to make proposals on how to deal with their grievances. Eventually, considerable sums of money were spent on improving the housing situation of Moroccan Jewry. Youth clubs were established. Prime Minister Golda Meir even met with several leading Panthers for a discussion, and though it was a dialogue between deaf people, it helped their cause.

For the establishment these demonstrations, and above all the violence and the threatening rhetoric, came as a shock: these were obviously not the Jewish boys and girls they had known in the past. (They are not nice young people, Golda Meir said, having met a few of them.) The Panthers had not grown up in the youth movements, they were dropouts, many of them had not served in the army, and some had criminal records (and not just because of a little pilfering in the shops). They were radicals. Unlike their parents, they did not hesitate to voice their case, they were not politely requesting but demanding with the shake of a fist. They belonged to another culture.

Jacques Benhabib was well aware that, even within their own community, there was a great deal of skepticism with regard to the
Panthers. The older generation liked the slogans about the pride of the
Jews of the East, which had been wounded so often. They remembered
arriving to the port of Haifa, being transported in open trucks in the
rain to the Ma'abarot where tents were not yet made ready. Contrast
this with immigrants from Romania, who had been taken in buses to
a restaurant and only after a meal transferred to camps that were much
nicer. Why did immigrants from the Anglo-Saxon countries get pref-
erential treatment? When they looked down from their homes in the
Katamon to Rehavia, they saw new Israeli neighborhoods built for the
"Anglosaxim," or immigrants from the English-speaking countries.
And what a tremendous difference between these luxury buildings and
the "asbestonim" of the Moroccans, comprised of a room and a half
(twenty-four square yards altogether) for a family of six or more. After
a few years, they would be given slightly larger apartments of two
rooms (forty-two square yards) in high-rise buildings, but often there
was no elevator in these buildings, not to mention a great deal of
dampness and noise.

These were real complaints shared by most immigrants from Arab
speaking countries. Be that as it may, many within the Moroccan
Jewish community were still suspicious of the Panthers, who were far
too secular, seldom attended synagogue, and, generally speaking, did
not belong to the "old" tradition.

Jacques and his friends staged demonstrations throughout the
summer of 1971. They also published leaflets and a journal of sorts.
But within a year the impetus petered out. The Panthers remained a
protest movement confined to Jerusalem, in fact limited to only two
or three neighborhoods. Its leaders were the heads of local street
gangs; those outside Jerusalem were not willing to accept their
authority.

Subsequently some of these militants were co-opted by the establishment, and some of their complaints were remedied. There were quarrels and splits among the Panthers. The Matzpen militants from Café Ta'amon were disappointed by the outcome of the Panther revolution, and the social workers were not happy either. After one year it was all over. A few years later the first dissertations about the Panthers were written by the sociologists at the Hebrew University. It had become a historical event.

The tension in the Moroccan neighborhoods persisted. It was expressed in different ways. There was the *Ohalim* (Tents) movement in the 1970s, which did not engage in violent major demonstrations like the Panthers. Unlike the Panthers, it was not an ethnic movement but rather a group engaging in social protest arising out of an acute housing shortage. It attracted support from a few Jerusalem artists and actors (there was for a while a street theater), but students did not become involved. At the same time, there was a criminal element in the Moroccan movement that despite heroic efforts on the part of the social workers, resurfaced from time to time.

By the time Jacques was nearing his thirtieth birthday, he had married and was father of three children. The family had moved to one of the better parts of Katamon. They could afford a three-room apartment. He had found employment in the Ministry of Interior, which had accepted him despite certain stains on his record. The lean young man had become far more substantial; he still had his mustache, but was wearing fewer rings and bracelets. He was now an ardent supporter of Betar Jerusalem, the leading local football club, and like most people around him, he voted for Begin in 1978 and for other right-wing parties in subsequent elections. Labor scored little more than 10 percent in these neighborhoods. Why the support for the right, which was doing little for the disadvantaged? Because the right, even though led by Ashkenazim, was considered to be more friendly to the

Moroccans, and because the patriotic slogans appealed to them much more than those of the elitist peaceniks, virtually all of whom were middle class Ashkenazi.

In 2001, the thirtieth anniversary of the Black Panthers was celebrated with many articles in the media, and later there was a long television documentary with Charlie Biton, Shemesh Cochavi, and Sa'adia Marziano as the guides. What had become of the leaders? They were still chain-smoking and they had not aged well. Biton had joined Rakach, the Communist party, and had been elected to the Knesset. He could be relied upon to cause the occasional scandal, such as chaining himself to a microphone in parliament. But such behavior did not generate much sympathy in his community or in his party. His attachment to communism did not last; his political allegiance changed several times. Having been a staunch advocate of the Palestinian cause, he was now identified with the right wing. He had married an Ashkenazi schoolteacher and owned a house. Interviewed thirty years after the fact, he still insisted that one day there would be a bitter struggle, perhaps an armed struggle, between the downtrodden and the establishment, though he would not venture to say when such a battle would break out or where.

Shemesh Cochavi went with a small delegation to Moscow to protest the Soviet decision to permit hundreds of thousands of Russian Jews to leave for Israel. Cochavi said that their absorption would cost one hundred billion dollars, and that the Israeli Oriental proletariat would suffer as a result. Later, at age fifty, he began to study law. Marciano supported left-of-center parties, whereas Reuven Avergil was almost the only one of the leading Panthers still politically active along the old lines—within the framework of a "rainbow" group called Keshet Mizrachi. Some of the Panthers became very religious; most found a niche somewhere. On various occasions, the former Black Panther leaders protested against the frequent arrests and prison sentences meted out against young Moroccans for drug dealing.

Some of the Matzpen leaders were integrated into Israeli society. One became a well-known commentator with the daily *Ma'ariv*, a few left the country. But there were others to take their place, such as Michel Warshawski (also known as "Mikado"), the son of the chief rabbi of Strasbourg, who became one of the main spokesmen of the cause of the Mizrachim and a bitter enemy of Zionism in all its forms.

As for Jacques Benhabib and his friends, their resentment against the Ashkenazim lingers. True, it became more difficult to complain about political discrimination when several presidents of Israel came from an Arab-speaking country, as did subsequent ministers of foreign affairs and defense, chiefs of staff of the army, government ministers, and secretaries-general of the Histadrut, the trade union confederation. In fact, these days being of Mizrachi origin has became something of an asset. When in trouble with the police or the media, Mizrachi politicians harp on their North African background, which they think entitles them to a certain immunity from the law.

Some of the wealthiest people in Israel and some of the key figures in the economy are now of Mizrachi origin, and not just old wealth such as the Recanati, but people who had spent their childhood in the tents of Ma'abarot, like Zadik Binu, a leading investment banker; Jo Elmelih, prominent in oil prospecting; Jossi Chachamshvili and Shlomo Eliyahu in insurance; and Eli Papu, who owns a chain of hotels. Iraq-born Efraim Sadka trained as an economist at MIT before becoming an economics professor in Tel Aviv University. Subsequently, he managed Kupat Holim, a leading mutual fund, and then became both head of the America-Israel bank and chairman of Housing & Construction Company. One could not fly much higher. Yossi Rosen, also born in Baghdad, became head of the Israel Corporation, prominent in chemicals, navigation, oil refineries, and semi conductors. Lev

Leviev, born in Uzbekistan, was chairman of the board of Israel-Africa, a company with worldwide interests in diamonds and many other fields. His name figures in the list of the five hundred richest people in the world. The Nimrodis, originally from Iraq, made money in the arms trade and later acquired a media empire. It was difficult to find big corporations in which people with a Mizrachi background were not represented.

But it is also true that most of these wealthy Mizrachim came from Iraq and Egypt, from the Caucasus, Turkey, and Greece. Only a few were Moroccan. As one observer noted, it was not enough to be a Mizrachi. A Moroccan background was also needed, and few of these had made it into the front ranks. At the same time, unemployment, particularly in the development towns, is still considerably higher than among the Ashkenazim, and the average income of a Moroccan family is still less than that of the Ashkenazim. There are even indications that the income disparity between Moroccans and other groups is increasing (except for the ultraorthodox). The reasons are twofold: Ashkenazi families are considerably smaller than Moroccan; the disparity began to decline only in the 1980s. What persisted, however, is the educational lag: far fewer Moroccan children graduate high school, and the difference in the number of those who go on to college or technical schools is even more striking.

So there still was not that much of a common bond between the Benhabibs of the world and the average Ashkenazi, nor indeed with Iraqi Jews who had been relatively well-off in Baghdad. The latter integrated much more easily into Israeli society and rose to positions of prominence in the economy, the administration, and academia. Most of the leading academic ideologists of the Mizrachi revolution in Israel were not of Moroccan origin. There were Ashkenazim among them and quite a few middle-class Iraqis, but the few Moroccan Jews to be found writing articles and books lived in France, Canada, or the

United States. There was a rising number of mixed marriages between Ashkenazim and Mizrachim but again, less so with Moroccans than with other Sephardim.

Eli Benhabib, Jacques's cousin, was born in Katamon. He attended a religious school. This was not at all that unusual because in the 1970s, when Eli grew up, the ultraorthodox, and above all the Lubavich, made a great effort to attract children from Oriental backgrounds. While the emphasis in these schools was on religious subjects, the education was far more intensive, and a child who distinguished himself as Eli did could be singled out for special treatment and promotion. In fact, once having entered the Orthodox orbit, his whole career seemed to be predestined. He was away from home most of the day, and at the age of eighteen it was suggested to his parents that he should attend a Lithuanian *yeshiva* in France where he could study to become a rabbi. This would mean that for years there would be one less breadwinner in the family, but it was an honor and the pressure brought about by their own local rabbi was so great that they agreed. When Eli returned from Paris in 1983, he married a very distant relation living in Beersheba. At the same time, his career got under way— but not as a rabbi.

Until this point, Eli's interest in politics had been limited and his views conventional. According to the education he had received, it was up to the leading rabbis to decide how their followers should vote. He had felt a certain unease for years towards his Ashkenazi mentors. He acknowledged their wide Talmudic erudition, but he resented the condescension with which he and other Moroccan students were treated. They were needed by the Ashkenazi rabbis of "Lithuanian" persuasion, but they were neither liked nor trusted. Behind their back they called them "Frenks," and the Ashkenazi ultraorthodox would not eat or drink with them for fear of violating the ritual laws. Intermarriage with Moroccans was definitively discouraged.

Eli was approached after his return by a small group of slightly older Moroccan activists of whom he knew by reputation. They said the time had come to organize and get involved in the coming election to Jerusalem municipality. Their words fell on eager ears. Eli did not know it at the time, but he was present at the creation of Shas, which for a while became the third largest political party in the country. The Jerusalem militants who had insisted on putting forward a list of their own (three of them were eventually elected, one became deputy mayor of Jerusalem) pioneered the emancipation of the Mizrachim from the tutelage of the Ashkenazi ultraorthodox.

Eli was asked to undertake two missions, which he did with both considerable enthusiasm and brilliant success. One mission was to secure the approval and endorsement of leading Sephardi rabbis, because without their blessing the whole enterprise was bound to fail. His second assignment was to drum up support in the election campaign of 1984 in some of the development towns where there was a strong Moroccan element. Despite his youth he showed good political instincts and a capacity to organize. In Rechasim, Netivot, and Kiryat Malahi, Eli's districts, Shas polled between 35 percent and 45 percent of the vote, far above the national average. Eli Benhabib was too young to become a national figure, but it was predicted that sooner rather than later he would attain a position of leadership—either as a member of parliament, or as head of a leading *yeshiva* or foundation. Even the wife of Rabbi Ovadiah Yosef, who strictly controlled who was to have access to her venerable husband, took a liking to the young man who now lived with his young family in Har Nof, the same Orthodox neighborhood in which Ovadiah Yosef lived.

The establishment of Shas had a far more lasting impact on Israeli domestic politics than did the Black Panthers. Shas expressed the complaints and the aspirations of the new underclass that had come into existence with the immigration of the Moroccan Jews. Shorn of the usual rhetorical exaggerations, there is no denying that many of their complaints about inequality in income, education, and many other issues were justified. The Moroccan Jews resented the fact that the Ashkenazim, many of them just a generation or two removed from the ghetto, felt themselves culturally superior. They did not want to mix with the Moroccans and regarded them as savages, with their specific cults and religious traditions. The Mizrachim felt themselves oppressed and exploited, second-class citizens. They had their own cultural traditions, which the Ashkenazim belittled or despised. They had been sent to development towns in which the quality of life was inferior to the bigger cities and where economic prospects were exceedingly limited; they depended on a few major factories, and were these to close there would be mass unemployment. If the government failed to respond fully to their demands, they complained about neglect. If the government did help, they accused it of paternalism. True, they became a leading political force. David Levy became foreign minister, and Moshe Shahal, president of Israel. They started their careers in the development towns. But the success of a few did not compensate for the failure of the many. As they saw it, it was all the fault of the Ashkenazim, who had brought them to Israel. That a lack of initiative, ability, and ambition on their part might also be involved seldom occurred to them.

The transplantation of a premodern community into a state that was (and had to be) modern was bound to create enormous, perhaps insurmountable, difficulties. The Palestinian Jewish community before 1948 (the *yishuv*) had been to a large extent an elite that had consciously turned against the Jewish tradition of Eastern Europe. The Moroccan Jews were anything but an elite. They wanted to preserve their traditions. Zionism had been very weak in the Oriental countries; Herzl and other prophets of Zionism had envisaged the establishment of a Jewish state for the Jews of Europe who they believed were in acute danger of extinction. They had known little about the Oriental Jewish communities, and what they knew had not inspired them with enthusiasm. This was true with regard to the left as much as for the right. Jabotinsky, the guru of the maximalists and later of Likud, had been as scathing about "Levantinism" and the "Oriental spirit" as Ahad Ha'am, the cultural Zionist and prophet of pacifism. The European Zionist leaders were hardly saints, but they firmly believed that the future Jewish state should have high moral standards.

Once the state came into being, it quickly became apparent that these hopes were to some extent misplaced. Some Ashkenazi ministers, and even a president, were found to be dishonest. Such charges led invariably to their resignation and in some well-known cases to suicide. Still, corruption was not the norm among the Ashkenazi. Among many of the Mizrachim, a different mentality prevailed. When Arye Deri, the young leader of Shas, went to prison for corruption and embezzlement in 1998, the great majority of his supporters argued that the court (even though headed by a Sephardi) had been illegitimate, and that the secular state had no right to judge one of them. Many thousands accompanied him on the way to prison. They compared him to Alfred Dreyfus, and there was even talk of civil war.

The early Zionist leaders were not racists in the biological sense; in fact, they hoped, as Ben-Gurion did, that there would be plenty of Oriental Jewish PhDs and generals in the very near future. But they firmly believed in the superiority of European culture and they were convinced that in a Jewish state, Oriental character was neither desirable nor viable. Racially, that is to say genetically, North African Jewry might be close to European Jewry, but the cultural differences were tremendous.

Why did Zionism undertake such desperate efforts, and invest so much energy and money persuading Oriental Jews to immigrate to Israel? Why did the hotheads among the emissaries from Israel sometimes engage in questionable practices to expedite immigration? There was the unfortunate doctrine of the ingathering of the exiles (the transplantation of the Ethiopian Jews was another example of misguided ethnic solidarity). The Zionists believed that since European Jewry, which should have been the main reservoir of man- and womanpower to build the new country, had been destroyed, and since Russian Jewry was cut off, Oriental Jewish communities had become the main—indeed, the only—hope for building the new state. In addition, it was genuinely believed that these communities were in immediate physical danger.

Seen in retrospect, both assumptions were questionable. There had been pogroms in the Arab world during and after the war, notably in Iraq, Libya, and Morocco. It is doubtful, given the rise of violent nationalism and xenophobia, that Jewish communities in Arab countries had much of a future. The fate of all foreign communities in Egypt under Nasser was symptomatic—they were expelled. This is true for the Jews of Iraq, for instance, but it is not at all certain whether the Jews of Morocco (two hundred seventy thousand in 1948), a more tolerant country, could not have stayed there. It was certainly not faced with the same question of life and death as the Jews of Central Europe before 1939. Even if they did have to emigrate, it is not at all certain that Israel had to accept everyone save the educated middle class that made its way to France, as most of the one hundred thirty-five thousand Algerian Jews did.

In 1948, Israel was a small country of six hundred thousand Jewish inhabitants with very limited resources. The fact that within a few years it absorbed a far greater number of immigrants was probably unique in history. But would it not have been more honest to state openly that the country at the present stage was not capable of absorbing all of them? Israel was not in a position to offer immigrants anything but the most primitive conditions, and this should have been made clear at the outset. But it was not. Would it have been morally wrong if the Israelis had insisted on more stringent criteria for admitting immigrants? And was it evil on their part to insist on a policy of population dispersal so that not all immigrants would congregate in greater Tel Aviv, which would have been unable to cope with the influx? Spokesmen of North African Jews often said in later years that they did not share the ideals of the European (political) Zionists. They claimed to be the true (religious) Zionists. If this were truly the case, having waited for the return to the Holy Land for so many centuries, they might have waited a little longer. They also felt themselves heirs to a great cultural-spiritual tradition. It is not clear why they should have given this up by leaving the country of their ancestors, where, as so often claimed, they had been treated well.

Would Israel have survived without the influx of North African Jews? Fifty years after the fact, some spokesmen of the Mizrachim claimed that the Ashkenazim had brought them in simply to fill the country because there were not enough other Jews left. Is this really true? The two hundred seventy thousand who came in the 1950s and who multiplied rapidly were not a decisive factor for the existence of the state. On the contrary, their arrival involved a diversion of resources that could have been used for the better absorption of previous immigrants. True, there were difficulties in accepting other Oriental immigrants, but not nearly as many. The Iraqi community had a considerably higher educational background (as did the Egyptian Jewish immigrants). And even though there were many complaints about initial discrimination, their absorption was infinitely less difficult. Only about one hundred twenty thousand Iraqi Jews went to Israel, yet today about 12 percent of Israeli physicians are of Iraqi origin, and Iraqi Jews are more strongly represented among teachers, in parliament, in the government, and the upper echelons of the army than one would expect on the basis of their representation of the general population.

In brief, a strong case can be made that both Israel and those who were to complain in later years about exploitation and degradation, would have been better off if all those who had initially come had genuinely wanted to participate in the building of the state and knew that the way would not be strewn with roses. In 2000, Israel would have counted a million or perhaps a million and a half fewer inhabitants, and the ultraorthodox parties would have considerably less power, as would the right-wing nationalist parties. Many Israelis would have regarded this as a blessing, even though in an age of political correctness it was unthinkable to say so.

In 1998, Ehud Barak, who was then the leader of the opposition, publicly apologized for the neglect and discrimination against Oriental Jews during the years after their immigration. He should have also apologized for the overambitious and misguided attempt to bring so many of them to Israel at almost any price. The integration of the various branches of European Jews in Palestine and Israel had been a difficult enough process. The German Jews, to give one example, had also felt discriminated against and established their own political party, but they had not insisted on maintaining their specific old way of life and cultural traditions. The marriage with North African Jewry was bound to be a rocky one, and the question persists whether it was a good idea in the first place.

Back now to Eli Benhabib and the seemingly unstoppable rise of Shas, the Sephardic-Orthodox party. It first participated in the parliamentary elections in 1984, but neither that year nor in 1988 or 1992 did it poll more than 5 percent of the total. But in 1996, it almost doubled its votes, and eventually it added another third—with nineteen seats in the Knesset it became the third-strongest party in the land. It appealed to the Israeli underclass on one hand as well as to those trying to maintain a religious, traditional way of life. (Such combinations have not been uncommon in the Arab world and elsewhere, such as in

Iran.) Shas showed from the beginning considerable creativity and initiative in strengthening its position. Given the Israeli electoral system, even small parties have an inordinate influence and blackmailing power.

Shas was primarily interested in financial allocations from the government; ministerial posts were of secondary importance. It was founded on an educational system that was different from state education, and not only because it mainly taught religious subjects. It kept children in school the whole day, and it provided a free hot meal and schoolbooks. Such an education did not give the children a good start in the labor market, but it fulfilled basic needs, and above all it created a sizeable group of people dependent on the party. It also provided an income base for the party, just as the Shas mayors in the development towns would forward part of the government allocations to the party budget. All this was of course illegal, and many Shas activists were brought to trial, but they usually claimed that they were acting according to traditional norms.

At one time Eli was head of a foundation for the preservation of Moroccan Jewish culture that received subsidies from various government ministries. He very nearly became involved in such an affair but got away with a warning. He had been advised by more experienced people in his party not to invest too much time in accounting. The fewer figures there were, the more difficult it would be to prove wrongdoing.

What accounts for the spectacular rise of Shas? On the central question confronting Israeli society—war and peace—Shas had no strong and consistent opinions. Yes, it was permissible from a religious point of view to give up territory for peace, but no, there is no room for concessions on Jerusalem and, generally speaking, Arabs can no more be trusted than snakes, as their guru, Rabbi Ovadiah Yosef, had said. Even though Shas gravitated towards the nationalist right, its policy is to maneuver between the secular parties, indeed, to blackmail them so as to strike the best deal.

Its appeal is based on an interesting mixture of ethnic solidarity, pride in the traditions of Moroccan Jewry, and the self-interest of a new stratum of young politicians eager to get their piece of the pie.

I have been using the word *Moroccan* somewhat indiscriminately. What is true for immigrants from Morocco is also true to some extent for newcomers from other Oriental countries, and the political militants have certainly tried very hard to include in their ranks members of other North African and Middle Eastern communities. This has been only partly successful, for the differences among them are considerable. The majority of the Council of Sages, their supreme spiritual authority, is not Moroccan in origin nor is Rav Ovadiah, but most of the younger generation of activists, such as Eli, and most of the rank and file are.

The ideology has been provided by Ovadiah Yosef, in his younger years an authority on the Talmud and the kabbalah, who promised to restore the old glory of Sephardi Jewry. For the less educated among the Shas supporters, an older rabbi named Yizhak Kedourie was the central figure. He had no known record of outstanding religious knowledge and what he said was literally inaudible and unintelligible, but the amulets he produced to protect the believers were important in the election campaigns. In the final analysis, the difference between Ovadiah Yosef and Kedourie was not that great, for Ovadiah Yosef also promised that those voting for Shas would enter paradise, but Ovadiah Yosef and his spokesmen used more modern methods to spread the message.

Eli was too intelligent not to understand the deep inconsistencies and weaknesses of Shas. He knew that the core of Shas, its educational system (*ma'ayan*), was deeply flawed—the concentration on religious subjects perpetuated in many ways the existence of a Mizrachi underclass. We cannot look into his heart; perhaps he thought that gradually this might change. Perhaps he was convinced that the more talented (like himself) would make their way in the world in any case. Nor do we know what he really thought of the state and its future. He must have known that the rigor of the Ashkenazi Orthodox had no future, and, in any case, was not in accordance with the North African Jewish tradition. He believed in the need of a religious renaissance for his community, and he was not overenthusiastic when he saw his congregation proceed on Sabbath from the synagogue to watching a soccer match, but he would not put up a fight against it or ban television. He was happy when Ovadiah Yosef in defiance of the "Lithuanians" decided in an *ex cathedra* judgment that the use of microwave ovens on the Sabbath was permitted.

Is Eli Benhabib a Zionist at heart? Inasmuch as the real existing state of Israel and its official ideology are concerned, his attitude is at best one of reserve. But at the same time he asserts that he and his friends are the only real Zionists. State and society have to be religious, even theocratic, in character based on the Bible, the Talmud, the Shulkhan Arukh, and Zohar, not on Herzl and the secular thinkers.

It is safe to say that these fundamental questions do not cause many sleepless nights to Eli Benhabib and his family in Har Nof. Like other Shas militants, he is so much preoccupied with daily affairs that not much time remains for giving thought to the deeper issues. He was firmly convinced for years that Shas had a great future and that its message would prevail. But then he began to have his doubts, not only because of the results of the elections of 2001 in which Shas heavily lost. His early optimism was not really justified, because the base of ethnic politics is somewhat brittle. The rise of Shas had depended too much on the presence of one charismatic rabbi, and the party had not been an outstanding success in improving the economic situation of the Mizrachim.

It is unlikely that basic ideology attitudes will change, that the Moroccans will turn against their religion and tradition. But there could be an erosion and splits at a time of social or political crisis; the disappointment of its supporters has already brought about a decline of its political influence. The rise of the Mizrachim in Israeli politics and, to some extent, the Mizrachization of Israeli society, are irreversible. But the changes will not be one-sided, and Mizrachi solidarity is bound to weaken in the long run.

I recently visited Musrara, where the Black Panther movement was conceived. It has not changed much, but it is no longer a slum. On the contrary, estate agents say it is one of the up-and-coming neighborhoods in view of (I quote from their advertisements) the friendly and hospitable atmosphere. They praise the Oriental character of the Arab houses surrounded by gardens with old olive trees. A Musrara penthouse is going for $430,000, the average apartment for more than $250,000, which is the same, or slightly more than, in Har Nof where Rav Ovadiah Yosef and other Shas leaders live. Where have all the Panthers gone? Most of the leaders no longer live in Jerusalem, and most of the followers have moved to the outskirts of the city.

Meanwhile their rabbis continue to preach, and their popular holidays (like Maimouna that concludes Passover), are celebrated as eagerly as ever before. The Shas members in the Knesset, though diminished in number, continue to fight for the interest of their electorate, and the postcolonial professors in Israel and abroad have not given up their hope for a Mizrachi revolution. The present president of Israel, Moshe Katsav, is of Mizrachi origin, and so are the foreign minister, the defense minister, and many other leading figures. The Mizrachim certainly have had a major impact on Israeli politics and society. This has contributed to making Israel more similar in character to other Middle Eastern countries. For a long time, well-meaning people all over the

world have argued that Israel de-Westernize itself and become culturally part of the area in which it is located. This has indeed happened
in recent decades, but it has not been a blessing, nor has it contributed
in any way to a solution of the conflict.

CHAPTER 13

SERFATY, CURIEL, AND THE DILEMMA OF THE JEWISH COMMUNISTS

THE ARAB-ISRAELI CONFLICT PLAYED A CENTRAL PART IN the lives of Abraham Serfaty and Henri Curiel, two Jewish communists who dreamed of revolution in the Middle East and believed that Jewish militants could play an important role in this struggle. Both became legends in their own lifetimes, even though neither ever visited Israel.

Abraham Serfaty was born in Casablanca in 1926 into a middle-class Jewish family. He remembers boyhood debates about the Spanish Civil War and World War II when power in Morocco passed to the Vichy authorities. After the war, he studied geology, mineralogy, and mining in France, and in 1951 he went to work for the Moroccan government as head of a phosphate mine in the north of the country. He joined the communist party while a student in France, and because of his political activities was exiled from Morocco to France together with other members of his family. He returned to his native country in 1956 when Morocco became independent, and he continued to work for the Ministry of Mines until he was dismissed in 1968. After years of political activity, partly underground, he was arrested as a dissident in 1974 and served the next seventeen years in Moroccan prisons, mostly in the Saharan desert.

In 1991, he was deprived of his Moroccan citizenship (the family held dual Brazilian and Moroccan citizenship) and again was deported to France together with his French wife, Christine, who had been active in mobilizing public opinion for his release from prison. A man of imposing stature and presence, widely educated, and courageous, Serfaty's case had attracted much attention among left-wing circles all over the world, especially in France. The Moroccan authorities were only too happy to get rid of him.

What makes the case of Serfaty so interesting from an Israeli-Palestinian point of view is the fact that he spent much of his time in prison (and later in French exile) thinking and writing about Moroccan Jewry, and lamenting their sad fate in Israel. He also wrote a series of books against Zionism and Israel. This was no mean achievement, considering the fact that he had never been anywhere near the place of action. Add to this the fact that the books and newspapers his friends and well-wishers supplied him with provided only part of the story. But he felt passionate about the subject, and his hostility to the state of Israel was vehement. When a Moroccan government minister once called him a Zionist, he brought a libel suit against him.

The struggle against what Serfaty saw as Israel's racist, chauvinist, and imperialist policies was one of the uppermost issues in his thinking, together with opposition to Moroccan occupation of the western Sahara and its struggle against the Polisario, an independence movement subsidized and supported by Algeria. This was considered not just unpatriotic but treacherous as well by the Moroccan authorities. As for Serfaty's campaign against Israel, however, they had few objections.

That a Marxist-Leninist opposed Zionism and Israel is not a matter of great surprise. But it is fascinating that his campaign became a central issue for an inmate of Kunitra Prison, which is two thousand miles from Jerusalem. One might expect him to have been preoccupied with affairs nearer home. He certainly did regard Morocco as his home; he was a patriot who always defined himself as a Jewish Moroccan.

This situation reminds one of Klemperer, Hitler's hostage who would become famous following the posthumous publication of his diaries. Klemperer was confined to a so-called Jew house in the city of Dresden during World War II. He suffered all the humiliations and persecutions that were the lot of German Jews. He witnessed the deportation of Jews to Polish camps, and he knew that they would be murdered there. Klemperer expected to be arrested by the Gestapo and share the fate of his fellow Jews. And yet in the middle of the war, he confided to his diary that the most urgent challenge facing him was to write a book against Herzl and Zionism. Strange are human reactions in extreme situations.

Serfaty's story had a happy ending. After the death of King Hassan II in 1999 and the ascension to the throne of King Muhammad VI, a more liberal policy prevailed in Morocco. Serfaty was not only permitted to return to Morocco, his reception befitted a national hero. He got a government job, and a villa was put at his disposal. He was also sent to tour the country to familiarize himself with the new conditions.

All this was in stark contrast to his experience in earlier years. After his arrest in 1974, Abraham Serfaty had been tortured in prison; so was his sister, who died two years later. His son was arrested for a while. In the 1980s, his situation improved, and he was permitted to have a wide correspondence from prison, receive all the books and newspapers he wanted, and write articles for both the PLO *Journal of*

Palestine Studies and various French periodicals of the far left. He wrote books that found publishers outside Morocco. On one occasion, Serfaty said that he and his comrades in jail were perhaps the freest people in the whole country—no one bothered them as long as they did not escape.

Two of the questions that preoccupied him above all were the correct strategy to be followed by the Palestinian revolution and the fate of his fellow Moroccan Jews. When Serfaty joined the communist party soon after the end of the war, many young Moroccan Jews among the intelligentsia and the middle class were sympathizers. Indeed, the founder of the Moroccan communist party, Leon Rene Sultan, was a Tunisian Jew. But over the next years most of them dropped out, whereas Serfaty remained a militant. He was aware that the presence of Jews in the party was an embarrassment and that it was best for the group for them to keep a low profile.

But as Nasser-style pan-Arabism, and later Islamism, grew stronger in the country, the problem of Jews in Moroccan politics became even more acute; the party needed above all native, that is to say Muslim, militants. Thus to give one example, Serfaty was told that he should not sign articles for the party press with his real name. This syndrome was of course not specifically Moroccan. Trotsky, Kamenev, Zinoviev, and Radek had not been the original names of their bearers.

This edict annoyed Serfaty, but it did not undermine his belief in the party and his leader, Ali Yata. He never made a secret of his Jewish origins—which in any case would have been difficult to deny—and he was not ashamed of his family, his ancestors, and, generally speaking, of Moroccan Jewry. What did greatly pain him were the reports about the horrible fate of his brothers and sisters who, seduced by what he considered fraudulent Zionist propaganda, had foolishly immigrated to Israel. The women had no alternative to working as prostitutes or domestics. The men were the lowest of the low in this colonialist society. The entire country and its ideology were rotten; David Ben-Gurion wanted to establish an empire reaching from the Nile to the Euphrates; the military clique of fascist generals such as Motta Gur were the real masters of Israel; the kibbutzim were not at all socialist in inspiration and practice but fortresses of imperialism. The whole Zionist endeavor was based on deception—there was no "Israeli people." The so-called Sephardim in Israel, like President Yitzhak Navon, were not really Sephardim.

This led to a question: why had the misguided Moroccan Jews gone to Israel in the first place? Abraham Serfaty placed some of the blame on himself and his comrades. They should have tried to persuade them to stay in their native country instead of tacitly accepting the exodus. And so he said many years later in an interview with a friend, "It is my failure, my tragedy. I was a communist militant and my thoughts were focused on the class struggle. I did not take account of ethnic identities."

The first few years of Moroccan independence were a failure, and many Moroccan Jews believed they were facing a dead end. Marxists like Serfaty and his friends offered the Jewish masses only one way out—immigration to Israel—and that was, seen in retrospect, their great failure. When the interviewer argued that the economic position of Moroccan Jews in Israel was better than it would have been in Morocco, Serfaty agreed—this was more than fifteen years after he had argued that Moroccan women were being forced into prostitution. But he stressed that it was a moral, not an economic, problem, for the Moroccan Jews were living in Israel on the basis of an injustice committed against the Palestinians in 1948.

But what is the explanation for the Moroccan Jews in Israel taking an overwhelmingly right-wing and anti-Arab position? Why did they vote for Begin, Shamir, Netanyahu, and Sharon rather than the forces of peace? These questions bothered Serfaty as they troubled the postcolonialists in Israel. Was it a case of false consciousness? Eventually they thought they had found an explanation: The Moroccans were essentially not nationalists at all. Opting for the right-wing parties was simply a protest vote against the Ashkenazi establishment as represented by the Labor party. Serfaty found some comfort in the emergence of Shas and the declaration of Rabbi Ovadiah Yosef in 1996 that it was permissible, even desirable, to exchange land for peace, which was contrary to Likud ideology. But Ovadiah was an unlikely ally for a Marxist internationalist, and his subsequent declarations (that the Arabs were snakes and should be destroyed) must have come as a shock.

Given the fact that the state of Israel had come into being, what was the correct position for a revolutionary to take as far as the Israeli-Arab conflict was concerned? For many years, Serfaty supported the Popular Front for the Liberation of Palestine, led by Christian Arabs, which supported a secular rather than an Islamic religious policy. But these groups were weak and their Marxism did not go very deep. Like erstwhile communists in other Arab countries, many of their support-ers drifted into the Islamic camp. Serfaty had left the communist party in the 1970s to become a free-floating member of the extreme left. As far as Palestine was concerned, he now put his hope on the progressive, noncapitalist wing of Fatah (the Arab Liberation Movement), which in his view was still the most democratic of all Arab movements and gov-ernments.

Abraham Serfaty, a Moroccan patriot, loved the country of his birth—its people, its culture, its language and customs. This was the country where he belonged. He felt equally rooted, especially in his later years, in the Jewish tradition, especially enjoying the holidays such as Mimouna (celebrated at the end of Passover). These were among the strongest memories of his youth, and he did not regard them as religious at all.

Was this Moroccan-Jewish synthesis realistic? Those who had immigrated to Israel had fond memories of Morocco too, and there was a steady stream of Moroccan tourists from Israel longing to revisit the places of their origin. But it is also the case that even before Islamism became a stronger force in Morocco, there were many Muslims who thought that although Jews had the right to live in their country, they had no business interfering in public affairs and politics. Morocco, more than any other Islamic country, had historically shown more tolerance towards Jews; there had been Jewish ministers and ambassadors well before in Europe. But there also had been persecutions and pogroms. The country was by no means wholly secular. Intermarriage was almost nonexistent. A case like Abraham Serfaty, the prodigal son returned, was the exception even in this most liberal North African country.

Serfaty had mellowed over the years. He understood the reasons for the downfall of the Soviet Union and its satellites, and the decline of communism. He still believed in the struggle for a better world, but this belief was held by many others, not only Marxists. He accepted the changes for the better in Morocco and the likelihood of further liberalization. (He might have been a little too sanguine in this respect.) He realized that his enthusiasm for the cause of the Polisario had been excessive. Having to choose between an Algerian-dominated western Saharan independent state and one in which Moroccan influence was easy, he no longer believed the former was a better choice.

With regards to Israel, too, his views underwent certain changes. Initially he had been against the existence of the Jewish state altogether. Later he accepted that until a binational state emerged, two separate states would exist side by side. In an interview in 1999 he said that he thought it beneficial for humankind for there to be an Israeli state with a Jewish majority, provided such a state was secular and represented all its citizens, Jewish as well as Arab. Just as a democratic Morocco should not adopt Islam as the state religion, Judaism should not be the state religion in Israel. This was a far cry from the views he had voiced twenty years earlier, and his more extremist comrades were not altogether happy that the old revolutionary was now willing to make concessions to political reality.

At the same time, Serfaty kept a distance even from his beloved Moroccan Jews in Israel. He declined an invitation from the post-Zionists of Beersheba University to visit Israel. Oswald Spengler, the famous prophet of the decline of the West, was invited by Harvard in the 1920s to attend a conference on the occasion of some university jubilee. He had never been to the United States, but this had not prevented him from delivering *ex cathedra* judgments about this subject. He declined the invitation, arguing that having just written about America, it would never do to expose himself to a wealth of new impressions that might affect his thinking on the topic. Serfaty's refusal to visit the country about which he had written so much was no doubt influenced by similar motives.

Even though the story of Abraham Serfaty had a happy ending, it still leaves open the question whether with all the admiration for his courageous stand, the sacrifices he made (which affected, after all, many of those close to him) were necessary and justified in retrospect and whether or not developments in Morocco would not have developed along the same lines had Serfaty and his comrades never been politically active. Had he perhaps fought and suffered for a cause that was in many respect dubious—Stalinism and the imposition of repressive regimes? It is understandable that for communist militants far away from the Soviet Union these aspects mattered little; they were preoccupied with local conditions and the local struggle. But could he as a Jew, as an outsider, have had any significant impact on the political life of his country? Perhaps that is an unfair question, one that can be asked only after the fact. It seems to have occurred to Serfaty in his later years that he had accepted a heavy responsibility not just as far as his own life was concerned but also those close to him.

Abraham Serfaty was honorary chairman when French left-wing intellectuals met in May 1998 to commemorate the twentieth anniversary of the murder of Henri Curiel on a Paris street. The story of Curiel is in many ways a counterpoint to that of Serfaty; a young, highly idealistic intellectual who had many talents and wanted to fight for the revolution but had the misfortune to be born a Jew in an Arab country, who thought of himself as an Egyptian, a belief that was not however shared by other Egyptians.

The Curiels had come to Egypt at the time of Napoleon. Henri's grandfather had been a moneylender, his (blind) father a successful banker. They were by no means among the very richest Jews. Their house in Zamalek, a Cairo suburb, was not one of the grandest, but they still had some fifteen servants working for them.

Born in 1914, Henri went to a French Jesuit school and French was his first language. His knowledge of Arabic remained scant throughout his life. His brother, Raoul, went to France to study and became eventually a well-known archaeologist, specializing in numismatics. Henri was designated his father's successor and had to get his apprenticeship in the family bank, which he loathed. He was tall and very thin, and early on developed pre-tubercular symptoms. His interests at the time, and for years to come, were divided between radical politics, avant guard literature, and the arts. As his biographer Giles Perrault put it, he sought consolation in books and women, sharing his time equitably between the young ladies of his acquaintance and the Cairo whores. The former he gave Proust to read, the latter, Dostoevsky.

He shared these cultural interests with other young Jewish intellectuals in Egypt and Iraq. In 1943, Curiel founded (or rather, refounded) the Communist Party of Egypt. A small sect had been in existence in the 1920s under a suitable inoffensive name—the Egyptian Movement for National Liberation. A few years later, Arturo Schwarz founded the Egyptian branch of the Trotskyite Fourth International. But whereas Curiel, after some initial hesitation, stayed in politics, Schwarz, having been deported from Egypt, became a leading expert on surrealism and Dadaism, and an art dealer, as well as the author of many studies on André Breton and Marcel Duchamp, alchemy, the kabbalah, and Far Eastern religion. In 2001, he gave part of his unique collection to the Israeli Museum in Jerusalem.

Curiel was arrested as a communist after the end of World War II and spent more than a year in the Huckstep detention camp. He was deported in 1950 and went to France, where he established a group of Egyptian communist sympathizers in exile (called the Rome Group), which supported the coup of the young officers in Cairo led by Gamal Abdel Nasser. This group lingered on for a number of years and for a time was known as the Egyptian Democrats of Jewish Origin which, in view of the composition of the group, was certainly an accurate definition. Eventually Curiel's group in Paris dissolved, as did the communist party in Egypt, which became part of the semi-legal Arab Socialist Union.

Henri Curiel's interests from then on were focused on national liberation movements in the third world. The French Communist party considered him an outsider, useful in some respects but kept at arm's length. (He was rehabilitated by the party only many years after his assassination.) His main passion during the late 1950s was the struggle of the Algerian rebels against the French colonial authorities. Subsequently he became a supporter of the cause of Vietnamese, Cuban, Chinese, and various Latin American radicals, including those advocating armed struggle (that is to say, guerrilla warfare and terrorism). He was the founder and coordinator of the French anticolonial movement which was later called Solidarité.

The French authorities showed a great deal of forbearance towards the activities of a stateless foreigner who should not even have been in France. But in 1960 he was arrested and spent some eighteen months in Fresnes Prison. After his release, he continued his operations as before. He must have had powerful protectors on the French political scene. It is hard to decide what was more striking, his courage and idealism or his political naïveté. How could he have failed to realize by the late 1960s that something had gone very wrong in the communist countries of Europe? How could he have had illusions about the kind of regimes that were emerging in the third world after liberation from the colonialist yoke? Algeria should have been a warning sign, but such was his loyalty to the ideals of his early years that he refused to accept reality.

Curiel had not only admirers in Paris but also enemies, and they wondered where the money for his activities came from. His enemies wanted to know what kind of assistance he provided—moral support, false papers, safe houses, and other logistic assistance. It seemed possible that he even provided weapons through various foreign intelligence services. And to what circles did he extend his assurance—was it only to radical political movements or did it also perhaps go to terrorist groups such as Carlos the Jackal? After all, one of the most important Soviet spies of the cold war, George Blake (Behar), was his younger cousin. (Blake had stayed with the Curiels in Cairo when he was a schoolboy, but it is most unlikely that Henri paid much attention to him.) It is difficult to know for certain. Most of these activities are shrouded in secrecy to this day. For all one knows the importance of his group was greatly exaggerated. But he was treading on dangerous ground and thus became a victim, gunned down in the entrance to his Paris home in 1978.

Who killed him? This is no clearer now than twenty-five years ago. Some suspected the Mossad, but this is very unlikely since he was not considered an enemy of Israel, having been in agreement with the foundation of the Jewish state in 1948 and having initiated unofficial peace talks in Paris between Israelis and Palestinians. Others suspected Palestinian extremists who might have thought Curiel an Israeli agent. The fact that Issam Sartawi, a Palestinian leader willing to talk peace with the Israelis, was also assassinated soon after makes this appear somewhat more likely. Then again it is not impossible that the intelligence service of one of the countries in whose affairs Curiel had interfered had engineered his murder.

All we do know is that the life of this Jewish revolutionary ended in failure, and, seen in retrospect, was long bound to end in disaster. Jews have been in the forefront of the revolutionary movement of many countries in Europe and elsewhere, and it has been their fate to be discarded (and often branded traitors). This was the case in Russia and in Eastern Europe after World War II—one needs only consider Rudolf Slansky, Ana Pauker, Jakub Berman, Matyas Rakosi, and countless others.

What drove many young Jews to join revolutionary movements? Various explanations have been suggested, including the tradition of the Jewish prophets and the marginal status of Jews in society, which made them particularly sensitive to social injustice. But the Jewish religion features more conservative than radical tendencies and, in any case, the young revolutionaries had rejected the religion of their ancestors. As for their marginal place in society, this may have played a certain role in some cases, but not in others. In Morocco, the communist party offered young Jews a way to integrate themselves into society, but in Egypt as elsewhere in Africa there could be no illusions in this respect.

I can think of only one instance in which individual Jews earned some gratitude on that continent: South Africa under Nelson Mandela where Joe Slovo and his comrades served the new regime for some years after the end of apartheid. But this was a rare exception, just as Mandela was an exception, and it was clear that even for the most radical Jews there was no future in South Africa.

However, the position of Curiel and his Jewish comrades in Cairo and Alexandria was even more precarious than that of the Jewish communists in Europe simply because of the power of nationalism and religion in the Arab world. Trotsky had, to say the least, an excellent knowledge of the Russian language and was steeped in Russian culture. The Russian intelligentsia at the time was overwhelmingly left-wing, and willing to accept outsiders in their ranks. In the Arab countries, and in the third world in general, there was no such tolerant and cosmopolitan intelligentsia. In the early postwar years, some Arab and third-world intellectuals had dabbled with Marxism-Leninism but any incorporation of leftist ideology was seldom more than a superficial interest. It was fascinating to watch almost a whole generation of left-wing radicals first join the Arab nationalist camp and later Islamism.

Curiel and some of his close associates were accused for years of "Zionist deviationism" by other communists, which couldn't be farther from the truth. He had been in favor of the UN resolution of 1947 aimed at the establishment of a Jewish and a Palestinian Arab state, but this had been the official position of the Soviet Union and most Arab communist parties. Calling Curiel a Zionist was simply another way of asserting that as an individual of Jewish origin he could not sympathize with Arab nationalism, let alone Islamic fundamentalism, which were the main progressive forces in communist eyes.

This was true even in Egypt, the most liberal of the Arab countries. The story of Adel Hussein (1932–2001) is quite typical. A popular writer and journalist and a darling of Cairo intellectual society and the local bohème, Adel Hussein was the younger brother of Ahmed Hussein, who had been the guru and leader of fascism in Egypt during the late 1930s. But when Adel became politically conscious in the

1950s, fascism was out and communism in. He became a member of the party, was arrested, and spent altogether eight years in prison. After his release he continued to work as a journalist, specializing in anti-Jewish propaganda and denouncing the Zionist plans for economic hegemony (the title of one of his books). He also became secretary-general of the Socialist Labor Party, which was neither socialist nor supported by workers but was the legal front of the (illegal) Muslim Brotherhood in Egypt. He also took a leading part in attacking fellow Egyptian writers who, he argued, were too secular in outlook and whose books were not sufficiently respectful of fundamentalist Islam. Together with his nephew Magdy Hussein, he wrote a column in the newspaper *Al Sha'ab* denouncing even the Egyptian Ministry of Culture for aiding and abetting secular tendencies in Egyptian cultural life.

Within a short period this Marxist-Leninist had moved to an extreme right-wing position, and there were many like him in Egypt and North Africa. In the Arab countries proper, it was the fashion of people of this background to move toward the nationalist center rather than the extreme right. (There were, as usual, some exceptions, Arab writers and intellectuals who remained faithful to the ideals of their youth, but my concern in the present context is with the majority.) Given the political realities—the absence of a democratic system—even those erstwhile radicals of the left had to be extremely careful in airing their views.

Whatever the reasons for this trend away from secularism and democracy, let alone Marxism and internationalism, it was obvious that there was no room for Jews in Arab politics. Seen against this background, the amazing story of Abraham Serfaty was a rare exception, made possible only by the relative tolerance that has prevailed in Morocco.

Both Serfaty and Curiel belonged to the old, Marxist left. In the present post-Soviet, post-communist period, they appear as relics of an heroic past, revolutionaries, firmly believing in social justice and a more egalitarian society, willing to sacrifice their lives for the poor and oppressed. One looks in vain for their successors on the left among Palestinians or Israelis. Once upon a time there was a communist party in Palestine and later in Israel, but it split many times. The communists were influential among the Arabs in Israel at one time, but this was before the rise of the PLO and the Islamists. They have long since jettisoned their Marxist internationalist ballast and become a nationalist Arab party, and even so they have lost their influence.

Where is the radical left among Jewish Israelis? Certainly not in Jerusalem, which was never fertile ground for them. True, there are groups of "critical" academics, sociologists and historians who (at best) quote, on occasion, Antonio Gramsci, the Italian communist who decades after his death became a cultural hero of the New Left, serving as perhaps their only remaining link with historical Marxism. But their real inspiration comes from very different quarters; they are preoccupied with gender studies and the linguistic turn and, of course, "subaltern studies." In the nineteenth century there was a phenomenon in Central Europe called *Katheder Sozialismus,* the socialism of the professors, mainly economists, critical of laissez-faire liberalism and capitalism who developed all kind of theories, some interesting, some less so, but usually remote from social realities.

A similar socialism of the professors has now emerged in Israel as well as in other countries, more among literary scholars than economists, except that the connection with socialism is even more tenuous. Today's proletariat, the truly poor, are found among the ultraorthodox, many of whom do not work but who have big families. It is found in many of the development towns among the followers of Shas, mostly of North African or Ethiopian origin and nationalist-religious in outlook. The new working class has shrunk, consisting in part of guest workers from Africa and other parts of the world and also of Arabs from the West Bank. They tend to work in construction and agriculture and, in the case of Jerusalem, as hotel staff. These social groups are unpromising from a left-wing point of view, so some of the critical (and atheist) professors have looked for a rapprochement with the very traditional rabbis of Shas.

In contemporary Israeli political language, "left wing" has virtually nothing to do anymore with socialism or social class or the ownership of the means of production. It has nothing to do with rich and poor. It is a synonym for the peace party, whereas "right wing" stands for a nationalist orientation. Both camps consist of various disparate parts, radical and conservative and whatnot. If there still are ideological discussions, they are within each camp rather than between them. The anti-Zionists of the "left" attack the old Zionist left, not the religious-nationalist right with which they have nothing in common, not even a common language and concepts that could be the basis for a polemic, let alone a discussion.

In brief, the left has disappeared. There may be the need for a New Left, but so far it has not arrived on the political scene.

CHAPTER 14

DR. SOBOLEV AND THE RUSSIAN REPATRIANTS

NEIGHBORS IN PISGAT ZE'EV, A NORTHERN SUBURB OF Jerusalem beyond French Hill, talk with affection and respect of Dr. Alexander Sobolev. The neighborhood is a settlement of some thirty thousand to forty thousand residents. It is heavily Russian, and Sobolev is active in community affairs; his wife is the chairperson of the local Russian cultural circle. A physician at Hadassa Hospital, he is one of the "repatriants" who made it. On my way to his house I had to ask several times for directions and everyone I asked was able to help.

I first met Dr. Sobolev several years earlier in a Netanya restaurant called *Moskovskie Nochi* (Moscow Nights), and a conversation ensued. *Moskovskie Nochi* is an unlikely name for a restaurant on the beach of the Mediterranean. A reference to Odessa would have perhaps been more apposite. But the ducklings filled with apples and the *baklazhany* (stuffed, roasted eggplant) are famous among Russian immigrants from Dan to Beersheba and beyond. There also is (or was) an excellent, albeit small, dance orchestra and even a floor show.

Sobolev and his wife, Natasha, arrived with the first great wave of Russian immigrants in 1989–90 when Mikhail Gorbachev was still in power. He was then in his early forties, with a working knowledge of English. When I mentioned that I had often visited Moscow and spoke some Russian, the conversation switched, to my discomfort, to his language. It emerged that his father had also been a physician in the Russian capital. The family had originally come from White Russia, and the name had been Sobol or Sobelson. He and his wife, also a medical doctor, had worked in the same hospital in Moscow. She was a gynecologist, and he specialized in diseases of the digestive tract.

The status of doctors in the Soviet Union, except for a few at the very top, had not been particularly high, nor was the income, even though many saw a few private patients on the side. On the other hand, life in Moscow had many compensations. There was a rich cultural life, and the Sobolevs had a wide circle of friends. Their political involvement had been minimal. They had been neither dissidents nor Zionists, and even their interest in things Jewish had been limited. Sobolev's father had been dismissed from his job during Stalin's last days when the campaign against the Jewish doctors (the "poisoners") had been launched, but he was later reinstated. There had been occasional manifestations of open anti-Semitism, and they knew, of course, that as Jews it was virtually impossible for them to reach the top positions in their profession. But they had accepted this.

Then why had they decided to emigrate? Sobolev conceded that this question had occurred to them more than once in the years since. The brief answer was that many of their friends had suddenly left. Things in Moscow were changing, and not for the better. The fear of anti-Semitic attacks was not really the decisive factor. More important were the concerns about what would happen to their children. What prospects would they have? They decided to emigrate. The choice of

Israel was largely accidental. They did not have relations in the United States or Canada, otherwise they might have gone there. Did they regret their decision? Would they stay in Israel? There were many reasons for and against, Alexander said, and Natasha agreed. We went on to discuss some of these reasons, and it turned into a long evening, ending after midnight on a bench facing the seafront.

The following story emerged. The Sobolevs' first encounter with Israel had been disastrous. They had arrived one November day from the cold climate of Moscow, but the balmy air outside Lod Airport seemed to be the only positive surprise at the time. Perhaps it had been a mistake to leave their work, their cozy little apartment, and their friends in Moscow? They were sent to an absorption center near Haifa where they knew hardly anyone. (In this respect their story was perhaps atypical. Whereas most of the immigrants of the 1970s had been sent to absorption centers, most of those who arrived in the 1990s were given recently completed housing.) Nor could they make themselves understood to the Israelis. Their children were sent to a school more or less immediately, but they came home dejected and declared that they would not go there anymore. The Ashkenazi children were not interested in them, and the Mizrachim called them "stinking Russians" and beat them up. The teachers briefly welcomed them, but made no effort to deal with their special needs such as speaking more slowly.

Would the Sobolevs be able to work in their profession? A few weeks after their arrival they were interviewed by an official from the Jewish Agency. They learned that their chances were less than promising. Thousands of Russian doctors were arriving—eventually fifteen thousand would come during the decade. The Sobolevs' first step was to register with the Ministry of Health. But unless they had worked more than twenty years as doctors in Russia, they could register only if they took a special training course and passed an examination.

Alexander and Natasha had worked for fewer than twenty years. Their other problem was that the training course was in Hebrew, and they needed a minimum six-month intensive language courses, eight hours a day, six days a week, to become proficient. What were the chances of passing the medical refresher course? About 40 percent, the man from the agency said. And what about finding work once they had passed both the Ulpan (as the language school was called) and the medical course? About 30 percent. And how would they live while studying for the examination? This was entirely up to them. The state would not take care of them. They were relatively young and healthy. They were expected to look for part-time work, any work, and they should not give up, even if the odds were against them. After all, in America too they would not have been permitted to practice medicine without attending refresher courses. As an afterthought, the man added that they might want to look for a kibbutz willing to employ them for a year or two as outside workers

That evening Alexander and Natasha had a long talk. Alexander thought the odds against them were too great. He floated the idea that they should open a little shop or look for other work. But Natasha insisted. They had invested too many years of their life studying and practicing medicine to give up so easily.

The time in the Ulpan passed quickly. They studied the language earnestly, but it did not come easy to them. They then looked for a medical refresher course in the Greater Tel Aviv area and even found a kibbutz willing to accept them on a temporary basis. Alexander worked night shifts in one of the factories there, Natasha in the kitchen. In the beginning they felt very lonely, but gradually they made a few friends.

And how did the medical course go? Alexander admitted that he felt some resentment against the Israeli doctors. Why should they feel so superior? True, they had studied longer and were familiar with all the modern drugs and medical tests. But Israeli medicine also had its weaknesses. The Israeli doctors had little time for their patients and hardly listened to their stories. Specialization had gone too far. They were interested in one part of the body, not the patient as a whole.

Alexander said that the six months of the course were the most difficult time in the Sobolevs' lives. They had to get up at five in the morning to make it to the hospital on time. They were back at the kibbutz between three and four in the afternoon, but instead of resting they had to spend at least a couple of hours on their homework. After a hasty dinner, they worked for four hours in the factory and the kitchen respectively. They were never in bed before midnight, and saw their children for only a few minutes a day. When the examinations came, they had not regained all their self-confidence but were glad that the written part could be in Russian (or English or French) rather than Hebrew. They were ecstatic when four weeks later the official notification came that they had passed. They were more excited than they had been twenty-three years earlier in Moscow when they had graduated from medical school.

But this was just the first hurdle to overcome. They made the rounds of the various medical organizations and hospitals, but the first offer came only after many refusals. The situation was further complicated because they wanted work in the same general area. At first they got temporary jobs replacing Israeli doctors who went on holiday or who had fallen ill. Natasha had to work as a pediatrician, which was not her field, and Alexander worked in trauma medicine, as deputy head of a first aid station in a small hospital in the Negev, where few Israeli doctors wanted to practice. These frequent changes also meant that that they had to rent apartments, which were expensive, and that the boys had to change schools frequently.

I asked Alexander whether he thought his career in Israel had been typical for the thousands of doctors who had come from the Soviet

Union. He said that he and Natasha had been lucky—half of the immigrants had not found work in their professions. A quarter of Soviet doctors had not even tried to pass the refresher courses, either because they were too old, they couldn't learn the language, or their hearts had not been in the profession in the first place. Another quarter had tried but failed. However, most of them had eventually found employment in jobs that were close enough to their former profession, in medical or bacteriological laboratories, for instance, or as paramedics. One of their friends had become head nurse in a leading hospital, where she earned about as much as Natasha did.

After five years of such peregrinations, Alexander had been lucky. At a medical conference he met a professor from Hadassah Hospital who engaged in research on *heliobacter pylori*. For a long time it had been believed that peptic ulcer and other stomach diseases were mainly caused by stress and dietary factors, but in the 1970s it was discovered that in many cases infection also played a role. However, it was a long way from recognizing this factor to curing the disease. Tetracycline alone often did not do the trick, and it was in this context that Alexander made a number of suggestions based on his clinical experience. The professor from Jerusalem tested Alexander's ideas and found them valid, and they coauthored a number of papers that earned international recognition. There were trips abroad, and eventually, when a vacancy occurred at Hadassah Hospital, Alexander got the job. At this stage Natasha decided to work part-time, so that she could devote more time to the children and their new home. Finding a job in a Jerusalem suburb was not too difficult for her.

The Sobolevs' professional experiences are a success story. But as far as their cultural and social integration was concerned, the story was different. Most of the people they saw after work were Russian. They had few Israeli acquaintances. They had no particular interest in Israeli culture and they subscribed to a Russian-language newspaper in spite of its low journalistic quality and its sensationalism. They were worried about the political situation—during the second intifada, there had been shooting in their neighborhood of Pisgat Ze'ev. Alexander was a liberal by Israeli-Russian standards, and he thought the two Russian parties were useless. Natan Sharansky, who had been a true hero in the Soviet Union, spending years in prisons and defying the KGB, had been a sad disappointment in Israel, and what Alexander said of Avigdor Liberman, originally a sidekick of Netanyahu, is not printable. Alexander thought that Israel should have tried to reach a compromise with the Arabs even if it would have involved painful Israeli concessions. Natasha and their younger son, on the other hand, thought that the Arabs would never be willing to make peace. They had visited Moscow three times in recent years, but the thought of returning had never occurred to them.

What about leaving for a more secure country, such as America? They said with one voice that emigrating once had been a greater shock than they had ever imagined. They would not try a second time. They had visited New York and had also been to London and Paris. Was Pisgat Ze'ev now home? The answer was a reluctant yes.

What about their children? They had been ten and eight when the family arrived, young enough to face the new country with fewer difficulties. Their eldest had been in the army and was now studying computer science; the younger child was still serving in a sensitive branch of air force intelligence, which he did not want to talk about (apparently it was photo interpretation). They both knew Russian well, since the parents had insisted on this, but they had Israeli friends and girlfriends. They felt that their place was in this country even though they were quite critical of it. The older one took me back by car from Pisgat Ze'ev to the hotel in Jerusalem, and what I heard from him when we were alone substantially confirmed what his parents had told me.

How typical is the story of Alexander and Natasha Sobolev? To try to give an answer we have to go back in time a few decades. I had been deeply interested in things Russian since World War II and it became for a long time my field of specialization. Most of the early Zionist immigrants to Palestine, the men and women who had arrived just before and after World War I, had Russian backgrounds, even though their interest in Russian affairs and culture was limited. Having said this, they were convinced that they knew all there was to be known about the subject. So I was surprised when during a visit to Jerusalem in 1958, I received an unannounced and unexpected visitor.

I was in bed that day at our old home, the Kadima House, sick with of all things chicken pox and running a high fever. Having more or less pushed aside my wife, the visitor, a middle-aged man who seemed vaguely familiar, entered my room and, ignoring my warning about possible infection, announced that Ben-Gurion had sent him. He had been told that I knew a thing or two about Soviet affairs (which he found difficult to believe in view of my German Jewish background) and that I had recently been to the Soviet Union. Hence his question: Was it at all likely that Russian Jews would ever come to Israel in significant numbers?

I thought for a few moments and then delivered a brief and very general answer: It would be difficult and involve a long and concentrated effort. It would make the Russians angry, even though they were not particularly enamored of the Jews. For them it was a matter of principle—as far as they were concerned there was no Jewish (or indeed any other) national question. The Soviet people were all living in peace under the umbrella of a benevolent government in *druzhba narodov* (friendship among peoples). But to get significant numbers out of the Soviet Union was not a hopeless proposition and should be tried.

My visitor disappeared without further ado. He had not given his name, but I had recognized him. It was Shaul Avigur, Ben-Gurion's right-hand man for things that were best kept secret. I would meet Avigur on a few later occasions in London, Warsaw, and elsewhere, but our conversation of 1958 never came up again. What I could not have known was that Ben-Gurion had been contemplating whether to invest considerable efforts in establishing an international network to promote the eventual exodus of Russian Jews. A very small skeleton group had existed in the Moscow embassy since 1952, but it was now a question of expanding this section of the embassy, of appointing emissaries to major Western capitals and thus going public with the help of Jewish communities. This organization was originally called the Contact Bureau but became later known as Nativ. A few weeks after Avigur's visit, Ben-Gurion made two speeches, which I read only many years later. He said that in his view there was no long-term solution for Russian Jews except immigration to Israel, even though he thought that only half of them, a million or a million and a half, would come. Israel should be prepared to receive them. These predictions turned out to be quite accurate.

In subsequent years, I came to meet and admire the young people in the Soviet Union who were active on behalf of this cause, usually in complicated and dangerous circumstances: Lova Eliav, Nehemia Levanon, Joshua Prat, and others. It was dangerous not just because of the threat of expulsion for activities unbecoming a diplomat. There were constant provocations by the KGB, and there was always the possibility of a traffic "accident," or worse.

The results of their activities were meager at first. Some Jews were permitted to leave Russia under the pretext of "reunification of families." A mere sixty were permitted to leave in 1960, but their number rose to just over two thousand in 1967 and thirteen thousand in both 1971 and 1972, even though relations between the Soviet Union and Israel had been broken off after the Six-Day War in 1967. Israel families would send individual requests to Moscow and the authorities there would issue permits; the record years were 1978 (almost 29,000) and 1979 (51,000). There was a sharp decline for no obvious reasons after 1980, with a record low in 1986. These exit visas were by no means cheap—the fee was about the equivalent of two months' salary of a Soviet citizen.

With Perestroika and Gorbachev's rise to power, mass emigration got under way: seventy-one thousand in 1989; two hundred thirteen thousand in 1990; and one hundred seventy-eight thousand in 1991. During the l990s, the yearly number of emigrants varied between sixty thousand and one hundred ten thousand.

But not all chose to be repatriants opting for Israel. Even before 1990, thousands of those who had left the Soviet Union chose to go first to Vienna or Rome and wait for an American entry visa. In later years, many went to Canada, and later still Germany became a favorite destination. In 2002, more Russian Jews went to Germany than to Israel.

Today's Jewish communities in Germany are preponderantly Russian Jewish. This was a cause of disappointment to those who had worked so hard to make emigration possible in the first place, but it should not really have come as a surprise. Russian Jews were no longer organized after the Revolution of 1917: there was no contact with Jewish communities abroad, they were no longer religious, and they knew, at best, a few words of Yiddish and no Hebrew. Generally speaking, there was no great interest in things Jewish. There was anti-Semitism, to be sure, but this alone did not make for cohesion and the preservation of traditions.

America had been the destination of choice for their grandparents' generation, whereas Israel, as the early emigrants wrote, was a difficult country with fewer opportunities. Conditions were more primitive, there was the permanent conflict with the Arabs, and younger people had to serve in the army. Those who chose Germany as their new home, well, they claimed a cultural affinity, having read Schiller and Heine, and in any case contemporary Germany was not that of Adolf Hitler. Above all, the social benefits given to new immigrants in Germany were considerably better than in Israel, and the Germans didn't object to mixed marriages.

It has been estimated that up to 30 percent of the "repatriants" were not Jews according to the *halacha,* the Jewish religious law, and many were not Jewish according to any law. Since the rabbis were (and still are) so powerful in Israel, they could cause great difficulties to the newcomers, whom they did not recognize as Jews. Thus a new category came into being of individuals who could not marry (since there was no civil marriage in Israel) unless they chose to travel abroad and get married there, and they could not be buried in a Jewish cemetery— even if they were soldiers killed in action.

All this caused many émigrés to choose countries other than Israel. Some went to Israel but subsequently migrated to other countries, some migrated to and fro more than once. There are no exact figures; however, almost a million did settle in Israel even though the rabbis were unhappy about this influx. Their attempts to make converts among the repatriants were unsuccessful.

The Jews from Oriental countries were not overjoyed either because they had hoped to become a majority, and the influx of the Russians at the very least delayed the fulfillment of this dream. They also complained that a substantial part of the financial resources that should have gone to immigrants from Oriental countries now went to the Russians. The Russians were better educated than the Mizrachim, even if their command of the language was lamentable, and it was easier for them to find rewarding jobs. This too caused envy and tension especially in the development towns with mixed communities. Nevertheless, the great majority of the Russian Jews stayed on, and this caused tremendous changes in almost every aspect of Israeli life.

For a few months in the 1970s while teaching at Tel Aviv University, I lived next door to an absorption center near the Akkadia Hotel. There was a newsstand there, and I became friendly with the owner. Her own origins were Russian, and she knew of my interest in newcomers from the Soviet Union (and my interest in Soviet history), so she introduced me to an elderly woman, always very properly dressed in the fashion prevailing before World War II. It transpired that the woman in black was the widow of Adolf Abramovich Joffe, who had been deputy foreign minister of the Soviet Union in the early 1920s. But I knew that Joffe, a physician by training, had committed suicide in 1927 because of his disappointment with the state of the Soviet Union, the absence of inner party democracy, and certain trends in Soviet society. His widow had been a young woman at the time. She had survived prison, deportation, and the Gulag, and toward the end of her life found herself, probably to her surprise, in Israel. I met others who had remarkable stories to tell, and I learned a lot about this tragic generation that is not reported in books and archives.

My conversations with the Sobolevs and other Russian repatriants continued over the years, and I was careful to read the accounts of other immigrants to Israel which, by and large, chronicled experiences that were very far from what they expected. They had come expecting to find a mini-America, and were so disappointed. The first immediate experiences were often euphoric, usually followed by long periods of disenchantment and even despair, mostly connected with their inability to find rewarding work in their field of specialization. In the early years, this seemed almost an insurmountable problem: how could a small country absorb these thousands of doctors and violin players and engineers with competence in industries that did not even exist in Israel?

In 1991, 30 percent of the male immigrants and 60 percent of female immigrants were unemployed. And yet, most were eventually absorbed, though not without great difficulties. By 1997, the number of unemployed was down to 10 percent, which was not much higher than the Israeli average. (The number of unemployed among Russian Jews in Germany was much higher even years after they had arrived.)

The repatriants had grown up under a system in which the state more or less took care of everyone's professional career. If someone failed to find a job in one place, he or she was sent somewhere else. A wholly different system was bound to cause much disappointment at first. But once they had overcome their dejection, many immigrants persisted in their attempts to find a niche in this strange society. Even if there was no demand for the engineers among them, they still had a good training in mathematics (generally speaking the Russian school system was superior to the Israeli in various disciplines) and found it not too difficult to retrain in the field of computer science.

A variety of services were established catering for the Russian communities—a theater and newspapers, bookshops and food shops. There had been twelve major orchestras in Israel before the Russians came, but in 1996 there were thirty-six. Twenty-four hundred professional musicians came, giving an enormous impetus to the musical life of the country; Israel Camerata, the leading chamber orchestra, was one of their contributions. There was a considerable demand for artisans and repair workers, plumbers and electricians and what not, who were willing to come to their clients' homes. This kind of work was well paid and provided a livelihood for many. Substantial Russian communities came into being in places like Karmiel and Ashdod and at the outskirts of the big cities.

Social and cultural absorption was less successful. The Russians lived in communities of their own. Most of them had no Israeli friends and made little effort to learn the language of the country. They found the Israelis often boring, rude, and *nekulturnye,* and as for the recent immigrants from North Africa and Asia, they felt they had little if anything in common with them. Some of them felt that there was an invisible wall between them and Israeli society, even if they had a good knowledge of Hebrew. The Russians established a subculture of their own with several daily newspapers and countless weeklies and monthlies (most of them short-lived). On the top of Russian apartments and houses were satellite dishes that enabled them to watch Ostankino and other Russian television channels; later these stations were made accessible by cable. There was an Israeli television and radio program in Russian, but many Russians preferred to watch the familiar Moscow programs except in an emergency.

The Gesher Theater in Haifa offered countless Russian concerts and readings and amateur as well as professional plays. Some elderly Russians celebrated their own holidays, such as the Victory Europe day when the veterans of the great patriotic war could be seen displaying the order of the red banner and the red flag, and medals for participating in the defense of Leningrad and Stalingrad; and there was even the occasional hero of the Soviet Union with the Order of Lenin. They also celebrated New Year's Day rather than some of the Israeli holidays, which they regarded as too religious in character. They put great emphasis on keeping the Russian language alive, and there were many special courses for their children.

The food in the Russian food shops was more impressive than the books offered in the bookshops—the old Russian classics and the recent Russian bestsellers, including the inevitable *Pikul,* historical novels with a strong nationalist tendency. The majority of repatriants were not intellectuals; they produced no Bunin or Nabokov or Chekhov any more than Brighton Beach did. A gifted writer named Dina Rubina who wrote a very funny novel called *Messiah Is Coming,* describing among other things life in a Russian community near Jerusalem and work at a Russian newspaper in Tel Aviv. But there were not many like her, and the general level of discourse was not particularly high. The

Russians harshly criticized Israeli performing arts, such as ballet and the amateur theater, and there was much truth in this. It was also correct with regard to sports; Israeli athletes had never been world champions until the arrival of the Russian swimmers and runners and pole vaulters like Alex Averbukh—many of them non-Jews according to the rabbinical courts. They were not genetically superior, but their approach and their training methods were more professional.

The Russians were more enterprising and curious as far as their new country was concerned than the Mizrachim, let alone the Orthodox Jews. Whereas the horizon of the latter was usually limited to their hometown, the Russians were inveterate travelers as soon as they could afford it. They wanted to visit not only Paris and London but also, young and old, Upper Galilee and Lake Tiberias, the Dead Sea, and the Negev. It was touching to watch these groups of very elderly hikers who knew little of Jewish history and were not really Zionists in any meaningful sense advising their fellow citizens not to give up a single inch. For if they had learned a lesson in the Soviet Union, it was that nice guys finish last. Some of their ideologists even argued that the old Israel had become tired of fighting for its existence after decades war and terrorism and that it badly needed an infusion of new (Russian Jewish) blood.

There were conflicts in the development towns in which the Russians lived side by side with the Moroccans, and sometimes there was fighting. The more enlightened Mizrachim conceded that the Russians had greatly helped to build these cities, but many others disliked them just as they had been disliked by the Israelis forty years earlier, and as every group of newcomers is resented. They argued that many of the Russians were not really Jews—they ate pork—and that before the Russians came there had been little drunkenness (which was true) and hardly any crime (which was untrue). That the Orthodox did not like them goes without saying. Their attempts to proselytize among the Russians were unsuccessful.

Perhaps the weakest and most controversial feature of the Russian immigration was their politics. Many of them hated the Soviet system, but they were to a considerable extent products of this system. How could it have been otherwise? Their politics were primitive and confused; Labor Zionism had, after all, built the country, but by and large they considered it no better than Bolshevism. They abhorred socialism but demanded a welfare state and frequently argued that certain services had been much better in the old Soviet Union. They had learned from bitter experience in Russian that only force counted.

More than two years have passed since the foregoing was written. The mood of the Russians in Israel has deteriorated. They have suffered like everyone else from the recession, and many are unemployed. The percentage of their young men in the armed forces, particularly in the fighting units, is high (about one in four in the combat units), and more than a few were killed in terrorist attacks; the number of civilians killed was even higher. They still vote for Likud and even for Avigdor Liberman, who personifies perhaps more than any other politician so much that is detested by many Israelis. But at the same time, the number of applications for immigration visas to Canada, the United States and even Europe has been steadily rising. They are reluctant to talk about the underlying motives, least of all to outsiders, and one can only guess about the extent of this exodus—and how much it will grow in the years to come if the economy does not improve and if the security problems continue.

I am reasonably certain that Alexander and Natasha Sobolev will not emigrate. I am also sure about their children. But I am not at all certain about their nice neighbors whom I met over tea in their house and who asked me about living conditions and the price of apartments in the United States and Canada.

CHAPTER 15

BAEDEKER, THE HOLY SITES, AND THE JERUSALEM SYNDROME

JERUSALEM HAS ATTRACTED VISITORS AND PILGRIMS FOR many centuries even though it was not the easiest place to reach. But visitors need not only prayers and spiritual guidance. They also have to know about dangers and opportunities, what places to visit and how to approach them, what to wear and what not to eat. They face prosaic questions such as where to stay overnight and what to do in a case of emergency, medical or otherwise. Such literature first came into being about two hundred years ago, sponsored originally by travel agencies such as Thomas Cook or publishers such as John Murray, both in London. (Strictly speaking it is much older. Bernhard von Breydenbach's *Peregrinatio in terram sanctam* appeared in Mainz in 1486.)

Thomas Cook was among the first to organize trips to places such as Switzerland. But Palestine was farther away and more exotic, and while there has not been mass tourism to Jerusalem on the Swiss (or Italian or Spanish) scale until recent decades, there had been a steady and growing steam of visitors and pilgrims to Jerusalem, and those who came were in need of more detailed advice than visitors to Rome or the Swiss Alps.

When Baedeker, the father of a world-famous series of guidebooks, published his *Jerusalem and Its Surroundings* in 1876 (a truly amazing source of information), there was no railway yet from the coast even though there had been talk about building one for a long time. Two omnibuses ran between Jaffa and Jerusalem, and readers were advised that the trip took twelve hours. But since the road was in such bad condition it was not certain that this service would last; one earlier such service had to be discontinued after a short time. Thus, there are long sections about dragomans and horses and camels.

Until 1874, travelers had their luggage inspected at the gates of Jerusalem, and some articles were liable to duty or even seizure. However, it was said that in all these cases, a *baksheesh* of a few francs would generally ensure the traveler against molestation ("but it should of course not be offered too openly, or in presence of the superior officials"). After 1874, the main problem for the traveler who arrived late in the day was that all the gates except the Jaffa Gate were closed. As for hotels, there were only two the guidebook could recommend, the Mediterranean near Jaffa Gate owned by Moses Hornstein, and the Damascus owned by his brother Aron. In addition, there were various hospices for pilgrims, such as Casa Nova run by the Franciscans, and the Austrian and the Prussian hospice. The two hotels had the only European-style restaurants in town worth mentioning. Despite their claims, they were not really up to European standards; the first modern hotel was built by Theodor Fast in 1894 opposite Jaffa Gate. Fast was a Templar from the German Colony who had trained as a hotelier in Europe. This establishment remained Jerusalem's leading hotel up to the 1920s. The main competition was the Jewish Jerusalem Hotel on Jaffa Road (also called the Kaminitz Hotel). Some years later, Kaminitz was overtaken by the Grand New Hotel outside the Jaffa

Gate, which was mainly frequented by English and American visitors and where the daily rate for a room was not less than ten to twelve shillings.

The morning after arrival the traveler would take a walk about town. He was warned that he would be sadly disappointed at first sight. The degraded aspects of Jerusalem, its material and moral decline, formed a melancholy backdrop to the stupendous scenes once enacted there. A crust of rubbish and rottenness enshrouded the sacred places. The streets were narrow, crooked, dirty, and ill paved. The traveler was warned of the superstition, fanaticism, and jealous exclusiveness of the religious communities.

Detailed advice about "intercourse with Orientals" is given by Baedeker (and most other guidebooks), and there is not much difference between the editions of 1876 and 1906. The traveler is told that most Orientals regard the European as a Croesus and sometimes as a madman, since the objects and pleasures of traveling are unintelligible to them. *Baksheesh,* a gift, is therefore expected from those so much better off. Everything is to be had for *baksheesh,* but the traveler is advised to give it only at the last moment. The ceremony of visiting an Oriental home, above all of coffee drinking, is described in detail (the longer the host wishes to have the company of the visitor the later coffee is ordered, as the visitor cannot take his leave before partaking of coffee). Business transactions are long and tedious, as Orientals attach no value to their time; one of the favorite expression of dealers is "*khudu balash*" (take it for nothing), which means about as much as "*beiti beitak*" (my house is your house).

Familiarity, we are advised, should be avoided, for true friendship is rare ("still rarer in the East than elsewhere"). There is a united anti-European front based in large part on the common bond of religion but also on cupidity. The traveler at home in every country in Europe will speedily be wearied in the East, however familiar he may be with the language, by the stereotyped questions and artificial phraseology of the people with whom he comes into contact.

On the other hand, those who understand how to treat the natives will often be struck by their dignity, self-respect, and graciousness of manner, and strangers should therefore be careful to preserve a similar high standard of behavior. Baedeker also notes that the "degraded ruffianism" so common in more civilized countries is quite unknown even among the most destitute, and that the expression "street Arab" is inappropriate and an insult.

Such descriptions of Jerusalem and its inhabitants are considered scandalous by today's readers, typical manifestations of an arrogant European imperialism and colonialism. It's an odd stance to take given the fact that Jerusalem was not located in a colony, but had been in Muslim hands ever since the Crusades. In these descriptions of Palestine and its inhabitants there was no difference between the comments of arch-conservatives and liberals. (There were Western visitors who loved Arabs, but the objects of affection were usually bedouins, not city dwellers.) In their journalism for Horace Greeley's *New York Tribune,* Marx and Engels, who had never been to the Near East, only echoed general European impressions when they wrote that in comparison with the hoi polloi of Levantine cities like Jerusalem, the lower reaches of the plebs of ancient Rome had been a community of saints. Politically incorrect or not, there is unfortunately every reason to believe that the descriptions by Western visitors were quite accurate.

William Smith's *Dictionary of the Bible,* a nineteenth-century standard work of reference (last reprinted in 2003), reported that the accumulated rubbish of centuries was one hundred feet deep around the Temple walls and forty feet deep on the Hill of Zion. Eustace Reynolds Ball, who wrote a *Practical Guide to Jerusalem and Its Environs* in 1900 (second edition, 1912), says that it does not require more than a stay of a few hours to realize that one is "in a city of an effete and decadent power. The streets are not drained—few are wide enough for wheeled traffic. There is no water supply, no gas, no European shops, no postal delivery except through hotels, and an inefficient and corrupt police." This practical adviser also says that one should walk very discreetly through the narrow, malodorous alleys and lanes filled with garbage. But he adds that his comments refer only to the city within the walls and that, by and large, in view of its elevation and isolation, Jerusalem is a fairly healthy city as Levantine cities go.

The authors of the guidebooks such as Baedeker are no more complimentary about the Jews and other native communities. In their dress and manners, the Jews of Jerusalem are said to resemble the Arabs from whom they have no distinguishing marks. The Sephardim speak a Spanish patois, writes Barnabé Mastermann, author of *Guide to the Holy Land* (1907); the European Jews speak a "peculiar German dialect," and they were distinguishable by their sidelocks. On the holidays and at the Wailing Place (as the Western Wall was then called), they may be seen in heavy fur caps and mantles of brightly colored velvet. Mastermann gives the number of Jews in Jerusalem as forty-five thousand out of a total of sixty-six thousand inhabitants, which is probably a little too high.

Writing about the Wailing Wall in 1876, Baedeker says that the Jews were in the habit of repairing there as early as the Middle Ages to bewail the downfall of Jerusalem. He recommends frequent visits to witness the touching scene of men leaning against the weather-beaten wall kissing the stones and weeping. (Eustance Ball, visiting the site a few decades after Baedeker, also finds the scene very touching, remarkable, and pathetic, and upbraids those tourists who consider the sight a spectacle like the native dances at Jericho.) The men often sit here for hours reading their well-thumbed Hebrew prayer books. Many of them are barefooted. The Spanish Jews, whose appearance and bearing are often refined and independent, present a pleasing contrast to their squalid brethren from Poland. And Baedeker mentions the following litany chanted towards evening:

> Leader: For the palace that lies desolate
> Response: We sit in solitude and mourn.
> Leader: For the walls that are overthrown
> Response: We sit in solitude and mourning, etc., etc.

At one stage when I lived in Jerusalem, I collected comments on the city by nineteenth- and early twentieth-century literary figures—how Gogol got even more clinically depressed, how Flaubert had farted when entering the Old City through Jaffa Gate, how Thackeray and countless others were put off by the dirt in the streets, how Melville did not find any grace in the general decay, what Aldous Huxley said ("Jerusalem—the slaughterhouse of religions"), and so on. There were a few exceptions—Disraeli was young and enterprising and unlike Gogol did not look for any deep religious experiences in the first place. There were also some German and Austrian Jewish writers, now half forgotten, such as Alfred Kerr and Felix Salten (the creator of *Bambi*), who thought that the city and the country, though in bad shape, had certain attractions.

The impressions gained by Jewish travelers were equally depressing. Eliezer Ben-Yehuda, who had done more than anyone else to revive the Hebrew language, wrote about the turn of the century that the situation had greatly improved. But Chaim Weizmann, visiting in 1907, said that Jerusalem had been the most unhappy experience of his whole stay in Palestine, that it depressed him beyond words, that he remained prejudiced against the city for many years and even now (1949) felt ill at ease in it.

After a while I gave up my search. It was depressing and repetitive, and these travelers had written about the Old City, not the

Jerusalem I knew best. Furthermore, the landscape had changed. The Judean hills were no longer bleak and desolate, and even the Old City had been cleaned up—to a point. Arthur Koestler and Manes Sperber had been to the ultraorthodox in Mea Shearim, but much as I was impressed by some of their novels, they had spent only an hour or two there. What could they tell me that I did not know? But I was still interested in the reports on Jerusalem by Aleksander Borisovich Lakir, my ancestor. When he visited Jerusalem in 1859, he was so shocked by the state of the holy sites to such an extent that he decided not to comment.

Virtually all Jewish visitors of the nineteenth and early twentieth centuries were appalled not just by the indescribable dirt but even more by the moral degradation so widespread in a Jewish community dependent to a large extent on gifts from Europe (*halukka*). After a visit in 1891, Ahad Ha'am, the prophet of cultural Zionism, asked, "What destruction was greater, that of our land or of our people?"

Nahum Goldmann, subsequently a prominent Zionist leader, arrived in Jerusalem with a group of fellow students in 1913. He had grown up with the traditional stories of a Jerusalem with walls of marble and gates of gold through which messiahs would ride one day. But all he experienced walking in the city was great sadness and physical pain facing such squalor, neglect, and lack of culture. About the reaction of his fellow travelers, he wrote that no other station on their trip to Palestine had given them so little, and after four days their greatest desire was to get out of Jerusalem.

Goldmann even began to doubt whether the group of Jews in front of the Wailing Wall was really praying with as much devotion as it appeared. His mood was not improved when an Arab drove his braying donkeys through the site in front of the Wailing Wall, which, after all, was the holiest of the holy of the Jews. He felt inclined to kill the poor donkey driver but fortunately did not give in to this impulse. For was it not true that the state of affairs was above all the fault of the Jews themselves? What people are we to permit such degradation?

Goldmann felt nothing but infinite shame about his people exposed to the scorn of the whole world. Everyone around him (the moon included) seemed to mock him derisively, and he wanted to leave this horrible place as soon as possible. The shock of Jerusalem was all the greater since he had witnessed before something of the new Palestine, the agricultural settlements and the new kind of proud Jew growing up there. What a world of difference between them and the sickly and timid *yeshiva* students of Jerusalem.

The impressions of Jewish leaders from Moses Montefiore to Herzl, but also those like Weizmann who had come from Eastern Europe, had been the same. Herzl wrote in his diary that Jerusalem's evil-smelling alleys contained only the musty deposits of two thousand years of inhumanity, intolerance, and impurity. At the Wailing Wall he perceived only superstition and fanaticism on all sides.

The guidebooks of the period between the two world wars were mainly written by Jews, except a few authored specifically for Christian pilgrims. They were meant to be read by visitors from abroad curious to see for themselves what had been achieved by the Zionists. Other visitors, mainly after 1933, came to contemplate settling in Palestine. These books deal with the Jewish holy sites and also the main Christian and Muslim churches and mosques, but much of the stress is on the new Palestine. The authors, such as Ze'ev Vilnai and Joseph Braslavski (later Braslavi), had acquired knowledge of the country over a period of many years. Their guidebooks were published by book-sellers such as Steimatzky, at the time a small bookshop on Jaffa Road. (In 2003, Steimatzky had more than one hundred branches through-out Israel.)

More often than not these authors had a predilection for Jerusalem. Tel Aviv was said to be boring, one street was like the next ("few points of interest, streets are crowded, traffic is heavy, taxis are hard to find"). Tel Aviv was outstanding only for the concerts and theater, which centered there, whereas Jerusalem was the political as well as the cultural center, and above all "eternity—thy name is Jerusalem." But this disdain toward Tel Aviv began to change in the late 1930s.

The guidebooks mentioned that myriads of tourists came to cosmopolitan Jerusalem every year. But where were they staying? Jerusalem had the only first-class hotel in the country, the King David, built in the 1920s with two hundred bedrooms (one hundred twenty with baths), with running water, central steam heating, and tennis courts. According to its brochure there was also a winter garden, an excellent orchestra, dancing, private telephones in many of the rooms, competent chauffeurs, and a world-famous view. But during World War II, the King David hotel came to house mainly government offices. There was little or no tourism. The hotel housed a few expelled monarchs from Europe and Africa and senior staff officers of the allied armies in the Middle East. Then King David was bombed and half destroyed in 1946. It remained out of action for several years.

There was no other first-class hotel and barely any second-class. The Fast Hotel on Jaffa Road had eighty rooms (but "strictly first class" was a considerable exaggeration). It had a bar, a tea room, and a garden as well as a garage and, as it advertised, well-known cuisine. (It became a soldiers' club during the war and did not reopen after 1945.) All other hotels, such as the Eden, Goldsmith, Amdurski, Herzlia, Rothman, and Friedman, had fewer than thirty rooms; all stressed that they had running water, but most rooms did not have a bath. In addition there were the non-Jewish hotels such as the Citadel (with ninety bedrooms and central heating) at Jaffa Gate, the Majestic, and the YMCA.

Café Europe on Jaffa Road had not only a *thé dansant* but also daily musical afternoons and evenings, as well as "the nicest garden in

Jerusalem and newspapers in all languages." The "all languages" was a slight exaggeration, but the Jewish residents, especially the recent arrivals, were avid newspaper readers in the German and Viennese tradition. Newspapers were expensive and difficult to obtain, especially in wartime. In fact there was one café called *Bet Ha'eton* (House of the Newspapers) that kept scores of newspapers from all over the world and where the consumption of coffee, tea, and cakes was secondary to reading.

While the guidebooks of the 1930s concentrated on topics of Jewish interest in the city including the "national institutions" like the Jewish Agency, they did not (and indeed could not) ignore the many other sites and institutions from the Italian Hospital to the Scottish Hospice, the (Jesuit) Pontifical Bible School, the various monasteries and convents and churches as well as Al-Aqsa Mosque and the Dome of the Rock (Mosque of Omar). The descriptions were not very detailed and could not possibly be compared with the old volumes of Baedeker that stressed (to give one example) when writing about *Haram as-Sharif* (Temple Mount) that "we now stand on one of the most profoundly interesting spots in the world." This relative neglect (there was not much on Jewish holy sites and synagogues either) could have to do in part with the limited interest of a Jewish public that had come mainly to see the new Palestine, but there was also the fact that for years, especially during the riots of 1936–39, it had been impossible for Jewish visitors to move freely in the Old City.

Holy places are part of most religions, but why they became sacred is a difficult question to which neither students of religion nor of anthropology have wholly satisfactory answers. Holy places can be found among the Hopi Indians and the Australian Aborigines, in Mexico, Japan, and ancient Britain and Ireland. Sometimes these were mountains or waterfalls or rocks or trees or caves or simply mysterious forces of nature. Elsewhere the mountains were artificial, as were the pyramids of Egypt and Mexico. Graves and graveyards became holy places in various religions, but the practice of pilgrimage from distant places is usually of more recent date. Nor has it been universally accepted. The holy places predated the monotheistic religions, and were essentially pagan.

The decisive spiritual dimension that had been contributed by Judaism, Christianity, Islam, and Hinduism was not connected with stones and trees and even mountains. Some of the church fathers advised their followers that one could be a good Christian without ever having been in Jerusalem, for the center, the core of their religion, was not the place in Palestine by that name, but Christ and the heavenly Jerusalem, for "the kingdom of God is in you."

With the Crusades, the element of making a pilgrimage to the Holy Land, and even to be in physical possession of the sites believed to be holy, became much more pronounced. But after the Muslim reconquest, up to the age of mass tourism, the number of pilgrims was still relatively small. In Islam, the *hajj* plays a central role—it is one of the five main duties of a Muslim. However, the destination was Mecca (or, in the case of the Shiites, also An Najaf and Karbala) not Jerusalem; in the fourteenth and fifteenth centuries, all kind of new Muslim holy places emerged, but these were mainly in North Africa.

In the case of the Jews, there were the prayers about Jerusalem, particularly on Passover concerning an early return to Jerusalem and the rebuilding of the temple. But this was connected with the coming of the Messiah, and as the Messiah did not come, this became part of the ritual and very few Jews undertook the effort to pay a visit. When Zionism first appeared on the scene, it was precisely from among the Orthodox Jews that strong opposition emerged to settling Palestine, for it was regarded as a profanation of the holy.

Although the religious-political conflict over Jerusalem and the holy places became a major obstacle to peace only in recent decades, it has been a source of tensions, domestic and international, for many centuries. The conflicts were predominantly between the various Christian denominations, mainly the Latin (Catholic), sometimes supported by the Armenian, Copt, and other churches, and the Greek, assisted by the Russian Orthodox. There was constant bickering and even pitched battles among the monks as to who owned what part of what church (or had access or was entitled to make changes or repairs) in the Church of the Holy Sepulchre, the site of Jesus' crucifixion and resurrection. At various times, the Ottoman authorities had to dispatch hundreds of soldiers to keep the peace between the Christians, and more recently the Israeli police has been called in. As a result of the lack of Christian cooperation, the building is in an advanced state of disrepair. The damage, a result of the conflagration of 1809 caused by a drunken monk, has not been wholly repaired to this day, and a Christian guidebook describes the shameful sectarian turf war as a disgrace to the religion, noting the unpleasant atmosphere both inside and outside the church.

Other Christian holy sites include the Via Dolorosa with its fourteen Stations of the Cross, the Tomb of the Virgin Mary (one among several places believed to be her grave), Gethsemane, and the Mount of Olives where Jesus is said to have lived for a while hiding from the elders of the Temple. In the eighteenth and nineteenth centuries, the European powers became involved in these quarrels, each trying to fortify its physical presence in Jerusalem. Although these conflicts (about issues such as silver stars to be affixed or replaced on top of a church) were not the only cause of the Crimean War, they were certainly a contributing factor to the developments leading to the outbreak of the war. The Ottoman government, on the other hand, while insisting in principle on the strict observation of the status quo, tended from time to time to give special rights to one church (and European country) or another according to the international constellation and its political interests.

The situation was further complicated by internal quarrels within the various churches. While the Greek and the Russians had initially cooperated closely, a rivalry set in during the nineteenth century. Furthermore, the Greek higher clergy had alienated their Arab flock; most of the Christians in Jerusalem were Arabs, whereas most of the clergy, and all the high clergy, were foreigners, and this was true for the Latin (Catholic) patriarchate as well. While the Turks had usually preferred the Greek clergy over the Arabs, during the twentieth century pressure grew for leading posts in the Christian churches to go to Arab Christians. But the position of the Arab church dignitaries was weakened in turn by the exodus of Christian Arabs from Jerusalem and Bethlehem, first under Jordanian rule and later as the result of the Islamization of the Palestinian national movement. Until World War II, Christians were strongly represented among the Arabs in Jerusalem, Ramallah, and Bethlehem, but within the last sixty years there has been radical demographic change. The influence of Christian Arabs has greatly declined, and their dignitaries have predicted that if this trend continues, the only Christians left in Jerusalem in the near future will be church officials.

These quarrels and conflicts between the Christian churches have by no means ended. One of the most bitter is the conflict between the Coptic and the Abyssinian church over the possession of part of the roof on a certain monastery, which has gone on for decades. But they have been overshadowed in recent decades by the Arab-Jewish conflict over the holy places, especially the Temple Mount (Har Habayit, Haram as-Sharif). For religious Jews, the Temple Mount is the site of the temples of King David and Solomon and therefore the only remaining part of the Temple from which the spirit of God (*shehina*) has never disappeared. It is also, according to Jewish and Muslim legend, the place of the binding of Isaac by Abraham (*akedat Yizchak*).

The Wailing Wall has been a bone of contention for a long time, the main issue at stake being whether the Jews were permitted to blow the *shofar* and bring chairs and benches and a wooden partition (between the men's and women's sections) to be placed in front of the wall. This infuriated the Arabs and led to the riots of 1929 in which more than two hundred Jews and Arabs were killed. As a result of the war of 1948, Jerusalem was divided between Israel and Jordan. Virtually all the holy sites except those located on Mount Zion were in Arab hands and Jews no longer had access.

Then came the Six-Day War and the famous message of General Mordechai Gur on June 7, 1967: "The Temple Mount is in our hands." The chief military rabbi was blowing the *shofar* and published an order of the day: "The dream of all the generations has been fulfilled before our eyes." But even the paratroopers, most of them not religious, were awestruck—they sang the "Hatikva," the national anthem. One said it made him feel that the Jewish people were something special, another that the Wailing Wall symbolized the Jewish people's yearning for unity. This tremendous surge of emotions was clearly not the occasion to ponder the price that would have to be paid.

The whole of Jerusalem was now under Israeli control. But the one major change made by the Israelis was the destruction of the small Mugrabi quarter, which made access to the Wailing Wall difficult. (The only access was by way of a narrow lane through which Arabs drove their donkeys and other livestock, which had so irritated Nahum Goldmann in 1913.) Since then the Temple Mount has become "the ultimate disco of the ultraorthodox"—in the words of Professor Y. Leibowitz, an Orthodox Jew. The difference is that unlike in a disco, there is total separation between the genders; women are not even allowed to put on a prayer shawl or to read from the Bible. (They are permitted to pray but not to read the Torah.)

On the whole there was great caution as to any change in the status quo; Moshe Dayan ordered that the Israeli flag that had been hoisted immediately after the conquest in 1967 on the Temple Mount be hauled down. Minister of Religion Zerach Wahrhaftig declared that the best way to protect holy places was to stay far away from them. But later Israeli governments, eager to preserve the status quo, have insisted on the right of access by non-Muslims, on the condition that these groups not pray during their visits. This, in turn, has reinforced deep fears among Muslim believers that these visits were not innocent tourism but that the Jews were out somehow to destroy their Noble Sanctuary (Haram as-Sharif).

While the Israeli parliament passed a law annexing eastern Jerusalem, Temple Mount remained under the effective control of the Arabs, and Jews were permitted to visit there but not to pray. This was in accordance with Jewish religious doctrine, which banned walking in the area for fear of treading on and desecrating the ground on which the temple once stood. Some extreme Jewish sects, such as the Neturei Karta, banned visits even to the Western Wall because it was in the hands of the Israeli government, to which they were unalterably opposed. Successive chief rabbis have denounced the ascent to Temple Mount as "wicked." Yet other Jewish religious authorities, such as Shlomo Goren, the former army chief rabbi, claimed that since it had been destroyed, the site was no longer holy anyway. Lastly, there were the religious-nationalist fanatics who, ignoring the injunction of the sages, tried repeatedly to offer their prayers on Temple Mount and have had to be removed physically by the Israeli police stationed there.

Radical Jewish groups, some Orthodox, some religious-nationalist, have routinely attempted to enter Temple Mount on Jewish holidays and also on secular anniversaries such as Jerusalem Day. Some of them have been engaged in conspiracies to destroy the Muslim shrines there. In their view, the possession of Temple Mount is a precondition for the coming of the messianic age, and whoever controls Temple Mount has the control over the land of Israel (or even more far reaching: He who controls Jerusalem in the last days controls the world, according to the Book of Daniel). For these people, the building of the Third Temple is the commandment of the hour, and if it leads to a great war between the Jews and the Amalekites, the forces of evil, so much the better, for it would speed up the coming of Messiah and final victory.

These provocations on the part of a few have led to incendiary Arab sermons, violent demonstrations and riots; the Jews, it was claimed, were about to destroy all that was holy to the Muslim faithful. In addition, there have been attempts by non-Jews of unsound mind to set fire to the Mosque (the Australian Denis Michael Rohan in 1969).

Temple Mount has an irresistible attraction for all kind of religious and nationalist fanatics and madmen and has become one of the most dangerous spots in the Middle East. It is, in the words of Gershon Gorenberg, "the epicenter of Jewish-Arab tensions."

What we know about the location of holy sites in Jerusalem as in the whole of Palestine (and not only there) is not based on hard facts but on pious legends that over time assumed the status of facts for believers. In other words, holy sites were created, sometimes for political reasons, sometimes out of religious motives. An obvious example is the grave of Joseph, allegedly located in Nablus, which, for all one knows, was the grave of some seventeenth century Arab sheikh. However, after 1967, some extremist Jewish groups decided to make this obscure place into a holy site equal in importance to the Western Wall. (It was destroyed in an attack by local Arabs in 2000 and a mosque was built there.) Quite a few holy places were established in recent years by immigrants from North Africa in development towns mainly in the south of Israel. But with a few exceptions (such as the grave of Baba Sali in Netivot—a spiritual leader of Moroccan Jewry who lived from 1889 to 1984—which has become a center of pilgrimage for Jews from Morocco), they are of local importance only.

This industry, the fabrication of holy places, is relatively new among the Jewish religious nationalists. However, it has a hallowed tradition among Palestinian Muslims, where this genre of literature is called *fadha'il* (history of cities). It praises the virtues of Jerusalem and magnifies its importance. It came into being during the Crusades and perhaps even before.

Although Jerusalem does not appear by name in the Qur'an, it occupies a central position in Islam. According to this tradition, Muhammad went from Mecca to Jerusalem overnight, and the ascension to heaven (*qibla*) on his horse took place from a rock, which is now sacred. According to this literature, Jerusalem will be the site of the resurrection. All the pious will gather there on Judgment Day and will witness the appearance of the Messiah (al Mahdi). Muslim writers reject all non-Muslim exegesis of their traditions (and some Muslim interpretations too) as either imperialist or Orientalist or Zionist. They claim that there was virtually no Jewish presence in the Old City of Jerusalem until quite recently. These spokesmen are more liberal toward the Christians, who in recent times constituted less of a danger. They maintain that Islam was always tolerant of other religions and that Muslims built shrines to various religions in Jerusalem. Shiite historians are upbraided by them for suggesting that the pilgrimage to Mecca was discontinued under the Umayyads. But how to explain the fact that the seat of government and administration under Muslim rule was in Lydda (Lod) and Ramla rather than in Jerusalem? How can this be brought in line with the argument that Jerusalem always had the third most important place in Islam? The explanation given—that there was too much congestion in Jerusalem because of its annual fairs and markets—is not quite convincing.

Muslim writers reject the argument that for long stretches of history Muslim rulers did not attribute great importance to Jerusalem. They claim that in fact it was the early Zionists who were not particularly interested in Jerusalem, partly because they were secular in inspiration, but also because they feared conflicts with the many other religious interests involved in the city.

This is perfectly true. The strong political-religious emphasis on Jerusalem in Zionism occurred only after 1967. But it is also true that Jerusalem was never equal in importance in Islam to Mecca and Medina (or An Najaf and Kerbela as far as the Shiites are concerned). Jerusalem, on the other hand, appeared throughout the ages in many Jewish prayers, including grace after meals, and in turning towards Jerusalem in prayers (this was also the practice in early Islam but was soon discontinued). "If I forget thee, O Jerusalem" appears in the Psalms, it is recited by a father at the circumcision of his son and by the bridegroom at the end of the wedding service. The famous "Next Year in Jerusalem" appears in the Passover prayer. For the religious Jew there was an indissoluble bond with Zion and Jerusalem; for secular Jews this bond was, of course, much weaker, and Zionism, a secular movement, was indeed inspired by, among other things, the desire to distance itself from the tradition of mourning and wailing and thus also from the Wailing Wall. For the founding fathers of Zionism, Zion was not Mount Moriah but the land of Israel. They paid a visit to Jerusalem but had no wish to live there.

The Old City is not only the place where most holy sites are located, it is also a giant religious supermarket where holy water can be bought, as well as holy stones, amulets, and charms of every description and for every denomination not to mention unbelievably kitsch pictures and icons. Holy water (*aqua bendita*) comes in bottles and ampoules, scented and perfumed; the average price is between fifteen and twenty-five dollars. The stones, priced according to size, all come with a hundred percent guarantee. This kind of thing has been going on since time immemorial; the carrying home of various "blessings and indulgences" was reported by Egeria, a French lady pilgrim, one of the very first, who visited Jerusalem circa AD 380. The chronicler Felix Fabri reported in the fifteenth century that pilgrims were shaving off stones, wood, and even earth at places believed to be holy, for magic properties were attributed to them. They were thought to make fevers and headaches disappear, the blind to see, the lame to walk, and even helped alleviate toothaches.

There were reports of wealthy Christians willing to pay a fortune for the skeletons of the Holy Innocents, the children killed by Herod in his search for the newborn Jesus. Fabri laments, "Thus Christ's faithful believers are mocked and robbed of their money for the infidels know of our ardent desire for the possession of relics such as wood from the Holy Cross, nails, thorns, bones, and other such things." Baedeker in 1876 did not fail to mention the rosaries and crosses made of olive wood, black stinkstone, mother of pearl, and other materials sold in front of the churches ("As a rule one half or one third only of the price demanded should be offered"). These practices have been refined through the techniques of modern salesmanship. Furthermore there are CDs of *Jesus Christ Superstar* and similar music. Videos of Mel Gibson's film, *The Passion of the Christ*, are expected.

The purchase of amulets and charms of every kind is equally frequent among Jews, especially those from North African and Middle Eastern countries. They offer protection against the evil eye and other misfortunes, medical and otherwise. These amulets, now sold all over Jerusalem, are made of sterling silver and fourteen-karat gold, usually in the form of pendants with the mystical name of God (Shaddai) as protection against magic. The second line on the amulet is often a request for protection—*yishmereni* (will, or do, guard me). For many decades, the Jewish faithful have written their wishes and complaints

on small pieces of paper and put them into the crevices of the Wailing
Wall. (When the crevices are full, and God, it is presumed, has had the
chance to study them all, they are emptied by a special crew and buried
somewhere.) But modern technology has brought progress.

It is no longer necessary to proceed to the Wall for this purpose:
the message can be conveyed there by fax (02 561 2222), there is a
Western Wall Camera that makes it possible to watch it at any time of
the day and night, and at www.jerusalem.muni.il, you can type your
message to God, which gets printed out and placed on the wall.

The Islamic charms are quite often of pre-Islamic origin (ani-
mistic, ancient Egyptian, Jewish, or Christian). The amulets (*tamima,*
but also known as *audha* and *hijab*) are usually worn around the neck,
and there are also amulets for horses, camels, and even donkeys. They
are often made of metal, as the noise of metals charms is thought to
drive the demons away, but they also appear in the form of knots,
strips of paper with verses from the Qur'an (often used by taxi drivers), hair, and little bags of leather or cloth containing herbs, drugs,
or shells of snails. Sometimes these amulets are placed in the hollow
of a stick. They are meant to dispel diseases, chase away thieves as well
as mad dogs, protect children, obtain victory in battle, and improve
lovemaking.

These charms can be bought outside mosques, churches, and synagogues in Jerusalem as well as in other cities, and occasionally also
inside them. They are relatively harmless, belonging to the realm of
folk religion. Far more dangerous is the growth of religious fanaticism
in recent decades, more often than not combined with aggressive
nationalism. The growth of Islamic fundamentalism with its violent
manifestations, from the Philippines to Afghanistan, from Iran to
Egypt, has been the most spectacular expression of this phenomenon.
But there has been an aggressive fundamentalist upsurge also among
Jews. More young men now study in Israeli *yeshivas* than in the whole

of Eastern Europe before World War II, and no one can account for this development.

What if the territorial claims of aggressive religions clash? This was the case with the Taliban and the famous Ayodhya mosque in northern India. A mosque erected on the site of a Hindu temple some three hundred years ago was destroyed by three hundred thousand Hindu militants in December 1992. (There were earlier clashes at the site in the nineteenth century, in 1912, and in 1934 in which hundreds of people were killed.) Ayodhya is one of the seven sacred Hindu sites, believed to be the birthplace of Rama, the God incarnate and fountainhead of Hindu culture. It was a place of worship and pilgrimage for a long time, but the problem assumed critical proportions only when an extreme Hindu party (BJP) became the strongest political movement in the country. Ayodhya is now the central issue in this party's program. As one might expect, fanatical Hindus want to build a temple in Ayodhya right away, regardless of the consequences. But the majority of Hindus do not regard this as a matter of such paramount urgency and would like to reach an agreement with the other side.

Thus the Ayodhya situation resembles Jerusalem and the Temple Mount. But there is no flashpoint as dangerous as Jerusalem. Ayodhya is not a central issue for Muslims beyond the Indian subcontinent. Furthermore, India is a country of more than a billion inhabitants, and elementary prudence dictates caution in confronting a power of this size. Israel, on the other hand, is a small country that, some Muslims believe, can be confronted without great risk.

The danger from possible actions by the Temple Mount Faithful and similar Jewish sects is obvious, but there are equally predictable groups among Christian sectarian end-timers. The statement from the Book of Daniel cited earlier also appears in the New Testament (in Revelation), and various end-timer cults have taken it as an injunction to attack Muslim religious sites in Jerusalem, thereby precipitating Armageddon. Many observers feared that with the beginning of a new millennium there was a distinct danger of violent attacks with incalculable consequences. These fears were not borne out by subsequent events, but this does not mean that the danger has passed. The Jerusalem syndrome in a subacute form persists not only among lunatics; the unwillingness to share sovereignty over the holy places has become a main propaganda theme and even official policy.

As a result, the holy places have become a political nightmare. The Palestinians are not content with having civilian control of Temple Mount. They want full and undivided control over the Old City. The religious Zionists and the nationalists regard negotiation over these places as heresy and wholly unacceptable. What if an agreement were reached that gave religious Jews full access to the Wailing Wall and other places? Such an arrangement existed between 1948 and 1967 but is now a dead letter. There is little reason to believe that it would be more effective in the future.

Many excellent and some not so excellent guidebooks on Jerusalem have been published in recent decades in all languages. They provide information on every conceivable topic, such as where to jog and where to buy skullcaps to the best places to find good date syrup. You can find the alcoholic content of Israeli beers. They do not always agree as far as their advice is concerned. *Lonely Planet* says that in certain areas of Jerusalem sexual harassment is a constant problem for women travelers. "The majority of problems arise with Arab males, but Israeli men are not known for their respectful conduct toward women either." The Bradt travel guide *Palestine with Jerusalem* reports that blonde women may find themselves subjected to a fair bit of unwanted attention in the Near East, "although women I've spoken to say that the attention is far worse in Israel where the men are apparently more persistent and aggressive." However, women are advised not to let the reputation of Arab men deter them from visiting Palestine, since a quick "*imshi*—go away" usually does the trick. *Footprint Israel* mentions the "over-hormonal testosterone-heavy" Israeli male but adds that most instances of harassment occur in the Old City after dark, on the ramparts walk, in the Mount of Olives area, and outside the Tabasco tearooms. Those confronted with such a situation are advised to shout and make a scene. The outspoken Bradt guide also advises readers who find themselves threatened by trouble that the phrase "*mish yahud*" (I am not a Jew) could prove a lifesaver.

The new generation of guidebooks is distinguished by a desire to cover as many subjects as possible, including thumbnail sketches of Israeli literature, music, the Jewish religion, archaeology, political parties, and many other topics. As befitting a work of reference, most try to be fair rather than propagandistic. Some do not try hard enough. Thus we may find references to Deir Yassin, the Arab village on the outskirts of Jerusalem where the Irgun massacred one hundred or more Arab civilians during the war of 1948, but no reference to the Arab attack a few days later in which a convoy of eighty Jews largely consisting of medical personnel were killed on Mount Scopus. To be fair, I have also seen the attack on the convoy mentioned with Deir Yassin omitted.

Travel guides written by authors who are obviously not right-wingers have a tendency to use terms such as *right wing* rather indiscriminately. One guidebook calls *The Jerusalem Post* right-wing, which is, broadly speaking, correct, but no pejorative epithets are used when describing the orientation of the Palestinian publications mentioned. Another work calls the stall holders in the colorful Mahane Yehuda market right-wing and then adds that they were attacked by Arab terrorists who were even more right-wing, a statement which does not greatly contribute to the understanding of the political situation underlying the attack.

A fair amount of this literature shows a naïve bias of which not only the Israelis are the victims. One guidebook reports that the Palestine Authority's record on human rights has been abysmal, which raises the question: Compared to what? With Sweden and Switzerland, or with Syria, Iraq, Saudi Arabia, and Lybia?

The borderline between anti-Zionism and anti-Semitism is not always clearly visible. The *Footprint Israel* handbook's long entry on Yad Vashem cannot make up its mind whether this is a legitimate endeavor or mere manipulation and political propaganda that serves only to devalue the memory of the victims. It quotes at length a variety of witnesses claiming that the memorial is an instrument forged to manipulate foreign visitors, using the horrors of Auschwitz to influence the living for Israeli propaganda (i.e., oppressing the Arabs). In the last paragraph, the authors avow that this controversial institution is deserving of a visit after all.

The political orientation underlying these guidebooks (some more, others less) can usually be established by examining the brief section providing suggestions for further reading. If the emphasis is on authors such as Edward Said, there can be no mistake regarding its politics; it is unlikely that guidebooks on Britain or France give pride of place to works hostile to these countries or that a guidebook to Syria will recommend works written by professors at the Hebrew University.

But this statement too has to be qualified, because authors of works of reference are by necessity very busy people and seem not to have read some of the books they recommend, just as they could not have eaten in every restaurant or stayed in every hotel appearing in their work. So from time to time they praise a book they would not approve of had they read it. Baedeker certainly would not have made such mistakes. But his books were written before the age of mass tourism with far fewer hotels and restaurants to inspect, and fewer books to read.

Everything considered, the guidebooks do a reasonably good job. Ideally, they should steer clear of politics altogether, but this might well be asking for the impossible in a place so highly charged with political emotions, where even outsiders are irresistibly drawn into the melée.

This too could be a mild form of the Jerusalem syndrome. But who needs these guidebooks now?

There was a time when a steady and growing stream of tourists came to Jerusalem and the other places. Cook's *Traveller's Handbook to Palestine,* published in 1934, lists nine hotels in Jerusalem, as well as a number of hospices. In late 1999, there were sixty-nine hotels (thirty-six of them in western Jerusalem), with eight thousand four hundred ninety beds. More tourists came to Jerusalem than to any other city in Israel. But with the second intifada in late 2002, tourism came to a virtual standstill; the number of tourists in 2002 was only about 20 percent of the preceding year, and it consisted mainly of inland tourism rather than visitors from abroad. But Israeli tourists too began to prefer Elat and Antalya (in Turkey) to Jerusalem. Hotels were empty or had to be closed, the shops in the Old City made no sales, and the situation was not much better in the Jewish quarters. The guides to the Old City and the holy sites had to retool. Taxi drivers had to give up their jobs. Only very brave publishers will consider new editions of Jerusalem travel guides in the foreseeable future.

I Saw the New Jerusalem...

WHAT WILL JERUSALEM BE LIKE FIFTY YEARS FROM NOW? For the last hundred fifty years—there has been a Jerusalem municipality since the 1860s—it has not been, with two or three notable exceptions, very lucky with its mayors. While the Jews were a majority, both the Turks and the British thought that the mayor should be a Muslim, and thus during this period there were five Husseini, three Khalidi, and three Alami mayors of Jerusalem. Under Ottoman rule, some municipal services were introduced, but by and large Jerusalem was run down. Ronald Storrs, the first British Mandatory governor in the early 1920s, was an intellectual who quoted Dante and Euripides, but politically and as an administrator he was less gifted; he had all kind of ideas for the city but lacked the ability to carry them out. He insisted that Jerusalem buildings should be of yellowish stone, which gave the city its monolithic, monochromatic character. The Arab mayors were members of leading families. None of them caused great harm, but only one or two, such as Salim Effendi Husseini (1882–97) who introduced street lanterns, night watchmen, and even a few street sweepers, contributed to its development. The Jewish mayors after 1948 were public figures at the end of their career, honest and hardworking but lacking dynamism and enterprise. None of them carried much weight or added much to the city, and none of them stayed on the job for very long.

Then, in 1965, came Teddy Kollek, who was mayor for more than twenty-eight years. He had vision, he knew how to get things done, and he was a public relations genius, one of the great mayors of the twentieth century. He got up early in the morning and went on unannounced private inspection tours. He gave the city a museum, a theater, gardens, and the Jerusalem Foundation, not to mention the Teddy soccer stadium. In his time, Jerusalem became a cleaner and more beautiful place. Kollek had no ambitions as far as national politics were concerned (he had been originally elected on a personal, not a party, list) and was therefore free to concentrate on Jerusalem affairs. He was not an equally outstanding mayor for the Arab residents and should have done more for them. Politically, it would not have made much difference in the end; peace between the two peoples could not have been achieved on the municipal level.

Kollek later admitted that he had neglected the Jerusalem Arabs—they constituted 30 percent of the population but received only 11 percent of the municipal services budget. As a result, elementary services in the Arab part of the city continued to deteriorate while the Israeli government engaged in various forms of land confiscation, establishing an outer ring of Jewish settlements around Jerusalem in a futile attempt to preserve the demographic balance. As was so often the case, the Arabs acted foolishly by boycotting Jerusalem municipal elections. Given their numerical strength they could have influenced municipal policy, but they abstained and their voice was not heard. Furthermore, there was no help for them from the oil-rich Arab governments that were so eager to support the families of suicide bombers.

They could have bought land on the open market in Jerusalem and escaped their ghettoization. But whereas Orthodox and nationalist Jews received funds for this purpose from their well-wishers abroad, the Arab Jerusalemites received only moral support from theirs.

Since Teddy Kollek's days, it has been downhill almost all the way. Some major new roads were built, but the infrastructure has steadily deteriorated. The green space, such as the Jerusalem forest, has dwindled. The present mayor, Uri Lupoliansky, is ultraorthodox, as are fourteen of the thirty-one members of the municipal council. Lupoliansky served in the army as a medical orderly before he turned ultraorthodox. He is a pleasant and decent man according to those who know him; he lives modestly with his wife and twelve children in an apartment in the Sanhedria quarter. He began his professional life as an actor playing a minor role in *Fiddler on the Roof;* his brother is a circus impresario. There has been no religious coercion under his leadership, but he is wholly the creature of the rabbis who appointed him, and he seems daunted by the enormous problems confronting a city that is heavily in debt. It has been suggested that one way to start saving would be to dismiss some of the eight deputy mayors.

Present day Jerusalem is a city in transition—but transition towards what? The Turks paved a road from the coastal plain to Jerusalem in the 1860s in preparation for Emperor Franz Josef of Austria's visit the city, but it soon fell into disrepair. When I first arrived in Jerusalem, the journey from Tel Aviv took about three hours because the road was narrow and chances were good that one would get stuck behind a truck fully loaded with building materials moving at an agonizing pace along the hilly serpentine roadway. Today there is a motorway from Tel Aviv and the distance can be covered in fifty minutes (except perhaps in the rush hour). There were a lot of trucks when I first came but few private cars. The first automobile, a Ford belonging to Mr. Vester of the American Colony, appeared in 1910 to the awe and amazement of all. His pioneering spirit should be admired: Who was going to repair his Ford when it broke down; where was he supposed to get gas?

The municipal area of Jerusalem is now three times larger than it was before 1967. With more than six hundred eighty thousand inhabitants, it is the biggest city in Israel and also the poorest. Lewis Mumford, the great planner, wrote in the 1970s that in order not to lose its specific character, Jerusalem should not be allowed to grow beyond a population of half a million. Today many planners take a million as their baseline.

About 24 percent of the residents of Jewish Jerusalem live below the poverty line, more than twice the percentage of those living in Tel Aviv and Haifa. The number of Jewish families living in poverty is greater than it is in the development towns in the south, which are populated mainly by immigrants from the Middle East and North Africa. Only one city in Israel has a higher incidence of poverty, Bne Braq, also populated by ultraorthodox families where a large part of the male population does not work. However, if the Arab residents of Jerusalem are included in the statistics, it emerges that 41 percent of the population live below the poverty line, four times as many as in Tel Aviv and Haifa. In recent years, soup kitchens for the needy have opened in Jerusalem, distributing hundreds of free meals daily.

I have been living for many years in bankrupt cities. Washington is chronically bankrupt and forever needs to be bailed out by the federal government. Berlin, where these lines are written, has a debt of fifty-five billion dollars, more than half the total Israeli GNP. In comparison, Jerusalem's debt, a mere three hundred million dollars, seems almost negligible. But the burden is far heavier on Jerusalem because there is no wealthy government to bail it out as there is in the United States and Germany. There is little if any room for reducing expenses, and the tax base is very small. Above all, there is no hope for improvement since it is a genetically poor city and so many of its residents are neither gainfully employed nor pay taxes.

Most residents now live in areas that became part of Jerusalem only after the war of 1967, from Gilo and East Talpiot in the south to Pisgat Ze'ev and Neve Ya'akov in the north. Beyond the green line there are Ma'aleh Adumim, a city of about thirty thousand, national-religious in orientation; Orthodox and ultraorthodox Betar Elit (the fastest growing), with twenty-five thousand; Givat Ze'ev; and Efrata. West of Jerusalem in the direction of Tel Aviv there is Mevasseret Zion in the Jerusalem corridor, middle class, secular, with an impressive mall (including a kosher MacDonald's), large private homes, and gardens. Those living there more often than not escaped from Jerusalem and feel no great urge to visit the city; on the contrary, Jerusalemites on outings frequent the cinemas and coffee houses of Mevasseret. To the great chagrin of the residents of Mevasseret, bankrupt Jerusalem is trying to take it over.

Another new city is Modi'in, about halfway to Tel Aviv. It was planned almost fifty years ago but for a variety of reasons was built only much later. Prime Minister Yizhak Rabin placed the cornerstone in December 1993, and eight years later Modi'in became a city. Not really a suburb of Jerusalem, Bet Shemesh (population sixty-five thousand) has almost trebled in size over recent years and is the biggest of these new cities. Bet Shemesh has some industry, but most residents work in Jerusalem or Tel Aviv.

It has been the policy of successive Israeli governments, in particular of Likud, to surround Jerusalem with a periphery of urban settlements. Seen in retrospect, this policy has not been very wise. It has made a political solution infinitely more difficult, and it has not affected the demographic balance between Jews and Arabs in the city. The fertility rate of the Arab population is higher. In 1967, about 26 percent of the residents were Arabs; their proportion is now 32 percent.

There has been a substantial Jewish exodus from Jerusalem, in particular among young, secular, working people. Since 1990, about two hundred thousand have left Jerusalem and the number of newcomers has been considerably smaller. (Fifteen factories left Jerusalem in 2002–03.) Nor was the building up of a Jewish periphery a wise decision from a strategic-military point of view, for keeping the roads to outlaying settlements safe means tying down substantial military and police forces.

The capital of the state of Israel now has a non- or anti-Zionist majority (ultraorthodox, one hundred thirty-five thousand; Arabs, two hundred twenty-five thousand), a majority that is bound to grow. Seventy-nine thousand children attend ultraorthodox schools in Jerusalem compared to sixty-five thousand who go to Jewish state schools and sixty-two thousand in Arab schools. A clear picture emerges from these projections.

There are many aspects of Jerusalem I would like to be more familiar with, for instance, municipal or business affairs. I am woefully ignorant as far as the criminal underworld of Jerusalem, past and present, is concerned. I know a little more on Jerusalem as a sport center, but there is not that much to know about this subject. A sports club named Bar Giora was established in this city in 1906, and the Lemmel School was the first in the country to have physical education as part of its curriculum. But after that the initiative passed to Tel Aviv and Haifa as far as the Jews were concerned, and to Jaffa for the Arabs. There was an Arab soccer team in Jerusalem in the 1920s consisting mainly of members of the Greek Orthodox community. The Arabs refused to play against Jewish teams, but the Jewish sport clubs had occasional competitions with the Lebanese of Beirut. There were a few tennis courts but no decent sports ground in Jerusalem until the YMCA was built in the 1920s and, of course, no swimming pool. Even in Tel Aviv and Haifa, swimming contests at the time took place in the open sea.

I also am not an expert on Jerusalem today as a media center, though I know something about its past. The city now has the greatest concentration of foreign correspondents and stringers in the world, excepting only Washington, London, and Moscow. Once upon a time the Zionist leadership was very proud if the country got attention and they tried to get even more of it, but recent publicity has been focused almost entirely on negative events.

The Hebrew newspapers with rare exceptions (such as the Orthodox religious papers) appear in Tel Aviv, but *The Palestine (Jerusalem) Post* is published in Jerusalem, and the state radio and later the television stations are located there. Most of the Arab daily newspapers are also in Jerusalem.

There were radios in Palestine even in the 1920s, well before I came, but no local station—radio listeners had to tune in to European shortwave stations and Cairo radio. There was a private Hebrew station owned and run by an enterprising gentleman in Tel Aviv named Mendel Abramovich as far back as 1932. The number of radios was about twelve thousand (licensed sets, that is, with probably an equal number unlicensed) even before the first official local stations were opened; the Palestine Broadcasting Service (PBS) began to operate in three languages only in 1935–36. The first primitive radios to arrive in Palestine came from the Soviet Union rather than the West; among the politicians, Ben-Gurion was the driving force for establishing a Jewish radio service in Palestine. (Ironically, decades later Ben-Gurion was the main opponent of establishing television services in Israel.) But there were enormous difficulties, and the Mandatory government hesitated to give licenses to private stations. It was only under the pressure of world events—the fear of propaganda broadcasts from fascist and communist countries—that eventually made the British government take the plunge.

During World War II, there was also a Forces Broadcasting Service in Palestine to which many listened, and workshops began to produce radio sets for local buyers. When the British Mandate ended in May 1948, Kol Israel took over, making use of both the studios and the staff of the Hebrew Service of the old PBS. The transmitters were north of Ramallah, in Palestinian Arab territory, and could no longer be used.

The quality of radio in Palestine was high from the early days, much in contrast to television, which was launched relatively late in Israel, in May 1968 after the Six-Day War. Why radio should be more enterprising and interesting I do not know, but this seems to be true for quite a few countries. Israeli was one of the first to use FM, which at the time was rare. My connection with radio began either during the last days of the Mandate or very early after 1948—I do not remember. I do recall that I had a program on Friday after the evening news, which was the time almost everyone was listening. I gave short talks about the personality of the week in international affairs. Even decades later, people told me that they remembered these programs—there were few other entertainments at the time.

The main problem was the pronunciation of my name, which cannot be rendered phonetically in Hebrew (as often as not announcers called me Lakvir or Loker because vowels do not appear in Hebrew print).

One day I got a phone call from Prime Minister Moshe Sharett. I assumed he wanted to brief me on some important matter of state, but I could not have been more mistaken. Sharett was a Hebrew purist and he wanted to persuade me to change my name to Yakir. The idea did not appeal to me at all and I mentioned that Yakir had been a Soviet general who perished in the purges of the 1930s. He replied that Charette had been a French general who had lost every battle he fought. He also said that he had known my father (which was sheer fantasy) and that he was sure that my father would have agreed with his suggestion. In near despair I asked for a couple of weeks' grace to ponder his proposal. Two weeks later he was out of office and, in any case, I was working on a book, gradually detaching myself from journalism.

My office was in Jerusalem's Fleet Street (Hassolel, now Havazelet), a short and undistinguished street off Jaffa Road. Some transport companies were located there, but it was around two-thirty in the afternoon that the street really came alive, when the evening papers from Tel Aviv arrived and a regiment of very young boys descended on Zion Square, running from there in different directions shouting "*Ma'ariv*" and "*Yediot.*"

The office was on the second floor of *The Palestine Post* building—until that night in early 1948 when the building was bombed by two British ex-police freelancers. I had gone home early that night. One of my neighbors on the same floor was *Hamashkif,* the right-wing revisionist newspaper that supported the Irgun. Among the permanent contributors was Abba Achimeir, originally a Russian Labor Zionist who had moved to the extreme right; for a while he wrote a column signed "Fascist" and he had frequently been arrested by the British. He was a man of solid knowledge of European culture (he had an Austrian doctorate), and I sometimes walked home with him. He was always an interesting conversationalist, unless the subject was current politics, when he became shrill and incoherent—according to him, the leading labor politicians were all criminals and prostitutes. I found his nostalgia for the forests and rivers of his native White Russia surprising given his love for Zion.

I remember a pale and very shy young man, perhaps nineteen years old at the time who arrived after the war. It was the first time I saw an Auschwitz number on someone's arm. His name was Dov Yudkovski, and he became the most important Israeli press lord of 1960s and '70s. He showed uncommon journalistic sense, not so much in unearthing scoops but as an organizer, anticipating the taste of the reading public. The fact that he was a nephew of the owner of the leading afternoon paper might have helped, but only Yudkovski made the afternoon papers the leading force they later became.

Dominating Hassolel Street was *The Palestine Post.* Founded shortly after the end of World War I as *The Jerusalem News,* it later changed its name to *The Palestine Bulletin* and in December 1932 became a regular daily newspaper named *The Palestine Post.* After the establishment of the state it was renamed, needless to say, *Jerusalem Post.* (Jerusalem's first major modern cinema, the Edison, also opened in 1932.)

The founder of *The Palestine Post* was Gershon Agronsky (later Agron) who for a few years was the mayor of Jerusalem. He had come to Palestine at the end of World War I with the Jewish battalion of volunteers from the United States stationed in Egypt, and later worked in Jerusalem as a stringer for more than a dozen British and American newspapers. Another such stringer with even more connections was Julian Meltzer, a native of London, who previously had been a policeman. The interest of the world press in Palestine was limited at the time, unless, of course, riots broke out. But there were visitors who stayed for a long time, such as John Gunther who acquired great fame in later years for his "Inside" books, Vincent Shean, and even H. L. Mencken.

The backbone of *The Palestine Post* during the 1930s and World War II was German Jews such as C. Z. Kloetzel, a well-known journalist in the Weimar press; "Frango"(Goldstein), the art critic; and Eugen Meyer, a lawyer by training who was the literary editor. English was not the native language of these three men, but they were educated people who aimed perhaps a little above the horizon of the readership. The two pillars and main English stylists were Lea Ben Dor, who later became editor of the paper, and George Lichtheim. Both were of Central European origin, their parents had been leaders in the early Zionist movement, and they both had received part of their education in England. George was a profound and witty writer and brilliant analyst, who, as a student of the history of socialism, became quite famous in later years. His *Marxism* became a classic. Lea was a very fine editor.

From about 1945 on there was a "Column One" written mainly by David Courtney (Roy Elston), a non-Jewish former wartime employee of the British Mandatory government. In the 1920s and '30s he had written a dozen travel books sponsored by Thomas Cook in London. I also wrote "Column One" once or twice a week using a pseudonym during the first years, mainly writing about foreign policy, but Courtney was far more famous than me. He was an elegant writer who was very critical of British policy at the time, and *The Palestine Post* readers loved him. After the state had been founded, his popularity waned—he had little more to say. On foreign affairs he took a line similar to the British *New Statesman* or the American *Nation,* and given the growing anti-Semitism under Stalinism this was not a position easy to defend. Courtney returned to England and his traces were lost; I was told that he did not find employment commensurate with his talents and died not long after, a bitter and disappointed man. I stopped writing regularly for the paper in 1955.

The Palestine Post of the 1940s was a great newspaper, and it was certainly a wonderful apprenticeship for me. Having had to produce editorials and various other contributions at an hour's notice, I had little patience with students in later years who complained that producing a seminar paper within a couple of weeks was a superhuman task. Comparisons between the intellectual and professional level of *The Palestine Post* and *The Jerusalem Post* of later decades would be pointless: The newspaper of the 1940s, small as it was, was almost highbrow and intended for an intellectually elite readership. It could well be that most readers at the time were not natives of England and America, whereas the composition of the readership in the '80s and '90s was altogether different, with other cultural, political, and religious interests, many of them "national religious" from the United States.

Journalists, it is well-known, cannot exist without coffee houses, and there were half a dozen within a few hundred yards. (Tea with lemon, and cakes of all sorts, were supplied in *The Palestine Post* building on an hourly basis, but this never replaced the coffee house atmosphere.) Agron, I believe, held court in Café Wina on Zion Square (where the other major Jerusalem cinema was located—the square was named after the cinema, and not vice versa). Wina was a slight cut above the other places as far as design and furniture were concerned, but not necessarily the quality of the cakes to be had there. (It would have been unfair to expect much in wartime or during the years of austerity that followed; apple cake was usually the safest choice.)

Probably the most popular was Café Atara, one hundred yards up Ben Yehuda Street, opened in 1938 by Heinz Greenspan, a recent arrival from Germany whose earlier experience had been in clothing but who soon realized that given the climate of Palestine, the poverty of the residents, and the lack of formality, this was not a line of business to be pursued. Café Atara was frequented by both modernist writers and those in the classical tradition, as well as military (then Hagana) secret service people—and of course journalists. Atara was the only coffee house that employed middle-aged women as a matter of policy. A few years ago Greenspan's son announced that the coffee house would close, but second thoughts prevailed and today the place is managed by Uri, a third generation Greenspan, providing not only coffee and cake but also the legendary onion soup. However, eventually the branch in town was closed down and Atara moved to Rehavia.

Needless to say, there are many more coffee houses in Jerusalem than in the pre-state days, chains like Aroma, Hillel, and Na'aman as well as those in the main street of the German Colony such as Kafit, where once upon a time there was a single forlorn one, named Café Loy. (Kafit is at the corner of Masaryk Street; there are more streets in Israel named after him than in his native Czech Republic.)

Other coffee houses of the 1940s included Ta'amon, Rimon, Europa, Tuv ta'am, and Alaska as well as a few outside the inner city such as Café Rehavia. In Café Hermon one met politicians from the nearby Jewish Agency as well as literary figures; this coffee house appears in both Agnon's and Amos Oz's novels, and Aharon Applefeld has written a book on the subject.

A great deal has been written about the institution of the Viennese coffee house where people went for a great many purposes—if they felt dejected, or if they wanted to share a sudden good fortune with friends, to meet members of the opposite sex, to play chess or billiards, to read out-of-town newspapers. Drinking coffee was a secondary purpose.

The function of the Jerusalem coffee house was different. Jerusalemites were far busier than citizens of Vienna during the classic period of the coffee house, but on the other hand, Jerusalem apartments were small; there were no bars or other such places to meet away from home. A coffee house was neutral ground for journalists to meet their sources and exchange information.

The first modern Arab coffee house (al Jawahira) appeared around 1920, also on Jaffa Road near the Russian compound. Leading singers of the day appeared there and also Badia Masabni, a famous belly dancer from Beirut. This institution had disappeared by the time I arrived in Jerusalem. However, the combination of coffee house-cabaret, probably copied from similar establishments in Cairo and Beirut, was frequent in the Arab quarters. As a Palestinian Arab chronicler of the period has noted, the image of Jerusalem as a city entirely preoccupied with religion was not quite correct.

The fact that 30 percent of the Jewish population is ultraorthodox (and quickly growing) defines much of the local culture. The ultraorthodox do not venture near a theater or a concert or a secular bookshop; in fact there is not a single major bookshop in town that befits a city of this size. Secular newspapers are banned in Mea Shearim and the Jewish quarter of the Old City, where even owning a television set is a sin to be punished. But there are nine (illegal) ultraorthodox radio stations and one national religious television channel, not to mention close to one thousand synagogues, most of them very small, and some forty-five ritual bathhouses.

There is a university and a theater, but the schools are not nearly as good as they should be. The percentage of high school students passing the final examinations is lower in Jerusalem than in other Israeli cities. Tel Aviv and other cities spend four times as much as Jerusalem for the education of a child. Students from outside Jerusalem may come up for a guided tour of an exhibition in the Israeli Museum or Yad Vashem, and there is, above all, Ha'oman 17, a substantial discotheque in the Talpiot industrial area. Jerusalem is the religious but not the cultural center of the country.

I recently read a letter written by Helen Bentwich from Jerusalem to her mother in England just two months after the end of World War I. Bentwich was the wife of Norman Bentwich, an Anglo-Jewish senior civil servant in the British Mandatory government. In later life she became a Labor politician and at one stage head of the LCC, something like lord mayor of London. "My dear mother," she wrote. "Here I am in Jerusalem—such a Jerusalem as one could not have conceived five years ago. [She had visited the city just before the outbreak of the war.] Motor cars and lorries tearing through the streets day & night; clean & decent bazaars inside the walls, law & order everywhere, free access to the Holy Church & the Mosque of Omar both of which I visited today as easily as one goes into Westminster Abbey. It's a greatly improved place…"

When I first came to Jerusalem more than sixty years ago I entered the city as most travelers had done since time immemorial, by way of Jaffa Road, which led from the outskirts of the city to the Jaffa Gate at the Old City walls. Among the first buildings one passed was the Sha'arei Tzedek Hospital to the right, built more than one hundred years ago by an Orthodox German Jew named Moritz Wallach; it is now a modern hospital on a different site. Wallach, a native of Cologne, lived for the hospital. He never married and had a small apartment in the building where he stayed until his death at a very old age. The old building, after being empty for many years, has been refurbished and now houses the Israeli Broadcasting Authority. The old road was very narrow. It has been widened, and most of the old houses to the left and right are coming down. Some have protested against this, but they were so ugly that I find it difficult to muster much enthusiasm for their preservation. The Mahane Yehuda market, almost always crowded, had to be crossed to get into the center of town.

Once upon a time, one hundred forty years ago to be precise, this entrance to Jerusalem at the westernmost part of the city was called Bet Ya'akov. It was the first station at which the diligence (or horse-drawn carriages) from Jaffa stopped. (The main station was then opposite Jaffa Gate.) The market was not the most hygienic of places and its alleys were always crammed. But to this day it has the best olives in town, the best feta, the best herring, the best pita, and excellent fruit, and I go there whenever I am in Jerusalem. I have been attracted by the smells and sounds of the market ever I came to know it. True, the decibel level is high and in the year 2000 Jerusalem municipality passed a regulation instructing the traders to extol less loudly the virtues of their fruit, vegetables, cheese, and smoked fish. The traders circumvented it by commissioning a "Hymn of the Market," which announced that Mahane Yehuda was Jerusalem's heart as well as a visual pleasure. Who could ban such a hymn?

At one time, the British Mandatory government planned either to close it or to rebuild it. But these plans were never carried out, and the old market has outlasted both the Turks and the British. At one stage there was also an elegant coffee house with the unlikely name Casino de Paris, providing congenial surroundings for the aficionados of *shesh besh* (backgammon) and throwing the dice. The Central Bus Station was off Jaffa Road, and farther on one passed the central post office, the municipal buildings, and Notre Dame (another hospital) until one reached Jaffa Gate.

Jaffa Road was the main street of Jerusalem at the time. There was a great deal of neglect and dilapidation; even in 1938, it looked more like a street in a Turkish or Russian provincial town than the entrance to Jerusalem the golden. But there were a lot of people of every provenance in the streets, Orthodox black hats, Arabs, Oriental Jews, monks of every persuasion, British policemen, horses, donkey carts, motor cars, even the occasional camel. To the left and right, little food stalls were selling black coffee, and cold water and orange juice and pitas. There were the smells and sounds of a bazaar, and the small shops could have been in a Polish town. As for the building that had been going on in the Arab part of the city, Charles Robert Ashby, the first architect of note to arrive in Jerusalem after World War I, was appalled by what he called the "neo-religious commercialism" and the colossal and hideous convents and monasteries.

What was ugly but picturesque sixty years ago is now desolate. Many of the small shops selling toys, shoes, and haberdashery are still there. But more than a few are closed and display For Sale signs. The houses left and right look even more neglected. The Central Bus Station, which used to be in the very center of town is now (quite sensibly) at the entrance to the city. There has been progress. Traffic lights at the corner of Jaffa Road and King George Street, once the busiest intersection in town, have replaced the Arab policeman who once directed the traffic on a little island protected by an umbrella. The newsstands selling papers from all over the world have disappeared. In the side streets very young and very old newspaper vendors squat on the ground selling Hebrew and Russian papers. On Zion Square there are other squatters, mainly religious dropouts, it appears, from the United States.

A great deal of building work is going on. The central part of Jaffa Road will soon become a pedestrian zone with all private transport banned but with a light railway leading from Neve Ya'akov in the north to Malha in the south where it will meet the railway to Tel Aviv. Big posters show how some of the planners (mainly, it seems, traffic engineers) envisage the Jaffa Road of the future and what a wonderful sight it will be: "New Life to the town center," they announce, "it is not too late…" It is said that abroad, the city centers prosper more than ever where the pedestrian zones are full of flaneurs and window-shoppers, tourists, people sitting in sidewalk coffee houses, and of course serious shoppers. They say that even in the age of the shopping malls and the Internet there must be the human touch, people meeting other people.

It is a wonderful vision, and it is heartwarming that even at a time of grave crisis there are visionaries unwilling to give up. But even if money is found to finish these ambitious projects, even if peace on earth arises, it is not certain that the center of Jerusalem can be saved. It has been dying for too long.

It has been a favorite place for suicide bombers, but this has not even been the main reason for its steady decline. Jaffa Road as a shopping center has been dying because the pathetic little shops have not kept up with the times and modernized themselves. "How doth the city sit solitary, that was full of people" (Lamentations 1:1). Customers have moved out of central Jerusalem and in any case would not be able to park there. The shopping malls in the suburbs, which came into being some ten years ago, attract more and more of these visitors. Once one could hardly move on the sidewalks because of the congestion and one had to stand in line for ice cream or falafel. There is no need to do so now. The crowds have disappeared and the streets can be crossed without difficulty.

Jerusalem is now a city without a center—the pull of the periphery is too strong. Not long ago there were grandiose plans for mega-hotels, skyscrapers of thirty-three stories, and a sixty-two-story monument in Ben Yehuda Street (the "center of the universe"). Environmentalists issued dire warnings about the lethal coalition between power driven politicians, greedy land developers, and megalomaniac architects.

They need not have worried. The developers did not take into account politics and economics, just as the traffic planners seem to have forgotten the demographic factor—the wish to escape from the center on the part of all those who can afford it, the expansion of the *haredi* communities, and the poverty of the city. At a time of economic plight and reduced subsidies, there is a movement afoot in the ultra-orthodox community to promote the professional training of some of their young men. But many leading rabbis are opposed to this in principle, for they predict that it will lead to loss of faith, moral turpitude, and the disappearance of their traditional society.

The optimists among the planners could point to the fact that at the very end of Jaffa Road (Shlomzion Hamalka, once Princess Mary Street), something like a new center of Jerusalem nightlife has emerged. It is limited to a handful of bars and restaurants offering Chinese and Romanian food, "espresso gourmets," coffee houses, art galleries, and an antiques shop. Not everyone above the age of thirty is even aware of the new center of entertainment. Perhaps the end of downtown Jerusalem is not yet upon us? It is hard to say, and also rather premature to predict that a dozen swallows might indicate a new spring.

There is one new ominous new development: the security wall, also called the Jerusalem Barrier and, more euphemistically, the Jerusalem Envelope. It is bound to be the most dramatic change in the city since

1967, but it is impossible even to speculate on its impact because construction is still in progress and there are so many uncertainties. There was initially great support in Israel and there can be no a priori opposition to self-defense measures. The English had Hadrian's Wall, the Chinese their Great Wall, and there have been countless fences or walls all over the world in recent times—even in Palestine during the last years of the British Mandate. The issue at stake today is not the height of the wall, as some suggested, but where the barriers should be. Those who chose the course of the wall in 2003 achieved the seemingly impossible. They combined land grabbing and thus maximum political damage (generating permanent political pressure on Israel) and imposed a maximum of hardship on Palestinian Arabs with a minimum of security for Israel because the wall brought about the inclusion of tens of thousands of more Arabs into the state of Israel.

No great prophetic gifts are needed to understand that this partition will not last as long as the Great Wall of China. Perhaps one day it will become a tourist attraction like the Great Wall, but what until then?

Chandigarh in India is the only city in the world that serves as capital to two states, Punjab and Haryana (which were once one state), and it happens to be almost exactly as big as Jerusalem with six hundred fifty thousand inhabitants. But it is a recent city. It came into being in 1953 because after the partition of the Indian subcontinent, Punjab was a state without a capital and furthermore there were many thousands of refugees from Pakistan to be housed. Situated in the foothills of the Himalayas, it was Nehru's dream city, planned by Le Corbusier, one of the world's great city architects. It is the most modern city in India, with a university and Asia's largest rose gardens, an artificial lake, and a ban to erect statues of living persons. It is legally "union territory," but on both sides there have been voices claiming sole authority and there have been disputes about Punjab river waters. But it is unlikely that the status of

Chandigarh will change in the foreseeable future, even though the majority of the residents are Punjabis rather than Hindu citizens of Haryana. And despite the fact that a court has in principle awarded Chandigarh to Punjab, its fate as the capital of two states is unlikely to change.

Chandigarh is not contested as a holy city; there are a great many holy cities all over the world from Mecca, Medina, and Karbala to Lhasa in Tibet, to Mathura and the other five Indian holy cities. But even there the issue of being a capital does not arise. Only Jerusalem is in the unfortunate position of combining holiness (for some) with heavy claims placed upon it as a secular capital. It is one thing to have possession of the sites considered holy and having unlimited access to them, and quite another to establish the center of administration. For millennia, Jerusalem was not the seat of any government administration—under the Ummayads and Abbasids, Jerusalem was ruled from Baghdad, Damascus, and Cairo; under the Mamluks and Ottomans, Constantinople was the capital, and even the regional administration of Jerusalem district was in Ramleh and Lydda—the Jews, of course, did not have a state.

Unfortunately, the prospects of a Chandigarh solution in Jerusalem are almost nonexistent. It is far more likely that the exodus of the young, secular, and enterprising among the population will continue, and Jerusalem twenty years from now will resemble, at best, Ramot. Ramot is a big suburb of about forty thousand inhabitants to the west of Jerusalem, and can be seen from the road to Tel Aviv. It was predominantly secular in the beginning but has largely been taken over by the *haredim.* The houses are more modern than Mea Shearim, and it is not quite as dirty, but there is the same neglect of nature and the quality of life. Bne Braq is a wholly *haredi* urban settlement north of Tel Aviv, resembling Orthodox neighborhoods in Eastern Europe one hundred or more years ago.

If present trends continue—and there is little chance that they will not—the new Jerusalem could be a mixture of the Old City and the *haredi* quarters, old and new.

Why has a symbol become such a tremendous political issue? Whence the insistence on the part of the religious nationalists on keeping Jerusalem as the permanent and exclusive capital? And why the insistence on the part of the Palestinians on having it as their capital, which it never was in the past? Why are people who do not want to live in Jerusalem still willing to die for it?

Paris, someone once said, is a city for lovers, but Jerusalem is a city for visionaries. Is that really true? I have not met that many visionaries neither to the left nor the right of Jaffa Road, neither in Ge'ula, nor in Rehavia, not even in the Old City. It is not a vision so much as a powerful myth, part of the general global trend of strong nationalist religious impulses. The vision is not that of religious orthodoxy, because the most Orthodox sections of the Jewish population do not recognize the state of Israel and certainly do not want Jerusalem as its capital. The Temple Mount is of concern only to the nationalists among the religious Jews. The truly Orthodox believe that the Temple will be rebuilt by the Messiah at the appointed time. Any attempt to rush it is in violation of the ban of the chief rabbis (which forbids the ascent to Temple Mount) and would therefore be blasphemy. For the Orthodox, decisive importance lies not on the political status of certain sites (of the territory of Biblical Israel or Jerusalem) believed to be holy by the nationalists. Rather, of overriding importance is the study of the Old Testament. But the nationalist myth has gained in power, as for many believers the spiritual content of Judaism has given way to the adoration of land, graves, and former temples.

At one time groups of Israelis came to Jerusalem for a day visit, but their numbers have been dwindling. Most Israelis do not particularly like the city, and they certainly do not want to live there. But there is great reluctance to share sovereignty, because Jerusalem is a powerful symbol. Symbols are fine, but the real Jerusalem has come to resemble more and more that part of a negative Jewish heritage that the Zionists of Herzl's generation wanted to forget.

The resolution of the Israeli parliament of 1980 stated that a special annual grant would be given by the government to the city of Jerusalem and special priority to further its development in economic matters and other respects. There is an Israeli government minister for Jerusalem affairs and a Palestinian minister for the same purpose; at one time it was Yizhak Rabin (who temporarily had half a dozen portfolios) and on the Arab side Feisal Husseini, residing in Orient House. But neither has been able to do much for Jerusalem, nor has the ministerial Jerusalem committee or the Knesset committee with its special annual grant to help Jerusalem out of its financial misery. There is a Jerusalem Day (the 28th of Iyar) celebrated throughout Israel in commemoration of the unification of the city in June 1967, but less and less attention is paid to it.

The problem of Jerusalem is the most difficult on the road to peace. It was mainly because of Jerusalem that the Camp David negotiations broke down in 2000. In all negotiations since, the question of Jerusalem has been postponed to the end of the agenda as the least tractable. The hope, it seems, is that Jerusalem will never be discussed, that there will be a failure to agree on the other bones of contention.

Theoretically there are a variety of solutions for Jerusalem. Like Chandigarh, the capital of two states in India, it could be the capital of both countries. Or it could be the capital of neither, becoming again a *corpus separandum,* a separate entity, as envisaged in the partition plan of 1948, with unfettered access to all holy places. It is frequently forgotten now that in 1947, the Zionist leadership had been willing to accept the partition plan according to which Jerusalem would not have been part of the Jewish state, and this refers not only to the Temple

Mount and the Wailing Wall but the new predominantly Jewish quarters of Jerusalem, where, after all, some 15 percent of the total Jewish population of Palestine made their home at the time.

There may not even be the need to change the Basic Law passed by the Israeli parliament in 1980, according to which "Jerusalem complete and united" is the capital of Israel—for nothing in that statement precludes it being also the capital of another country. Is it likely that the religious-nationalist fervor that makes the problem intractable will diminish in time? Perhaps, but not in the foreseeable future. This may be difficult for Americans and Europeans to understand; few of them would mount the barricades to keep the center of administration in their present capitals.

Why should it be different in Jerusalem? Why declare Jerusalem the eternal capital of Israel in a world in which there is nothing eternal? (Even Rome is only the eternal city, not the eternal capital.) Is it a religious-political syndrome that can be found elsewhere too? An Israeli poet, at one time my swimming partner in the pool of the Moria Hotel, who lived nearby, opposite the city wall, wrote a poem about the air above Jerusalem being filled with prayers and dreams like the air above cities with heavy industry. But it is also filled with curses and evil passions and, as Yehuda Amichai wrote, "from time to time a new shipment of history arrives."

But is it right to put all the blame on the dead hand of history generating the passions of aggression and war? How to get rid of this deadly burden? Psychiatrists have offered advice on how to deal with the Jerusalem syndrome in the case of individuals, but they are powerless to deal with groups of people, especially if they fail to even begin to understand their predicament. Both sides will have to suffer a great deal more until readiness for a compromise can be achieved.

The prophet Isaiah said many wonderful things about Jerusalem— that for Zion's sake he will not keep silent, and that out of Zion will go forth the law. But he did not say that his right hand will forget her cunning unless the Ministry of Tourism and the Ministry of Health are located in this city. Jerusalem is mentioned six hundred fifty-six times in the Old Testament, but it is nowhere said that this refers to the Wailing Wall or that sovereignty on part of the city cannot be shared with others. According to Ezekiel, Jerusalem is the center of the earth; according to Jeremiah, the throne of the Lord; according to Zechariah, God will return to Jerusalem with compassion. And as Abraham predicted, Mount Moriah is the place where God will be seen.

The Bible relates the appeal by Abner, the army commander of Israel, to Joab, the head of the opposed camp: "Shall the sword devour forever? Do you not know that the end will be bitter?" (2 Samuel 2:26). This happened in the days of King David—the appeal was successful and led to an armistice, but it did not last; later on Joab killed Abner in Hebron. Eventually King David imposed some order, but King Solomon, when he came to power, had Joab executed. There is no eternal peace on earth, but there is no permanent conflict either. Fanaticism too is subject to upsurges and downturns. But this is true for the long haul only—historical waves of great length—and it is difficult to muster much optimism as far as the years to come are concerned.

At the beginning of this book I said that I would refrain from engaging in prediction and prophecy. I have deviated from these good intentions towards the end. It would not have occurred had I cared less about the city.

ACKNOWLEDGMENTS

MY RECOLLECTIONS ARE BASED PRIMARILY ON PERSONAL reminiscences and on conversations with contemporaries. To refresh my memory, I consulted the enormous literature on modern Jerusalem. Of particular value are the publications of the Jerusalem Institute of Israel studies, the Teddy Kollek Center for Jerusalem Studies, and the Ben-Zvi Center for Jerusalem Studies for information on various sections of the city, such as the Street of the Prophets, the Nachlaot, and Rehavia, and the *Jerusalem Lexikon* (2003). *Yerushalayim betkufat hamandat* (Jerusalem in the Era of the British Mandate), edited by Jehoshua ben Arye (Jerusalem, 2003), includes rich material on the period by historians and eyewitnesses. David Krojanker's books on the planning and architecture of Jerusalem in consecutive eras were especially helpful. Mr. Krojanker's splendid latest book on Jerusalem, *Rehov Yaffo: biografia shel rehov* (*Yaffa Road: The Biography of a Street*), reached me just in time to enjoy and to be of use.

For Arab Jerusalem, the literature is less rich, but useful material can be found in the publications of the Institute of Jerusalem Studies (sponsored by the Institute for Palestine Studies), such as the *Jerusalem Quarterly* (since 1998). This should not be confused with the *Jerusalem Quarterly* that was published in Jewish Jerusalem. Guidance for foreign correspondents visiting Jerusalem can be found on the Israeli government websites and, reflecting the Palestinian point of view, on the websites of the Jerusalem Media Communication Center.

The back files of *The Jerusalem (and Palestine) Post* as well as *The Jerusalem Report* were invaluable and, above all, *Kol Ha'ir,* the interesting Jerusalem weekly newspaper distributed free of charge.

There are so many recent books and even dissertations on all the subjects dealt with in this book, from archaeology to Yad Vashem, from the kibbutz to the *haredim,* that it would be impossible to list them in detail.

Mayors and deputy mayors from Ronald Storrs to Teddy Kollek and Meron Benvenisti have written about the city, as have countless travelers and city planners, twentieth-century European writers from Selma Lagerlöf and Pierre Loti to Arnold Zweig, Arthur Koestler, Saul Bellow, and, of course, the Israelis and the Palestinians.

Adina and Shlomit not only helped me to obtain materials that are not easily accessible but also provided detailed replies to many queries. I should also mention my interns at CSIS in 2000–01, above all Melissa Goldate. Without the help of Marek Michalewski I would not have been able to use the many possibilities of modern computer technology.

Chapters of the manuscript were read by my colleagues at the Wissenschaftskolleg Berlin (2002–03): Professors Mark Cohen (Princeton), Reinhard Kratz (Goettingen), and Leonid Zhmud (St. Petersburg), as well as Prof. Y. Baumel, Dr. Avi Barkai, Professor Steven Aschheim, Yo'av Karny, Shabtai Teveth, Irena Lasota, Dani Rubinstein, Larisa Silnicky, Alexander Lifshitz, and Barbara Green. It goes without saying that they have not the slightest responsibility for the views expressed in this book. I am particularly indebted to my friend David Boggis, who gave the whole manuscript a professional, critical reading.

INDEX

ABOUT THE AUTHOR

W ALTER LAQUEUR TAUGHT AT BRANDEIS, HARVARD, THE University of Chicago, Tel Aviv University, Georgetown, and Johns Hopkins. He served as the director of the Institute of Contemporary History and Wiener Library London from 1965 to 1992 and is the founder and former editor of the *Journal of Contemporary History* and the *Washington Quarterly*. He was the chairman of the International Research Council Center of Strategic and International Studies in Washington from 1969 to 2000. He is the author of an autobiography and numerous books on modern and contemporary history, some of which have become standard texts and have been translated into twenty languages. He is also a well known commentator on international affairs in the United States and in Europe.